AF531348

# INTERNATIONAL ENCYCLOPAEDIA OF SCIENCE AND TECHNOLOGY EDUCATION

Volume 7

**Popularization of Science and Technology Education**

*Editor*

**Dr. Digumarti Bhaskara Rao**

*M.Sc., M.A., M.A., M.Ed., Ph.D.*

R.V.R. College of Education

Nagarjuna University

Guntur–522006

Andhra Pradesh (India)

**DISCOVERY PUBLISHING HOUSE**

**New Delhi**

First Published-2000

**Reprinted-2011**

**SBN 81-7141-548-2 (Set)**



**DISCOVERY PUBLISHING HOUSE**
4831/24, Ansari Road, Prahlad Street,
Darya Ganj, New Delhi-110002 (India)
Phone: 3279245 • Fax: 91-11-3253475
E-mail: dph@indiatimes.com

*Printed at:*

**Mehra Offset Press**
**Delhi**

# Preface

Science and Technology have occupied almost all spheres of human life. The wonderful achievements of science and technology have glorified the modern world and transformed the modern civilization into a scientific and technological civilization. Considering the importance of science and technology, they have been incorporated in every stage of education.

This International Encyclopaedia of Science and Technology Education is developed covering a wide range of aspects related to science and technology education for the benefit of all those who are associated with science and technology education. This Encyclopaedia is consisting of eleven volumes, namely:

1. Science and Technology Education,
2. Science Education in Developing Countries,
3. Organizational Structure of Science,
4. Science Education in Asia and the Pacific,
5. Science and Technology Education for All,
6. Values, Ethics, Talent and Girls in Science and Technology Education,
7. Popularization of Science and Technology Education,
8. Science, Power and Society,
9. Information Technology,
10. Teacher Training in Science and Technology Education, and
11. Science Technology and Society—A Curriculum Framework.

I convey my cordial thanks to UNESCO-PROAP, Bangkok, Thailand; UNESCO-ROSTE, Venice, Italy; UNESCO, Paris, France; IIEP, Paris, France; Commonwealth Secretariat, London, UK; UNCTAD, Geneva, Switzerland, Queen's University, Kingston, Canada; and Alberta Education, Edmonton, Canada for their kind co-operation in preparing this Encyclopaedia.

DR. DIGUMARTI BHASKARA RAO
Secretary
Academy of Communication Culture Education
Science and Service
GUNTUR (A.P.)

# Contents

**Part III—Popularization of Science and Technology: Delivery Systems for Out-of-School Science Activities**

# Part I

# POPULARIZATION OF SCIENCE AND TECHNOLOGY

# 1

# Science for All People: Some Educational Settings and Strategies for the Popularization of Science and Technology

HARBANS BHOLA

## Introduction

The ideal of "Health for All by the Year 2000" was adopted by WHO is 1981. "Education for All by the Year 2000" will be formally put on the world's educational agenda at the International Symposium jointly sponsored by UNDP, UNESCO, UNICEF and The World Bank to be held in Thailand during March 1990. Why shouldn't "Science for All People", be part of the "Education for All" initiative?

In proposing "Science for All People", do not, of course, hope to make Einstein's out of all the world's men and women. What we do hope is that, while keeping the best of each of our indigenous traditions, we will also inherit the new scientific culture—that set of skills, understandings, and habits of mind to which all humanity has contributed, to some degree, over the span of human history. We must claim our total heritage of traditional values and scientific vectors.

**Why Science for All People?**

A case for "Science for All People" can be made on grounds both moral and material. There is something highly immoral about a world which denies most of humanity a significant part of the collective human knowledge called science; and keeps away from those scientifically and technologically disadvantaged populations, the full enjoyment of the fruits of technology of production, communication, transportation, and health made possible by scientific knowledge and technology.

The case for "Science for All People" is equally compelling on material grounds—for simple reasons of bread and butter. Since the post-War years, socio-economic development has been on the political agendas of all nations, developed and developing. Development will stay on the policy agendas, particularly, of developing nations for the foreseeable future. What is germane to our discussion is the fact that development today is impossible without science and technology.

Whatever the definition of development for a particular culture or nation state, development will be impossible unless science and technology can be put to work to produce the surpluses necessary for the eradication of poverty and hunger from among the burgeoning populations and to provide the necessary services in health and welfare. It is important to note that science and technology are needed not merely at the heights of the economy in its industrial and Hi-Technology sectors, but also in the informal sectors of subsistence economics. Indeed, science and technology are needed with much greater urgency in the informal sectors of the economies of scarcities in the Third World where farmers and workers may be able to use new knowledge and skills without having to wait for the political and economic structures to change first.

**The Nature of the Crisis**

The popularization of science and technology today is a necessity, not a frill—something nice to have! Science, and the technology that science have spawned, already define and totally permeate our environment. Science and technology are with us on the land, in the air and on water; in the desert and on hill-top; in the city and the village; affecting our lives at work, play and prayer; in our wakeful and sleeping hours; and in sickness and health, and in happiness and sorrow. There is no hiding from science and technology. Most humanity is benefiting from the fruits of science and technology. But many are being hurt. Some are dying in their encounters with technology for lack of knowledge to cope with the omnipresent intruder in their lives.

The problem is manifold:

- Without enough understandings of science and technology, and yet being forced to come in contact with it in daily encounters, thousands and maybe millions are getting hurt—physically, emotionally, biologically—and, sometimes, fatally.
- Without enough understanding of science and technology, human beings are unable to make a positive use of science and technology as a social good for their benefit.
- Without enough understanding of science and technology, human beings are unknowingly making decisions and undertaking actions that are destroying their physical environment and endangering the survival of their own progeny.
- Without proper appreciation of science and technology, many cultures and subcultures are unable to renew their traditions, by failing to join the wisdom of their cultural tradition with the wisdom of the scientific tradition.

The costs of lack of scientific knowledge are high indeed. In Kenya, for example, hundreds of farmers are dying annually being unable to take proper precautions in using the fertilizers and pesticides which they are advised to use by the agricultural extension workers. In misusing technology, farmers, workers and housewives all over the Third World are unknowingly collaborating in the pollution and destruction of their water, land and air resources. The scientifically illiterate are unable to use science and technology for their good as they continue to live lives ravaged by preventable diseases and brutalized by hard labour that could be eased by the simple technology of the wheel and the pulley. Finally, they are easily swayed by the unscrupulous politician in the name of tradition to continue to cling to the past and refuse to enter the future.

**Problems and Contraints**

Two major problems are implicit in the above discussion:

I. Political actors (sometimes abbetted by scholars) create an unnecessary conflict between cultural tradition and scientific technology, and then impose an either/or choice on honest and simple folks, thereby inciting people to reject science and to choose tradition.

II. There is a lack of trained scientific talent in most developing countries that could be used to promote understandings of science and technology and help towards a symbiosis of tradition—the old wisdom, and science—the new wisdom.

**The Continuities between Tradition and Science**

Unfortunately too many of us have been taught to put science in contradiction to tradition. Science and technology are somehow thought to be the death-knell of tradition, the serial of humanism. This is not true. Indeed, we should see and promote the continuity between tradition and science. What is tradition anyway?

It is the experience and wisdom of our forefathers handed down to us for our use and for use by future generations. Tradition is the old wisdom, wrapped in emotion. Science is the new wisdom, not yet internalized. Science is tradition in the making. Ideally there should be no conflict between them. The two should be continuous, one with the other. We do have to understand that traditions in fact die if not renewed, and traditions do hurt if not continuously and critically re-evaluated by each new generation. Also, we must accept the fact that all that is subsumed under the catch-all phrase tradition is not worth saving. No traditional knowledge was good for all people for all times. Traditions are good as anchors but should not is be allowed to become shackles to progress. Those who preach the love of traditions themselves make use of new science and technology. Priests run television ministries. Governments that govern in the name of religion and tradition do not hesitate to spend billions on buying highly sophisticated technology of war.

### Lack of Enough Trained Scientific Talent

The second problem we must face in designing educational settings and strategies for the popularization of science and technology is the lack of trained scientific talent in the Third World. There is a paucity of scientists, engineers, technologists and science teachers both at the college and school levels. Teaching materials are scarce. Science laboratories are non-existent. In the adult education area, scientific and technological content is rarely taught. Agricultural extension, health education and family life education can not avoid teaching some scientific and technological information but it is often taught superficially, without possibilities for transfer to other settings.

### Settings and Strategies for the Popularization of Science and Technology

The tasks before us are quite clear. We need to work toward a symbiosis between cultural traditions on the one hand and science and technology on the other; and to develop scientific talent for all the various sectors of the society, including the informal sectors of subsistence economies. What we are concerned about here then is not merely about writing science curricula but about creating scientific cultures built around the purified golden cores of different cultural traditions.

Dissemination theory tells us that the popularization of science and technology, within a reasonable historical time-frame, will require to use of all settings and all channels of education and extension. The settings for teaching and learning science and technology for the creation of a scientific culture are:

- formal education (FE), including alternative formal education such as distance education;
- nonformal education (NFE), which can also be delivered through distance education; and
- informal education (NFE) which can be equated with socialization.

The formal school offers the first but not necessarily the foremost setting. Indeed, experience with the popularization of science through schooling has been disappointing. Most schools do not offer science. Those who do teach outdated curriculum, and do not teach it will. When science is taught reasonably well, it is academic in organization and hinders transfer to real-life problems and setting. Important initiatives need to be undertaken to improve the teaching of science in schools.

On the other hand, the channels of nonformal education for the popularization of science and technology seem particularly promising. The possibilities of nonformal education are immense in agricultural extension, health extension, and family life education. Nonformal education can and should be used not only for the transfer of technology but for teaching how to think science and to do technology.

Informal education in science and technology should begin at home. Of course, we have a problem here. Most parents in the Third World do not have scientific knowledge. This shifts our attention to how to break this vicious circle. Of course, we have radio and television that have entered many homes all over the world. Business can play an important part in teaching science by teaching about safe uses of their products and instead of simply instructing they can explain. Again, we will have a problem here when dealing with the illiterate.

Institutional settings for the popularization of science and technology should go beyond typical institutions of adult nonformal education and should include business and industry, the army and indeed religious institutions.

The media should include folk media, print media, and the electronic media of film, radio and TV. That should point to the need of paying special attention to the teaching of writing on scientific subjects in our training programmes for print journalism and telecommunication.

**Scientific Knowledge through Functional Literacy**

The concept and practice of functional as one form of nonformal education seems tailor-made for popularization of scientific and technological knowledge. The concept of functional literacy first proposed at the Unesco Conference of 1965 in Teheran, Iran is indeed rooted in the assumption of teaching modern skills at work, both in the formal and informal sectors, whether one is growing vegetables in the small kitchen garden or working on the power loom in a textile factory. The concept of functional literacy, initially limited to economic concerns has now been generalized to the use of scientific knowledge at work, at home, and to the health of self and family.

Experience with functional literacy programmes has already thought out at least two useful lessons:

1. That important knowledge of science and technology when taught in the context of farmers' and workers' daily lives is easily understood and is actually utilized, if personal resources and surrounding context permit.
2. That scientific and technological knowledge taught in the context of work does transfer to other settings, especially if possibilities of such transfer are brought out in the course of teaching. Adults who are taught science and technology in functional literacy classes also disseminate this knowledge to other people in the family and in the neighbourhood.

**Assuming a Mission, Planning for Actions**

If discussion and debate have to lead to actions and operations, a mission must be assumed, initiative defined and action planned without loss of time. The following steps should be taken immediately:

(a) Establish an adhocratic organizational arrangement to be responsible for keeping the momentum going; and to serve as a point of crystallization around which multiple initiatives can be defined, professional networks created and appropriate actions taken.

(b) Publish a usable report (or reports) on the International Conference and disseminate it/them widely to appropriate audiences.

(c) Establish a newsletter on "Science for All People" which at some time may become a professional periodical.

(d) Establish a committee of the concerned to work on a curriculum for science and technology for use in adult education and functional literacy projects. A beginning could be made with the monograph, Towards Scientific Literacy by Thomas and Kondo published in 1978 by the Unesco/Iranian Institute for Adult Literacy Methods in Teheran, Iran.

**Other Actions to Follow**

The list of actions above are those that we can undertake right here or agree to follow upon, on our own, with minor rearrangement of our own currently available resources. There are other actions, however, that we must actively lobby for:

1. Unesco should be asked to pay special attention to the popularization of science and technology through nonformal education, and particularly functional literacy programmes. The proposed emphasis on "Adult Science Education" should be duly formalized through inclusion in Unesco's programmes of discussion and publication.

   1.1 Such a commitment should be demonstrated by UNESCO by making "Science for All People" an important thread in the "Education for All" initiative of UNDP, UNESCO, UNICEF and the World Bank already under way.

   1.2 Unesco should establish formal linkages at a programmatic level with the WHO project on "indigenous science" to help in the emergence of a symbiosis between traditional wisdom and scientific knowledge.

   1.3 Unesco should convene a group of scientists to develop a universal core of human scientific experience for universal dissemination.

2. The International Council for Adult Education (ICAE) as an international association of non-governmental associations should also be persuaded to complement their focus on culture with another focus on science and technology; and through its programmes and publications to promote "adult science education".

3. Unesco should be advised to ask all member states to establish within appropriate national ministries and departments, Units for "Science for All People". Such Units should:

   3.1 Promote analysis of traditional knowledge with scientific and technological implications and its synthesis into indigenous science to be integrated with modern science.

   3.2 Encourage scientists to become interested in dissemination of scientific knowledge within schools and through-out-of-school education and at the same time encourage adult educators to become interested in science and technology.

   3.3 Establish committees and groups to develop science and technology curricula for the dissemination of science to different groups in diverse settings through use of all the different media available within a society.

   3.4 Wherever possible, use appropriately, the institutions of religion, army and business to collaborate in the dissemination of science and technology.

   3.5 Invent and establish community level institutions such as Vigyan Mandirs (Temples of Science) in India to promote science and technology at the local levels.

**Conclusions**

Some important things have already happened in regard to the mission of this Conference. The Conference itself will be seen as an important milestone on the road to progress. It must have already given some visibility to the idea. Some important practical ideas have been generated during our discussion and deliberations that we need to build upon. Finally, a network of those concerned with this important issue has come about and is ready to be extended and strengthened. What we need now is to stay committed and to continue the work.

## REFERENCES

1. Bhola, H.S., "Scientific Literacy for Adult Learners," Bulletin of the Unesco Regional Office for Education in Asia, Number 18, June 1977, pp. 235-242.

2. Science for All Americans: A Project 2061 Report on Literacy Goals in Science, Mathematics, and Technology. American Association for the Advancement of Science, 1333 H.Street, N.W.Washington, D.C., 20005, 1987.

3. Thomas, Frederick J. & Kondo, Allen S. Towards Scientific Literacy. (In: Literacy in Development: A Series of Training Monographs. H.S.Bhola, Series Editor). Teheran, Iran: Unesco/ Iranian Institute for Adult Literacy Methods, 1978.

# 2

# Nonformal Education: A Hinge Between Science and Culture

CAMILLO BONANNI

In this paper the term Education is understood to mean the laborious process by which human beings acquire an awareness of new goals, the freedom of making choices in relation to them, and the intellectual and technical skills required for attaining them, while the term: Non-Formal Education is a conjunct, dynamic in its nature and flexible in its modes, consisting of socio-education activities leading to cultural adaptation to change as well as of non-structured, non-graded, non-sequential learning experiences.

These socio-educational activities and learning experiences are offered to groups and individuals involved in a transformational process so that they could possess that knowledge, those skills and those abilities which are indispensable for the implementation of the practices required firstly for achieving and then for keeping their new standards of life.

This compound of socio-educational activities and learning opportunities is particularly necessary in those geographical areas where economic development projects are taking place and a marked educational deficit exists.

Previous experiences (Panama, Tanzania, Thailand, India, Cuba, China, Vietnam) have shown that the main aims of developmental projects were attained more easily in situations where an acceleration in the rhythm of social change was produced by an educational action.

Now, if we take into consideration the fact that developmental processes are put in motion by a dialectic contraposition between tradition and modern science and technology we ought to assign, without any hesitation, to the expression: "Popularization of Science", not the meaning of scholastic lectures on scientific themes, but that of a process of endogenous transformation from old traditions into new practices, tributary to a scientific approach to the reality.

Health and nutritional developmental programmes, sanitation and water supply schemes, projects aiming at increasing basic grain production, agrarian reforms, resettlement and employment plans, establishment of agro-industries, etc. : all of them, every where in the world, narrate the story of an unceasing journey of mankind from tradition to science and technology.

How exactly does a Non-Formal Education action fit within this journey?

We think that a Non-Formal Education intervention will facilitate and accelerate any process of change, not imposing new values, but contributing to the regeneration of the existing ones, on the basis that traditions are not immutable paradigms but, on the contrary, they themselves are vectors of transformation. By its action local communities will be surely lead to modernize their living conditions, smoothly, harmonically and without traumata.

To substantiate the abovementioned statements we would like to introduce the hypothetical case of an Health Non-Formal Education Scheme, addressed to rural communities, aiming at transforming magic and religious traditions, inherent in health and diseases, in new preventive and therapeutic practices, based on scientific criteria.

The traditional medicine is ruled by three basic principles: the first attests that the human being cannot be separated from his social, religious and physical environment; the second one is that human body is a whole and must be cured as a whole and not only in some of its parts or organs; the third one is that the natural milieu, being panteistic, i.e. having life and intelligence, does permit the transfer of an illness from a free or from an animal into a person and vice versa, this consequently leads to the belief that the reestablishment of the environment's harmony, through purification, group-ceremonies, animals' sacrifices and dancing performances, will no doubt, send away all diseases from a community.

Together with these cultural performances the traditional medicine often adopts also individualistic curative measures such as that of administering vegetal potions, which are made of roots, seeds and leaves of certain plants having therapeutic qualities.

The modern medicine, on the contrary, being focused mainly on the individuality of each patient and based on the recognition, as causes of diseases, of pathogenic agents, generally prescribes cures consisting in dietary rules and in the supply of chemical medicaments.

It should be clear that to improve the health at the well-being of the rural communities many of the old traditions, no longer in line with the complex present reality, need to be transformed in modern concepts and practices, congener to science and technology.

This, however, has to be done without undermining the intrinsic structure of the social groups and their expectation of continuity, as well as without opposing in a strong way traditional beliefs, which alone ensure the efficient relationship between human beings and their natural environment.

Let us see, in the following paragraphs, by which progressive steps a Non-Formal Education Scheme could contribute to the attainment of the abovementioned targets.

Operators of the scheme ought to be a health educator, a social animator and an advisor in popularization of science.

They should elaborate, in the beginning, a design, which should be articulated in the following successive phases.

The first phase will be the preparatory one and it will consist in:

(a) The acquisition of knowledge and understanding on the social structure of rural communities, on their value system, on their traditional views vis-a-vis health and diseases, on their demographic characteristics and on their anthropological and ethnographic roots (the findings of these investigations should be then presented to the attention of the communities, so that their members could feel that their own traditions were considered of great value by the Non-Formal Education operators);

(b) The making of an inventory of the substances employed by the local pharmacopoeia specifying their qualities, so that the phyto-therapeutic partimony of those communities will be known;

(c) The identification of the traditional rural institutions that already exist in the area, selecting among them those which possess a potentiality for adaptation to new concepts and practices;

(d) The motivation of those members of the communities whose role is that of upholding traditions, such as local healers, civil judges and elected or hereditary leaders, so that they could be induced to become the main agents of change within their communities.

The second phase will be the participatory one. It will consist in making people sensible to the new approaches to health and this target should be attained by organizing group-discussion, panels, A/V presentations, questions-answers exchanges in the course of which an ensemble of new concepts on health and diseases should be conveyed to the groups, favouring their absorption by dialogues and conversations.

All the information on scientific and technological concepts should be given in non-structured, non-graded and non-sequential ways and should be close to the life experiences of the members of the communities. Moreover bridges should be built in order to establish direct communication lines between scientists and people.

The third phase will be the operational one. It will consist in introducing to the groups new hygienic, preventive and curative practices leaving them free to select those which are better commensurate to the existing cultural and social structure of their communities.

Successively, according to their choices, modern medical facilities and provisions should be put at the disposal of the rural communities and integrated, little by little, into the endogenous health system.

This seems to us that it is what Non-Formal Education can do in guiding traditional societies towards to understanding that, to face the problems of the present time, their old partimony of knowledge and behaviours should be adapted to the methods of modern science.

In conclusion, in the analyses of the role which can be played by Non-Formal Education in popularizing sciences we do realize that it can contribute not only to the infusion of science into cultures but also to the transfer of certain cultural aspects, elicited from the traditional experience of the people's life.

These latter can emerge during the preliminary anthropological and ethnographic investigations, or the maieutic exchanges of opinions between scientists and members of the rural communities as well as from the manifestations of the creative spirit of the people.

For example, remaining in the field of health, we can acknowledge the following ones: the ecological consciousness linking and interrelating human beings to their natural environment; the strict social integration among members of the same groups; the value and the effectiveness of the phytopathologic traditional pharmacopoeia and the comprehensiveness of basic existential concepts, like the concept of "water", which is not limited, as it is for us here and now, to that of a physical commodity, but comprises the relationships between water and health, water and diseases, water and sanitation, water and religion, water and the social structure of the community, water and life.

Consequently Non-Formal Education can surely play a crucial role in overcoming the dichotomy, peculiar to all process of change, between imported science and technology on one hand and cultural partimony of traditional beliefs and customs on the other hand.

In fact, while science encourages culture to adopt models that are innovative and enterprising, and this without undermining the cultural principle of identity, it can be, to its turn, enhanced by elements of traditional wisdom brought forward by culture.

If so, the people, made by education able to master the writing and reading skills, could not only autonomously open the book of science but also add to it additional chapters, containing cultural themes congenial to the needs of our current days.

Finally, it can be said, therefore, that Non-Formal Education may deserve to be designated as a hinge between science and culture.

# 3

# The Popularization of Science and Technology From an Educational Designer's Standpoint

FRED GOFFREE

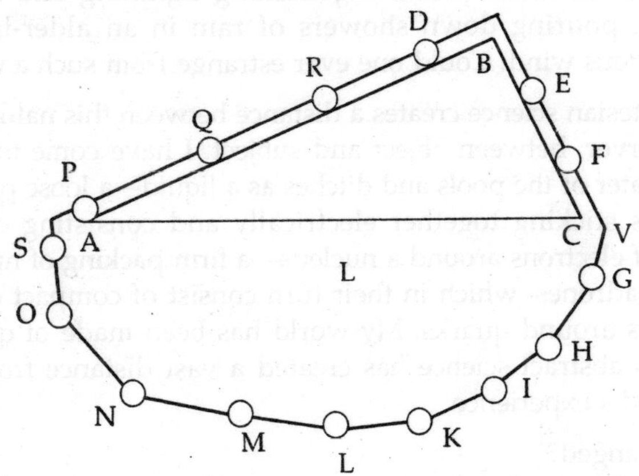


On the sides AB and BC of the vertical triangle ABC are the physical points D and E equal weight G, connected by a cord which has passed on a pulley at T. What is the proportion between the forces by which D and E are pulled down along the sides AB and BC? We imagine that D and E form part of a string, on which physical points of weight G have been threaded at mutually equal distances, and ask what this string will be going to do. When it begins to move it will after having moved, look exactly as it did at first, so that the movement will continue. So perpetual motion is created, which must be regarded as absurd. So the string will remain in rest; this rest will not be disturbed when the pending part at A and C is removed. From this it follows that the part of the string at AB keeps that at BC in balance. Now, as the number of points along both sides are in proportion to the lengths of these sides, the forces at one of these points along either side will be universely proportional to the length of those sides (Simon Stevin's Clootrans proof, 1586).

With thanks to the National Institute for Curriculum Development SLO, who through their technical and financial support enabled me to perform this study. SLO, Enschede, The Netherlands.

'As a little boy I got to know nature in a world of fermenting peat and stiff reed rustling in the eternal wind, of silent pools and ditches with incessantly ripping water, and of drifting clouds passing quietly overhead in constantly changing shapes, or at times producing flashing lightning and rolling thunder, pouring down showers of rain in an alder-lashing tempestuous wind. Could one ever estrange from such a world?

Cartesian science creates a distance between this nature and the observer, between object and subject. I have come to think of the water of the pools and ditches as a liquid—a loose packing of atoms sticking together electrically and consisting of thin clouds of electrons around a nucleus—a firm packing of nuclear-bound hadrones, which in their turn consist of compact clouds of gluons around quarks. My world has been made of quarks. And this abstract science has created a vast distance from my childhood's experience.

Estranged?'

(Andriesse, C.C., De Diefstal van Prometheus (Prometheus's theft, only in the Dutch language, Amsterdam 1985).

### 1. Determination of Standpoints

The author studied mathematics and later pedagogics. In the intersection of these two areas he performed didactical research and development work. The results had to be made accessible to teachers training in mathematics. Now the question was how to use the developed materials in the classroom and how to add the scientific knowledge acquired to the maths teacher's professional skill. The answering of these questions again led to an educational design: a Mathematics & Didactics curriculum for teacher training.

Meanwhile his attention was drawn to educational designing. Mathematicians have throughout the ages made more or less successful attempts to explain mathematics to others, laymen and colleagues alike. Each explanation, each attempt to make a mathematical invention accessible to others, is an educational design in itself! If a certain part of science can catch on with more or less outsiders depends on numerous factors. Just remember the problem with which János Bolyai was faced in the 1830s when he was trying to draw the experts' attention to his invention, Non-Euclidian geometry. To be able to understand the new theory, it was necessary to know not only the language of science and Latin and to have insight into mathematics, but also to abandon the established world view.[2] Something like this happened in the beginning of this century when physicists began to study the structure of matter. The quantum theory resulting from this study was incompatible with the classical image of mechanics which was developed by Newton and others. The determination of classical mechanics gave way to uncertainty, expressed in the uncertainty principles of Heisenberg and Schrödinger's equation. The developments in this area, from Rutherford's atom model to such applications as laser, compact disk and the tunnel electron microscope, were recently (April, May, June 1989) made accessible to a vast public via the 'From Quantum to Quark' course on Dutch educational television (Teleac). The author or the present paper was one of the participants in the course. He experienced personally what it meant to make acquaintance with natural science in a popularizing way. The total course comprised 10 TV and 10 radio lessons of half an hour each and a beautiful designed course book. Educational material providing a reference basis for the realization of an essential 'learning project', as was described by Allen Tough in the 1970s when a growing interest was shown in adults education. But the ideal the author had in mind with respect to adults education, could not be properly realized.[3] What actually was lacking in this course from this point of view was the interaction with others, in which the knowledge acquired could have been shared, weighed and discussed with those others. With the above considerations as a background, the author started the preparation of the present paper. The situation regarding the popularization of Science and Technology in the Netherlands was made the object of a brief study. Educational designing, adults teaching, mathematics and physics, in this order of importance, determine the plan which affords the author a certain amount of safety.[4] He is well aware that Science and Technology constitute an essential part of daily life in the Netherlands, and also that making them accessible to a vast public will also be followed attentively by the scientific world and could unduly get out of hand under pressure of commerce.

So he started out as an educational designer in the border area between two cultures. On the one side the (sub)culture of scientists speaking their own language, where the work is bound to strict rules of conduct, where publicizing has become of vital importance. On the other side there is the culture of all those others who at least tolerate the scientists, perhaps encourage or even stimulate but certainly pay them and put their confidence in them or not. So they went in search of opportunities to materialize the interaction between these two cultures. Interaction based on information, communication and education in non-formal settings and with informal methods. In the following section the author from his background reflects on the theme 'popularization of science and technology' and on the question 'what can non-formal and informal education do?' A number of ideas came up, which enabled him to take a targeted view of the situation presenting itself in Netherlands.

## 2. Reflections on the Theme

### *2.1 On the Popularization of Science and Technology*

In the Netherlands it is mainly the scientific journalists who determine the image of popularization. The profession of scientific journalist is still in its infancy; in the early 1970s the impulse was given by the scientific world itself.[5] In the beginning it was limited in particular to popularizing, elucidating and explaining the research, but it was not long a critical standpoint was assumed. The so-called broad public debate on nuclear energy in 1978, initiated and subsidized by the Government, fits well into this picture. It was not only a matter of understanding better what was going on, but one should be able to join the discussion on the whys of the developments and the possible consequences thereof.[6] A matter that is often ignored in the discussion, is the fact that 'the public' must have at least some basic knowledge of the matter in question and must have learned how to use the information supplied in practice. In this connection one could speak of cultural literacy.[7] Against the background of cultural literacy the following characterization of 'popularizing' gets a clear meaning: the image of scientific knowledge is simplified in such a way as to make the outsider understand the consequences, although he cannot reconstruct it himself. It is, of course, a question of how one wishes to interpret 'understand'. In mathematics didactics it is customary to distinguish between the various kinds of understanding. A distinction which could possibly also be useful in the popularization of scientific knowledge, viz.:

1. receptive understanding: one has been able to follow the argumentation, but cannot retell anything thereof;
2. reproductive understanding: one can reconstruct the argumentation, but the knowledge acquired is insufficient for application in a new situation;
3. productive understanding: by applying the newly acquired knowledge one can solve problem and even extend one's knowledge.

There is also another approach to 'understanding' in mathematics didactics which may be useful when thinking about popularization. It was the English mathematics teacher-psychologist Richard Skemp who, following the Norwegian teacher trainer, Stieg Mellin-Olsen, put forward another difference:

> Instrumental understanding versus Relational understanding. In the first case one understands only 'what must be done'. Each problem with an algorithm for finding the solution. Teachers can also give an instrumental explanation: tackle the problem in this way and you will get the correct answer. The real study of

mathematics asks for more, for insight into relations and answers to why-questions. In this case we speak of relation understanding, one has insight into the matter one grasps the mathematical structure and can proceed on the basis thereof.

If popularizing of scientific knowledge in intended to weave that knowledge into the existing culture, we must overstep the boundaries of receptive and instrumental understanding. Reports from the scientific journalistic world support this consideration.[8]

With levels of understanding, everything has not been said, however. It is also a matter of how science is understood in society. This means that not only scientific knowledge should be popularized and didactized, but also capita from the philosophy of science. In Dutch society, where scientific knowledge is regarded as the principal source of education, for example, there is the interesting question of how to make large group realize that the old scientific ideal, viz. finding 'the truth', has meanwhile been abandoned. And also that a large number of the choices made within the scientific society, are not only based on internal and rational considerations, but inter alia also originate from ethical considerations or political pressure.

Science is the work of humans; this is the idea which, despite the enormous achievements in our century, stands out clearly. How these (sometimes ingenuous) people did their scientific work, what personal elements influenced the work, how progress was made and which role was played thereby by the interaction with colleagues, constitute the elements of a story that cannot be retraced in any scientific report whatsoever. It is a story which none the less should be told, like all those other stories in which culture is transmitted from one generation to another. Here we may expect interesting contributions from scientific sociologists.[9] Information from ethnomethodological research in the places of scientific society where interesting work is performed, whereby use is made of conversations, logbook notes and interviews, are as many aids in the writing of these stories.

In addition to philosophy and sociology, the history of science can also be a rich source for those having made popularization their aim.[10] Alan Bishop, a renowned mathematics didactician in the UK breaks a lance for the history of mathematics in his recent book 'Mathematical Enculturation'. Whoever wishes to see mathematics as part of our culture and starts organizing education in mathematics along those lines, will not be able to get around those who invented mathematics and their stories. Now the personal acquisition of mathematical knowledge and skill requires more than just taking cognizance of stories about the origination of mathematics. Mathematics, as Bishop puts it, is 'a way of knowing'. In current terms it is to be regarded as a technology, notably a symbolic technology. Mathematics is a toolbox as well as the skill to use it in all kinds of situations. A person wishing to make the technology his (intellectual) property, will have to practice mathematics himself and make (re)inventions himself. Although this demand exceeds the objectives of popularization, the approach of mathematics as a subculture and the proposals he makes to get an enculturation process going, can also contribute to the popularization. The more so as a global movement has recently been started which has chosen 'ethomathematics', as they call it, as a starting point for mathematics education. Which means formal mathematics education founded on informal procedures and intuitive concepts. This observation takes us to the following section, in which we shall try to develop some insight in regard to non-formal and informal education, to what we could understand by this and what opportunities such settings offer in regard to the popularization of science and technology.

### *2.2 What Non-formal and Informal Education Can Do*

A person elaborating scientific knowledge for educational purposes is called a (specialist or general) didactician. The didactician's activities can best be indicated as 'didactizing'. Those performing the same work on behalf of groups in society that do not acquire the information via formal education, are called information officers, whose task it is to popularize. The difference between didactizing and popularizing is found in the different objectives. Also the possibilities and impossibilities of the settings (formal and non-formal) in which the results of didactizing and popularizing are developed, are different.

If we take adults education as formal education[11], the difference will fade, in particular if we consider the basic level of cultural literacy.

The levels of understanding of the foregoing section perhaps provide some clarity here. They lead to the distinction of levels in regard to didactizing and popularizing. Levels which on clear formulation of the objective and the target groups, become distinctly visible. In this case we would limit ourselves to the schematic drawing shown below.

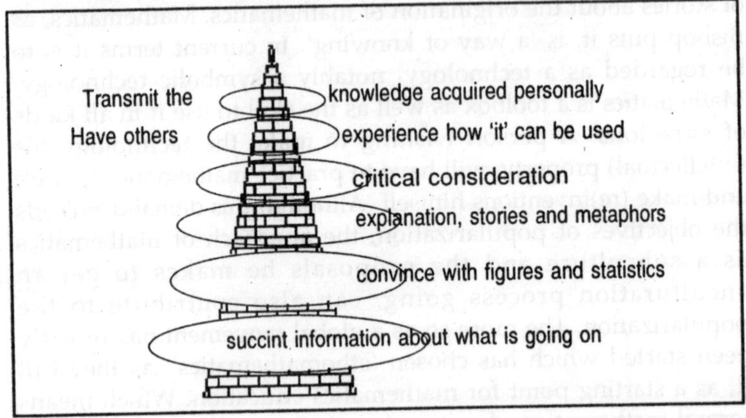


Levels of popularization and didactization and the extend of the target groups.

For the introduction of a new technology the lowest level (with the largest target group) can be translated into 'making users-friendly'. A problem will arise if the utilization of the technology has negative results, for the environment for example. To large groups of users the critical discussion at one of the higher levels in notably inaccessible, with the possible consequence that those concerned refuse to consider other ecologically sound approaches. In the Netherlands this kind of risk is recognized, but little is done to improve this. New technologies can easily be introduced via informal education.

Trade and industry have shown the possibilities in regard to numerous household utensils and implements and even to the introduction of home and personal computers.[12] The apparatuses and the daily environment offer as many opportunities to learn more efficiently than one can from the best educational course. In fact, non-formal education is at its best.

Is this also as easy in regard to information about scientific knowledge? As long as the lowest levels are concerned at which the learner need not participate himself actively in the information (learning) process, there is no reason to assume why this should not be so. That informal education can do more was described by the Dutch author Klaas Schippers form his own experience, in booklet published on the occasion of the Boekenweek (Books Week) 1989, entitled: 'Het White Schoolbord' (The White Blackboard). In this booklet he describes how, as a ten-year old after the great void of World War II, he got to know a new world via the white cinema screen. While formal education in the classroom continued as if there has been no liberation at all, he got, in the non-formal settings of the Amsterdam cinema theatres, 'informally' acquainted with many aspects of 'his own' culture.[13] Led by what was offered by the films of that time, he learnt to see his environment from a different point of view. He saw much more, also more to learn from. The opportunity of watching films turned Klaas Schipper's own environment into a learning environment. It is curious to read which details of the pictures he still remembers. The informal education apparently left deep marks. So, what informal education can do is creating opportunities which can change the environment of daily life to a learning environment. In the Netherlands this insight is being translated into concrete measures. The 'Bibliotheekproject' (Library Project) of the Amsterdam University, commissioned by the 'Nederlands Bibliotheek en Lectuur Centrum' (Dutch Library and Reading Centre), is an example of this. It led to a 'Gids voor bibliotheek en mediagebruik' (Guide for library and media usage), whereby the utilization of all resources offered by the library is made more attractive and easier for a wider public. The following section tells about the ways in which an increasing number of organizations and institutions are giving shape to the ideas referred to.

A remaining question, however, is what induces the general public to avail themselves of the opportunities offered. Like in education, the problem of motivation plays a role here. Klaas Schippers was intrinsically motivated to learn from 'the white blackboard'; the spirits moving him were stirred up only from the outside. Was it perhaps the design of the learning environment or the stories with accompanying pictures, or possibly just the space allowed to him to put his own fancy and imagination to work that made this informal education so successful? Further investigation would seem useful here.[14] In the foregoing, the idea of individual competition was already tacitly assumed. How can the individual, participating in today's society be informed about and be involved in the results of science and technology? That is how the definition of the problem could at any rate be regarded. It was also one of the questions presenting itself in adult education. This question otherwise made the designers of material for adult education stick closely to the rigid scholastic approach of education despite their criticism on regular education. In response thereto Mr. De Zeeuw, professor of methodology of adults educational research at the Amsterdam University, suggested a change of views. Against individual competence he poses the idea of collective competence, instead of the (traditional) introductory model he suggests the participation model.

Let us now closely follow his thinking. By way of example we take the field of arithmetic in the context of a camping shop at the cote a'Azur in the south of France. Competent arithmeticians are a common phenomenon. They are capable of making mental calculations in virtually every situation. They something choose playful methods just for the fun of it, which lead even more quickly to good results. They calculate in a relaxed manner and cannot be put off their stroke by lookers-on. They often also see something special in numbers which others do not notice. They see, for example, that the number 37 has something particular: multiply by 3 it figures out at 111. And when ask to multiply 24 by 37, they answer: 888, without hesitation. Competent arithmeticians feel up to any arithmetical problem; they calculate skilfully, efficiently, relaxed and with pleasure. They do a lot of 'mental' calculating and know exactly when the moment has come to resort to pencil and paper. At times they can also be seen using calculators.

The cash girls of the camping shop always use the adding machine, which even indicates the change to be returned to the customer. When she is running out of small coins, she does the calculating herself. For example, the customer owes an amount of Frs 31.35 and offers a Frs 50 note, upon which the girl asks:

have you got Frs 1.35? If he has, she keys in 'Received Frs 51.35', and reads out: 'Return Frs 20.00'. These girls are highly competent to make calculations, although a great deal of the competent mental arithmetician's performance remains a secret to them.

Some school masters in the Netherlands are rather fussy about this; as they see it, these girls are not competent to do arithmetical work at all. There are even adults who had not properly learned arithmetic at school and who primarily refuse to use a calculator. They want to learn what they missed at school and regard the calculator more or less as a prothesis to offset a handicap. Now back to the camping shop. Sometimes one of the cash girls must assist at the bread counter in the back of the shop. The croissants are put in a bag and the shop assistant notes down on the bag the amount to be paid. One croissant costs Frs 3.20 and the number of croissants bought is somewhere between 1 and 16. This takes a lot of figuring, with the cash desk so far away! No way! At the bread counter they have a table with the prices from 1 u/i 20 croissants, which is continually consulted.

Mr. De Zeeuw would say that the girls in that shop are competent arithmeticians. And he observes that the arithmetic competence has got a new face, a different character due to the presence of the apparatus. To many members of society, however, the possibilities of the calculator still remain hidden. In this regard De Zeeuw speaks of the background of a competence. He then declares that in certain cases it can be very useful to change the character of a competence by changing the background, by finding possibilities in it. This applies not only to arithmetic, but also to motoring, planning a journey or preparing a meal, to mention only a few things. New knowledge and new technology may change the nature of competences. To this end changes must be made in the backgrounds of the traditionally defined competences and one has to learn things that the different from those one was used to. Thereby problems can present themselves as schoolteachers showed in the case of the pocket calculator. The fact that things in the non-formal atmosphere of the camping shop apparently went well, is encouraging and demonstrates the importance of the influence of the context on the motivation to learn.

De Zeeuw goes even further. He observes that in our society the opinion is held that those 'entering' society must have achieved competence in regard to a certain supply of knowledge. Hence the school for juveniles and brush-up courses for adults who in some way or other missed the boat at school. Those who hold this opinion, base their ideas on the so-called introduction model. Education, schooling or training precede the introduction of any part of society whatsoever. One can also take a different view by not beginning to think in terms of the minimal individual competence which everyone should have to be able to function properly in society, but by finding out to what extent the collective competence of society can grow. Together people have a vast amount of knowledge and know-how at their disposal and it is advisable for individuals to profit from it and, if possible, to contribute to it. This can be realized by participating in activities in society. Those who wish to buy a motor-car, make inquiries at the Automobile Club, the dealers and the exchange, the traveller can avail himself of the opportunities offered by the travel agency, and cookery books, cookery columns in the papers and Cooking with Nelly on TV make a real cook out of the culinary amateur. In order to make the vast amount of knowledge and know-how accessible to a wide public, opportunities must be provided for many to take part in activities. De Zeeuw in this connection therefore speaks of the 'participation model'. Changing the drawbacks of competences, giving elucidations to it and enabling inspiring activities to be performed is what can be done informally.

In the following section an insight is given into the Dutch situation. We can then also evaluate the chances of the participation model in the Netherlands.

## 3. Popularizing in the Netherlands

### *3.1 Random Choices From History*

The Netherlands have a rich history in the field of natural sciences and in attempts to involve major groups in society in the development thereof. This history is described in detail (and in a popularizing way) inter alia in the book 'In Stevin's footsteps' by Prof. K. Van Berkel (Amsterdam, 1985). Simon Stevin (1548-1620) can indeed be regarded as a shining example.

He lived in a period when science and the (often technical) applications thereof were regarded as a whole. This led, amongst others, to the circumstance that he on the one hand gratefully availed himself on the brainwork of such classical scholars as Euclid and Ptolemeus, and on the other hand aimed at major user groups through his work. The peerless didactician (see also the clootcrans proff on the cover of this paper) wrote in the national language (and not in the language of the scientists) and paid every attention to the presentation. Of his works we mention 'Beginselen der Weegkunst' (1586) (Principles of the Art of Weighing) about statics, and 'De Thiende' (1585) (The Tenth) in which the introduced decimal fractions and their application to 'stargazers, land surveyors, carpet measures, wine measurers, body measurers, mint-masters and all merchants'. Science was an 'engineers' science' also in the centuries thereafter. In 1736 it was the physicist Petrus van Musschenbroek (Apparatus of Musschenbroek, the pyrometer), who made an attempt to make the Newtonian physics and Bacon's ideas about 'experimental physics' accessible to a wide public. He wrote 'Beginselan van de Natuurkune, beschreven ten dienste van de landgenoten' (Principles of Physics, written on behalf of fellow-countrymen). The state of affairs in physics in this 18th century was such that popular scientific readings were held throughout the country. An essential condition was the possibility of demonstrating physical tests. For instance Deniël Gabriël Fahrenheit, who came from Danzig and settled in Amsterdam in 1718, showed all kinds of variants of barometers and thermometers. An interesting incidental fact was that there was question of an interaction between the 'scientists' and 'the public', because also amateurs from the public made contributions to the development of science, as is now the case again with the computer science in our era. In the second half of the 18th century 'learned societies' (such as the Wiskunding Genootschap (Mathematical Society)), which until this day have developed certain activities for a small group of interested persons and also the Dutch Society of Science were formed. From that moment popularization was institutionalized. Prize contests are held, discourses are published, natural-scientific collections are built up and lectures are given. What the Society wished to promote was practical science. The formulation of the first prize contest (1753) is a good example of this: 'To what extent have the Dutch rivers got bogged down since the beginning of this century? In what way can the sand and mud flats that have settled on the bottom be removed and bogging down be prevented?'

Due to the interactive nature of the popularization and the dominance of the Societies over University science-practising, popularizing could also have an adverse effect on the development of science. What formerly was easily 'explainable' via demonstrations, for example, were subjects from optics. But the abstract mathematics of Newton, Bernoulli and Euler did not offer these possibilities. Therefore the core of Newton physics, the mathematical description of natural phenomena, had to be passed over. This to a certain extent applied equally to the growing complexity of the experiments. For example, Antonie van Leeuwenhoek's microscopy could not be made accessible to a wide public because of the inimitability of the observations. As a result, interest of science dwindled. The bottom fell out of it, so to say.

Gradually university science was getting more chances to develop, and from then on a new (sub)culture came into being. Scientists began to withdraw into the 'ivory tower' and hardly bothered to respond to 'outside' rumours. Every now and then the general public hears something of which the essence and sometimes also the ready-for-use results remain hidden. In the second half of the present century, as already observed, the necessity of giving information and of interaction with society stood out clearly. By and by the Government economies which in particular also affected the universities, have given to information a commercial aspect: he who can credibly 'sell' 'his' science can be assured of the necessary subsidy.

One interesting moment from the history of popularization should not remain unnoticed here. It was way back at the end of the 18th century, at the time when the aftermath of the French Revolution was beginning to make itself felt in the Netherlands. Before 1795 each region had its own weights and measures, which were strongly determined by the various contexts in which measuring was done. The names of the weights and measures had a 'couleur locale' and were hardly interchangeable. From the point of view of the national authorities this was intolerable and at the time of the French Oppression measures were consequently taken to introduce the 'Metriek Stelsel' (Metric System). In 1802 Johannes Henricus Van Swinden, professor at Franeker and Amsterdam, was commissioned to write a 'Verhandeling over Volmaakte Maten en Gewichten' (Treatise on Perfect Weights and Measures). Although Van Swinden had been chosen for his extensive expert knowledge and didactic qualities, this did not work properly. In 1809 Louis Napoleon therefore dictated the introduction of the metric system. Even this did not work and in 1812 also the old measures were again allowed in official documents. It was not until 1820 when the metric system was definitively introduced. Although even till this day the old surface and contents measures are occasionally still being mentioned in rural regions.

What does history teach us within the scope of popularization and education? First of all that, where technology and science go together, the provision of information is facilitated. This is strengthened further as soon as it becomes possible to give demonstrations with apparatuses and equipment. It is, however, rendered more difficult if the application of abstract symbolises such as mathematics becomes necessary. If giving information alone is no longer sufficient and a wide public must be convinced that they have to change to other customs, other educational tunes should be changed to. If, moreover, a symbolic technology is concerned, such as the introductions of the metric system (and at an earlier time the introduction into Europe of the Arabic figures to replace the Roman figures), it is very much the question if the limited possibilities of informal and non-formal education are indeed sufficient.

### *3.2 The Current Situation in The Netherlands*

Here, too although to a lesser extent than regard to history, we have to limit ourselves to some striking examples. Of particular interest are the example in which invisible elements of science and technology are brought to the fore for a wider public to enable changes to be made in the backgrounds of competences. They contribute to a better insight into the aforementioned participation model and the idea of collective competence.

*3.2.1 Non-Specialist Publications*

In the radio lessons 'Van Quantum tot Quark' (From Quantum to Quark) by the Nederlands Educative Televisie (Dutch Education Television) 'Teleac', a number of non-specialist books on quantum physics were discussed. 'The Dancing Wu-Li Masters' by Gary Zukav and 'QED. The Strange Theory of Light and Matter' by Richard Feynman (both books translated into Dutch) are outstanding example of publications which can show up well within the scope of an informal course. To any person interested they offer an opportunity to develop the work of the course into a substantial 'learning project'. This applies equally to several other publications available in the Dutch language. As examples of books given for a birthday present to the interested laymen in the Netherlands we would mention in this respect: Rudy Rucker: The Fourth Dimension, 1984; Hoffstätter: Gödel, Escher, Bach, 1979, and Nigel Calder, Einstein and the Universe, 1979.

*3.2.2 Educational Television*

In 'Teleac magazine', Spring 1989, were announced: De Twaalf Provincien (The Twelve Provinces) (geography of our own country), Geschiedenis van Rusland (history of Russia), de Trojaanse Oorlog (The Trojan War), De Jaren Dertig (The 1930s), de Planeten (The Planets), Van Quantum tot Quark (From quantum to Quark), zelf Mode Maken (making Your own Fashion), Grafische Technieken (Graphic Techniques), Financieel Management (Financial Management), Effectief omgaan met Conflicten (Effective Handling of Conflicts), Rechtswijzer (Law Guide) (practical information about laws relating to persons and families), Ouderen Wijzer (Guide for the Elderly) (practical information for persons of and over the age of 55), Meer Culturen en Erflaters (Multiple Cultures and Testators); three language courses: Taal van allegad (Everyday Language) (elimination of illiteracy), Latin (Roman language and culture) and Andiamo (holiday course in Italian). For the next season a Dutch version of the American programme 'The Mechanical Universe' has been announced in addition to other programmes. Besides Teleac, also the Radio Volks Universiteit (Radio Adults University) presents popularizing programmes. On August 8 the Dutch TV viewers could see a one-hour programme in which the latest novelties in the field of 'electronics in the household' were shown. In this programme three families were followed in their own households (with a.o. telephone, video recorder, video camera, magnetron, computer, modern, electronic shopping, CD player); they visited a 'house of the future' and commented on it.

*3.2.3 Informal Course Work*

The abovementioned RVU originates from the long-reputed Dutch Adults Universities. They offer an extensive range of courses: To suit all tastes. At present local, often Municipality-subsidized courses are held, from elementary English to philosophy, from illiteracy elimination courses to art history. And, within the scope of popularization, also informatics for women.

*3.2.4 Technique Museums*

The big cities of Amsterdam, The Hague, Rotterdam, Utrecht and Eindhoven each have a more or less well-known technique museum. The Evoluon at Eindhoven (the place where the cradle of the Philips concern stood), the Amsterdam technique museum 't NINT, the Utrecht University Museum and Museum at the Hague are doing their utmost to create a kind of interactive science and technology centres according to a British model. So more workshops than comic strip, with the object of making the public occupy themselves (inter)actively with science and technique. They also make use of technique themselves, audio-visual media in particular, to show the exhibited objects in many subtle distinctions. But the context of a museum, with its casual and often unprepared visitor, is hardly suitable for intensive acquisition of complicated knowledge. Only if the possibilities of a museum as a workshop can be utilized in a wider scope, can a certain amount of profundity be achieved. The museum may be said to bring otherwise invisible objects to the fore, but changes in the background of certain competences require more energy than is in general invested in a visit to the museum.

*3.2.5 Federation 'De Jonge Onderzoeker' (The Young Researcher)*

In 1967 a Dutch broadcasting corporation according to the US Science Fairs model organized a contest for young researchers. Two years later the Stichting 'De Jonge Onderzoeker' (the Young Researcher) was established, to which Prince Bernhard, husband of the then queen Juliana, was appointed honorary chairman. In the years between 1970 and 1985 the Foundation issued a periodical of its own and organized local 'juvenile laboratories' in particular. (The first in 1969 at the Evoluon at Eindhoven). The Foundation has meanwhile been changed to a Federation of the local foundations which are kept going through sponsoring and municipal contributions. Until this day the periodical 'De Jonge Onderzoeker' has been published as a quire of the popular-scientific periodical 'Mens en Wetenschap' (Man and Science).

The activities of 'De Jonge Onderzoeker' may be regarded as popularization of science and technique for young people, the activities are performed in non-scholastic settings and inspire an indeed small group of youngsters to make major intellectual efforts on different levels. Things that remain hidden in the education programmes of the various schools (mainly creative occupation with concrete material in projects) are limelighted in the juvenile laboratories. For a few years now attempts have been made to rouse the interest of girls as well ('Techniek 10' for girls only and the Foundation 'Jeugd en Techniek' for girls and boys alike). Annually, contests are organized as well as the 'Dutch Science Week' for Juvenile European researchers, but also contacts are established with other countries: young dutch researchers are sent to workshops abroad and assistance is rendered in the equipping of juvenile laboratories (of which there are twelve in the Netherlands and where one or more of the following subjects are being studied: chemistry, electronics, geology, model-making, biology, photography, computers, physics, rocket construction and video), whereby the Government assists in developing a curriculum for the subject 'Techniek', which will be introduced before long in secondary education.

### 3.2.6 *The Subject 'Techniek' in the Secondary Curriculum*

Although with this subject we have entered the field of formal education, this must not remain unmentioned here.

Formally, 'Technique' featured only in the curricula of vocational schools, and physics teachers of the other school types hardly got round to technical applications. Not well-known utensils are becoming subjects of technical studies, both practically and theoretically. If this subject fulfils what it promised, all Dutchmen will get a certain degree of technological literacy, which will at least facilitate and hopefully encourage the digestion of popularized scientific information in extracurricular settings. What has so far been developed in the curricula for technique is, however, making a very schoolish impression. This is inter alia the result of the elaboration in non-interesting details of lists of objectives. It has appeared to be still impossible to include in these. lists the 'creative room' of De Jonge Onderzoekers.

*3.2.7 Dalta Expo*

Different from the Technique Museum in the Netherlands are the visitors' centres, which give an introduction to a nearby phenomenon. They are found in nature parks and nature reserves, e.g. the wadden Sea in the far North of the Netherlands. A special place is held by Delta Expo in the Netherlands, of which a substantial part lies below sea level, and which has of old fought a heroic battle against the water. Dikes were built, the dunes along the seashore were strengthened, lakes were converted to fertile polder land, a large dam was constructed in the north of the Netherlands and vast parts of the then closed-off sea were impoldered. After the devastating flood of 1953 a new and ambitious plan was made to protect the North Sea shore in the Southwest Netherlands for ever against the sea: the Delta plan, which received international attention. One of the last major feats was the construction of a flood barrier to protect the coasts against the violence of the waves during the numerous autumnal storm tides on the one hand and to regulate the water level flexibly up to a large distance on the other. In the vicinity of this product of technical expertise and scientific thinking a permanent exhibition was established where at three different levels historical, hydraulic, geographical and ecological knowledge can be acquired. The implements, (scale)models, pictures, outlines, diagrams and sounds presented on the floors of the exhibition space, are shown in practice when one looks out of the window or, even better, if one takes the time to visit the flood barrier by round-trip boat. The designer, Jan van Tooren, based this project on a very special philosophy. One of the ideas developed therein is that visitors should be enabled to form their own opinion on this technology and its consequences in regard to society. This is to a certain extent in contradiction to what the principal, the Public Works Department, had in mind.

Visitors centres worldwide can give particulars about intensive-information methods. The idea that the visitor should be enabled to plot his own 'educational path' through/on/in the phenomenon. It is not inconceivable that 'visitors centres' present a good metaphor for popularizing science and technique at one of the higher levels.

*3.2.8 Daily Papers*

In 1981 one of the principal dutch daily papers, 'De Volkskrant' (People's Newspaper) was the first to insert a special quire 'Wetenschap en Samenleving' (Science and Society). In 1986 it appeared to be worthwhile to compile a selection of 50 articles from quires of the previous year in 'Jaarboek 1986. Wetenschap en Samenleving' (Yearbook 1986. Science and Society). In June 1989 this book was obtainable in a supermarket at 6.5 per cent of the original price. The 50 articles feature 11 main subjects: astronomy, space travel, landscape, hydraulics (a.o. 'De faalkans van de storm-vloedkering' (The chance of failure of the flood barrier)), energy, environment, medical developments, physics (a.o. 'Kijken in het binnenste van een atoomkern' (Looking into the inside of an atomic nucleus)), biotechnology, computers and miscellaneous subjects. What is keeping scientific journalism busy at the moment? To get an idea of this, we consulted another well-reputed daily paper, NRC-Handelsblad. This paper also has a weekly quire: 'Wetenschap en Onderwijs' (Science and Education). It as a rule consists of a small number of leading articles, an extensive book review, the typification of a certain instalment of a popular scientific periodical, a larger number of short informative reports (from a.o. textile dyeing, chips for navigation systems and the problems concerning potable water) and occasionally an in-depth discussion of an interesting dissertation. Also the irregularly appearing column 'Reken Maar' is highly interesting because people are made to think about and to make calculations based on quantitative data which are usually accepted as a matter of course.

The following enumeration of titles of some leading articles in the quires of June 13 to June 25 (1989) inclusive could perhaps give an impression (mind that a holiday period is concerned here):

Mathematical models with the computer

Jaw-bone inflammation and antibiotics

Aids and other veneral diseases

The academic debate

DNA fingerprints under fire

The history of transvestism

Flying kites with satellites

The problematic place of natural science in society

Video camera and its significance for anthropology

Abortion pill works, but may not

Pausiana's travel guide for Greece re-instated

Exotic plants and animals in the Netherlands

Life after the construction of the flood barrier

Herman E. Daly and his Plimsoll line for economy

Information of Central Statistical Office too expensive

Prions are perhaps not very rare

First gen therapy with man meets substantial opposition

Characteristic of the leading articles of both daily papers is that:

- they have been placed in a social-economic context
- numerical data are preferred as eye-catchers
- attention is paid to possibilities of application
- future developments are anticipated
- explanations in outline of problem definitions and principles are given

- also information about the history of the development is given
- sometimes brief theoretical remarks are inserted (leV=..)
- functional or non-functional illustrations are inserted to enliven to article
- the motive is often found in a forthcoming congress or a controversial article, sometimes it is the scientists themselves who seek publicity.

On account of the prescribed small extent of some articles in daily papers and the lack of foreknowledge of the general public, the article usually have to be limited to 'information in outline'. Yet the authors must also reckon with expert readers, not only by avoiding mistakes, but also as regards the contents of the information. In certain articles both levels can be recognized; they are real examples of expert didactization.

*3.2.9 The Stichting Publieksvoorlichting over Wetenschap en Technologie (Foundation for Public Information About Science and Technology)*

This foundation was formed in 1986 on the initiative of the Dutch Government. In the Netherlands of the early part of the 1980s it was planned to give science and technique a broad social basis for innovative reasons. For the first 5 years of its existence the Stichting will provisionally be subsidized by the ministries of Onderwijs & Wetenschappen an Economische Zaken (Education & Science and Economic Affairs) to an annual amount of Hfl 5 million; it has an independent status. Honorary chairman is Prins Claus, queen Beatrix's husband. The other Board members are experts from the world of science, the media and trade and industry. There are 12 office workers.

The purpose of the foundation is to promote the provision of information to a wide public about developments in the fields of science and technique and to promote independent formation of opinion through all kinds of activities. An interesting thought is the idea that in certain cases this will succeed better 'by explaining why and how science and technique have produced a certain thing than by explaining exactly how it works'.

The Stichting has also chosen the following lines of approach: scientific, social, cultural, human (the developments are mainly determined by persons) and global (with the consequences for the Third World). The planned activities for 1989 include: stimulation of radio and TV programmes (the programme 'Van Quantum tot Quark' was subsidized with Hfl 170,000), releases of agendas of activities to the press, issuance of a Newsletter, insertion of articles in door-to-door papers, assistance in arranging exhibitions, setting up a data bank, co-operation with other institutions in this field, giving information to scientific journalists, organization of workshops and study tours for journalist, assistance in organizing press conference, organization of public days, programming of the National Science Week and maintenance of the 'Science Line': any one having a question in the fields of science and technique can phone 06-821.2144 at Hfl 0.20/minute. Information is also supplied in writing.

In arranging the activities the arrangers go about in a target group-oriented manner. They expressly do not aim at motivating non-interested persons and those with a low educational level, or at providing a cultural literacy basis. This is the task of regular education, they argue. As the Stichting is still in its infancy it is impossible to give a characteristic of its work as yet. In 1991 an evaluation will be made in connection with the possible continuation of the Stichting. PWT co-operates with inter alia NOTA, a government organization engaged in investigations concerning the possible social consequences of the introduction of new technologies.

### 3.2.10 *Science Policy*

Since 1978 the Government has issued the periodical 'Wetenschapsbeleid' (Science Policy) in six editions per year. As stated in the colophon, it aims at 'promotion of the knowledge of and formation of opinion on science policy in the Netherlands. In this quality the publication contributes to the propagation of information about this subject and is intended to contribute to the discussion on the science policy to be conducted.' So information is given about the Government's doings, and also articles with opinions of others are included. The main purpose is to keep the discussion in the Netherlands going on basis of correct and factual information.

**4. Conclusion**

The foregoing is not the result of a thorough study, because the time available therefor was too short. Yet the cursory study in the Dutch territory has revealed some matters that may offer a contribution to the practice and theory of popularizing.

First of all there is a low interest in basic insights, skills and attitudes 'the public' need to be able to profit from science information. In and outside the normal education patterns the propagation of a cultural literacy can be engaged in. The Dutch development in regard to De Jonge Onderzoekers and the new subject Technique indicate a possible direction. The idea of 'room' for personal fantasy and creativity is important. But also on the level of information it should be possible to do more in the Netherlands. In the centre of this will certainly be the motivational problem: how to persuade people of that target group to participate.

Secondly, a more detailed elaboration of the participation model would be useful. The objective is to change the appearance of competences by making changes in their background. Here the stories fit in of those who are already following the right track, richly illustrated stories with which one can identify oneself.

Next, those who are willing should be enabled to materialize thorough 'learning projects' in their own surroundings. Opportunities to acquire knowledge must not remain hidden, lucid information on this point is essential. Local 'public welfare' and public institutions should attune their offers to each other so that the information flows could strengthen each other.

In non-specialist articles the stories of scientists as 'ordinary people' with all their hopes and doubts, should also be inserted. But also what is actually being performed in the field of science, what is so special about it and the possible consequences should not remain unmentioned. Popularizing in this case means telling stories, giving explanations and opinions.

Finally the visitors centre, as can be seen in many places worldwide, is an inspiring metaphor for educational designers for the higher levels of popularizing. Here A RISC TRIP is made possible in natural surrounding converted to a 'learning environment'.

**Literature**

Van Berkel, K., In het voetspoor van Stevin. Geschiedenis van de natuurwetenschap in Nederland 1508-1940 (In Stevin's Footsteps. History of natural science in the Netherlands 1508-1940), Boom, Amsterdam/Meppel, 1985.

Bishop, A., Mathematical Enculturation. A Cultural Perspective on Mathematical education, Kluwer Academic Press, Dordrecht, 1988.

Goffree, F. and H. Stroomberg (eds.), Creating Adult Learning, Theoretical and Practical Communications on Educational Design for Adults, SMD, Leyden, 1989.

Nieuwendijk, G. (ed.) Jaarboek 1986, Wetenschap & Samenleving (yearbook 1986, Science and Society), De Volkskrant, Omniboek, The Hague, 1986.

NRC Handelsblad, katern Wetenschap & Onderwijs (Science & Education quire).

13-6-'89 u/i 7-8-'89, Rotterdam, 1989.

PWT, Werkplan (Planned Activities) 1989 and Jaarerslag (Annual Report) 1989, Urecht 1989.

De Zeeuw. G., De Verborgen Vaardigheden (The Hidden Skills) in Van der Zee a.o., Volwassenenducatie. Dilemma's en Perspectieven (Adults Education, Dilemmas and Perpectives), Boom, Meppel, 1984.

**NOTES**

1. Great impression is made by the subject that enable non-experts to help thinking expertly on the subject. David Hilbert (1862-1943), for example, designed a magnificent science fiction story to explain the concept of 'infinite' and in 1884 the Victorian schoolmaster Edwin Abbott wrote a 'Romance of many Dimensions' (Flatland) to give an even larger number of readers than Hilbert had in mind, an insight into 'the fourth dimension'.

2. More generally known in this connection is the tragic history of Galilei who, with his concrete observations and intelligent interpretations did not succeed in convincing the seventeenth century's theologists that only Copernicus's vision on the solar system was correct.

3. This idea was described earlier in the introduction of the recently published book 'Creating Adult Learning'. The substance of it is that adults should be enabled to arrange their own learning as 'A risc trip' through a learning environment. 'A RISC TRIP' as a symbolic abbreviation (acronym) stands for Activity (the central issue of learning), (taking) Risks, (being) International, (making) Selections and Constructing (new possibilities). To this effect the educational designer creates Tasks, the possibility of Reflections and Interactions and stimulates the making of Productions of one's own.

4. He realises also, however, that he notes down these rules with the aid of the 'Words' word processing programme of the screen of the Apple Macintosh Plus, that the discussion on the construction of an increasing number of motorways because of the excessive growth of the car fleet is also his concern, that the information of the Scientific Annex in his newspaper on the just established dioxine poisoning of milk concerns his own environment, that the consequences of the Tsjernobil calamity are still noticeable also in the Netherlands, that Tsjernobil cannot be included in the results of the totally fallen-through 'broad public debate' which was started in 1978, on nuclear energy, that information about Aids is also addressed to his children and that the sale of CD players, video recorders, walkmans, personal computers, alarm systems and more of these technological wonders are far beyond expectations in the Netherlands. But also that in consequence of the Government economics all Dutch scientists have to sell their products as well as possible to society and that commerce has meanwhile shown how you can sell 'whatever' or 'whomever'.

5. A milestone is the inaugural lecture held by Prof. Dr. B. Smalhout, anaesthetist, entitled: 'Death on the table', in which in fact for the first time in the history of medical science a vast public was informed about errors made in the operating room. The principal daily papers in such cases give increasing space to scientific information until in the 1980s insertion of weekly quires was proceeded to: 'Wetenschap en Samenleving' (Science and Society) (De Volkskrant) and 'Wetenschap en Onderwijs' (Science and Education) (NRC-Handelsblad).

6. One if the best known scientific journalists in the Netherlands is

S.Rozendaal (Elsevier). He quotes a statement of the antibiotics researcher Rene Dubos, in which the task of scientific journalism stands out clearly: 'The kind of scientific knowledge that the general citizen needs is not the technical knowledge of the professional scientist, but a general conception which helps him to recognize and evaluate the social consequences of science and technology and which enables him to anticipate it to a certain extent. For if this conception is not anticipate it to a certain extent. For if this conception is not forthcoming, people will increasingly have to reconcile themselves to the tyranny of the expert, who thus becomes a person taking decisions without being answerable to society. Participation of the public in the decision-making process concerning scientific problems is probably essential for the coherence of the democratic societies and for the survival of their institutions.'

7. In the Netherlands this is meanwhile also being done in the discussions on the final terms for basis formation. Basis formation (only recently invented, not yet fully flashed out and by far not yet realized is education in which all Dutch citizens should participate and which is completed at about the age of 15. In the curriculum of this basis formation the subject 'Technique' has, otherwise for the first time, been included.

8. For making the new technological products accessible, matters may be a bit different. I understand my word processor instrumentally, but I do not know what to do within narrow scopes. If something unexpected happens against when, for example, a piece of text suddenly seems to have disappeared, I am on the verge of despair because I have not the slighest relational insight. Still I have a feeling that I am reasonably happy with this technology; with the aid of the guide book I can even make footnotes!

9. It is they who since the 1970s have also drawn scientific knowledge itself into their considerations because (a.o. since Kuhn's The Structure of Scientific Revolutions) the insight has taken root that the development of scientific knowledge is in particular also of social concern.

   It is not the (naturally determined factual) knowledge which determines the interaction among the scientific, but the interaction which to a substantial degree determines what scientific knowledge actually looks like.

10. At the moment it is being planned in the Netherlands to insert short stories from history (I am thereby thinking of such illustrious persons as Ampere, Archimedes, Boerhaave, Bohr, Boyle, Buys Ballot, Casimir and Copernicus, to mention only the As, Bs and

Cs) in door-to-door papers. The numerous readers of these papers, which are distributed in particular for product-advertising reason, will undoubted in particular for product-advertising reasons, will undoubtedly recognize the names of streets and squares that have been named after these celebrities. Curiously enough, these names do not occur in the history books at school and no more were the persons mentioned when the results of their scientific efforts were introduced as subject material in the classrooms.

11. Rather recently all activities such as illiteracy elimination, parents' retraining, women orienting themselves in society, arithmetic for beginners, etc., in the Netherlands were institutionalized and legally regulated.

12. Following the initially long-term study courses of programming languages or difficult word processors, one-afternoon instruction at the leader's home is now sufficient. And after the user has succeeded in mastering the principles, he gradually extends his knowledge further.

13. Thus, for example, not until two years after the liberation of 1945, he for the first time sees, via the famous Carol Reed movie The Third Man (starring Orson Welles), what and now World War II actually was.

14. Extensive experience with contemporary young persons and their dealing with the new technology has yielded sufficient wisdom to relieve research from the pre-scientific part. In the perspective of the problem formulation of this conference, investigations should be given the nature of development research. Then the question is: What does the practice of informal learning teach us in regard to the arrangement of non-formal learning environment? The answer should be given in form of instructions and clues for educational designers. Key conceptions are: learning-environment and action support.

# 4

# Patterns of Nonformal and Informal Education Effective for the Polarization of Science and Technology

ANA KRAJNC

During the last decade school system and adult education undergo very dynamic changes. The school reform was introduced on the secondary school level, in adult education and in higher education. As the feedback of this reform on upper levels, the primary school programme was changed afterwards as well. It's difficult and almost impossible to describe great changes which were brought in after 1976 by Act of education. It was a megalomanic swift, the blow which changed the school curricula (all programmes were made anew), many schools closed and many new opened. Names of the schools were completely changed and new terminology for educational area introduced. Man can easily ask, where all this energy and input comes from and what made people move so eagerly to confront the problems of education. The great need for new knowledge has pressed the politicians and public functioners, economists and developers. They realized the same what in other societies did, too; the school does not serve efficiently any more for the normal economic and social development. Worried were parents, too, and fear of what would their children know the future was dominant. The teachers shared the general opinion that schools should be renewed and modernized, but they were too much in the matter itself and therefore had difficulties to see more concretely what changes should be made in the school system. The political party was the power which carried on the school reform under the premises that technical and scientific knowledge of the population would be improved. Into school curricula were introduced new subjects (polytechnical education, working practice, computer science) and the previous subjects were revised. Officially was prescribed the ratio between technical students and others (70 against 30 in favour of the students of technical school) and all students were carefully streamed in so called new, reformed "directed (so called) education".

From outside it seemed as the carefully planned and well elaborated trial to match the formal school education with today world needs. From the reform on the education was and is still the hot issue of public discussions and many conflicts arise from there. Still the right solution has not been found yet, one could say, while the effects of education are unsatisfactory.

**From the School Reform to New Experiences**

The school reform initiated many new studies, analyses and observations of status quo and the development after the introduction of the reform during the last decade. There some important conclusions and discoveries derive from. The boom of the knowledge, world wide intensive "production of new knowledge", quick development of science and technology pressed our reformists to be engaged primarily with the quantitative dimensions of the educational reform.

The groups who were shaping the reform discussed primarily how to squeeze the great amount of knowledge which was recently produced in technology and science. The number of school hours, number of subjects and number of students became the central questions within the reformists discussions. But the needs for school hours were overwhelming and they were still not sufficient, when confronted with "quick jump" of technology and science. The school curricula dangerously expanded and in some schools the students had to stay in classrooms from early morning (7 a.m.) to late in the afternoon.

Some new space for new subjects in school curricula was made so that the previous subjects were reduced to minimum or some of them left out completely (classical languages, history, social sciences, art). This attempt swept away some subjects of general education, which gives the knowledge with highest capacity of transfer from one field of application to another. At the same time general education develops personal characteristics of the students, for most their interests, horizon, understanding of the environment, outlook, and independence in personal decision making and planning depend on it. The reformists were not aware that cutting down the subjects of general education (they called them as "unpractical", "not directly applicable", "historicistic burden") were looking primarily for practical benefits of schooling which can be seen directly and immediately in the practice. Such an accent on economic quick achievements and political goals made them "bind" for the losses and mistakes made. Instead of mathematics, physics, history of literature etc. were included the more applicable subjects like: electrotechnic, machinery, computer sciences.

But such changes the general knowledge which could fertilize the applicable more practical subjects was dangerously reduced, and the learned new knowledge remained static, paralized. The first generations of students who attended the reformed "directed education" were very unpractical in spite of their "practical and applicable subjects" in curricula. At most they were able to use their knowledge in the situation they were taught for, but the transfer and the flexibility of the knowledge was very low.

From these facts one could conclude that more important is to obtain the general wide education than the narrow (new) knowledge. Without it the students were not able to obtain new knowledge themselves or to create new knowledge. Their education made them static and predetermined. One could say that our reformists were "cutting the branch on which they were seating".

After one decade of practical experiences it is also observed that the reform relied too much only on "intentional education", on school curricula, and did not take into account the other nonformal and informal channels for obtaining knowledge. When it paid attention to other patterns of education (out of school education) the quantity, number of school hours etc. would be reduced easily and spontaneous learning in environment where the students live would make the school more pleasant and not so overloaded with subjects.

The reformists build reform only on one pattern of school education (which is most traditional and subordinated to clear planning), but loses its social and psychological roots, when treated so isolated.

As in many previous case in our school reform more attention was paid to planning, dissemination and input of formal education, and less attention was paid to the receivers, consumption of knowledge or output. Some analysis show that the results of such reform are relatively poor and not the right way to go today, when people have to consume so much new knowledge, the young ones and adults.

From our reform it can be learned that school cannot function properly without well developed adult education system. It is decisive for the school curricula, what will happen after the school. The patterns of adults' learning are complementary to children's previous formal and informal or nonformal learning.

**Drop-outs From the Schools and Informal Learning**

The drop-outs from the schools after the reform quickly grow in number. Surprisingly was that among them were very capable students with high IQs and talented, but they had difficulties to adapt to the hard rythm of the overloaded school programme. On average the drop-out grew up to 25-30 per cent of generation which entered the secondary schools. These young people had to enter work in one or another way very early and they had to learn if not in schools then in other patterns of nonformal and informal education.

The drop-outs were quickly and directly exposed to the new technology which was being introduced in enterprises when economically it could not be avoided any more. The equipment of factories is usually more modern from the school labs, and the information flow is fresh and current mixed with all kinds of domestic and foreign resources. Among the drop-outs the education shifts from formal to informal, from intentional (school) to functional education. No time is lost in between for educational planning and programming. The selection of knowledge goes in the parallel, and in the dependence with work and other social activities (entertainment, sports, health care, sociopolitical activities, cultural engagement, family life). So selected knowledge matches directly with the needs, because it is based upon the diagnoses and not the prognoses (upon which the school curricula relies upon).

The drop-outs followed in their job promotion show quick upward social mobility. They are especially successful in working or developing themselves small businesses, services and in tertiary section of economy. They are well informed and struggle for new knowledge (handbooks, short courses, professional reviews, asking specialists, travelling abroad and visiting foreign companies, trades and associations etc.) in most imaginative way usually very individual ways and methods.

Drop-outs operate as "freelanders", they have to find themselves their own way to the information they need. A lot initiative and imagination is involved in their activities they report about in some analyses made in our country during the recent 4 years. Comparing to the graduates from regular schools, who were before in schooling successful and stayed in the school to the end, the drop-outs prove some special characteristics and patterns of life still and social behaviour. They are must more imaginative in finding the proper solutions, through their behaviour they demonstrate much higher level of social independence. They operate with higher level of self-initiative. All these to the great surprise and mistrust of the teachers, who still remember then failures in the school. Teachers who met them earlier in the school treat them and approach them with a lost of mistrust and disagreement. The teachers do not believe in any other way and method of learning besides formal school education.

Our Act of Education enables the evaluation of knowledge obtained via nonformal and informal way, and after the evaluations made, the law allows even formal degrees and diplomas, which the candidates could obtain afterwards. In practice it never developed and the schools did not even name the proper commissions for evaluation of nonformally obtained knowledge. The teachers mistrust is some patterns of learning had negative consequences in our practice.

The formal education and the patterns of informal and nonformal education remain separated instead of the systematically integration, which could bring success in learning new technology and scientific development. Teachers is schools rely extremely upon formal education, while the others, who learn via nonformal education are left upon spontaneous resources of knowledge and the lack of systematization reduces their efficiency in learning.

In the described situation it is evident that "the differentiation of labour" in education did not take place yet. When this is obtained both formal and informal/nonformal education will obtain their own specific function, which should be complementary to each other.

Nonformal education of school children depends upon their possibilities for actual activities and when they are included in the real life to a greater extent, and they are not just observers of others (their parents, their teachers). Children's own actions make them learn spontaneously and matched with real needs.

**Adult Education and Learning of New Technology and Science**

Several researches proved that adults depend on nonformal and informal education in the process, when they have to obtain new technology. "Genotype" programming of school curricula, the whole methodology how to shape them leads to the static education, which obviously cannot follow quick changes in technology and science. The complementary function to the school education developed in adult education activities or "phenotype" education, which is matched with individual situations, and it is flexible, changeable and dynamic enough to guarantee the follow up with new technology and science.

In the researches made we structured adult education planning and programming into some categories according to the institutional (workers universities, factory educational centres, evening and correspondence schools for adults) and individual level of engagement:

Pattern 1: Fully institutionally prepared programme of continuing education, realization and evaluation remain within the adult education institution. Group Work.

Pattern 2: Semi institutional. Basic planning and programming done at the institution together with some in advance prepared educational means. Occasional group work. Over 70 per cent individual learning. When and how decides the learner himself.

Pattern 3: Individual learning with one basic (or sometimes two) educational mean (handbook which a person studies through). The educational means is popular, widely distributed, and used by learner as such. Learner does not search additional means. Main effort of learners, put into consuming the knowledge. The attempts to use new knowledge in practice appear in parallel with learning and immediately afterwards.

Pattern 4: Learner makes combination of many educational means, uses various resources (reading talking to experts, observing the activity and equipment, experimental use of equipment for training purposes, writing, drawing, travelling, consultations and instructions). Learner is crossword for several educational impulses. Conditions necessary are high motivation for education and ability for independent learning.

For the transfer of new technology and science among adults population is the initial animation, rise of aspirations for new equipment of methods and technology of work the unavoidable phase. It is necessary for all patterns of learning. It comes "in waves" in our social environment and it is at certain time common for most people. To illustrate this: it is possible to see in previous period that there was the time when people were interested in TV sets, it was followed with spread interest for dishwashers, later, Hi-Fi, and later video technic, and recently DC music in parallel with computers. The least interests were animated in private life needs. In parallel the technology of work has changed and computerized production is coming into the country over night.

The motivation for learning about computerized production is more existential, but still it divides the population of employees into two parts:

- the workers who struggle to obtain the necessary knowledge, they consider that their previous knowledge and abilities enable them to obtain the necessary skills and information, and they are very acceptable for knowledge,
- the other half of the workers (calculations are about 50 per cent) feel paralized by new technology. Most of them in this group are functionally illiterate. They were in school, but their professional/occupational training is industrial very narrow education, which in new area does not lead anywhere. They feel dependent from the social help and play roles of dependents. One after another such groups and loosing the jobs and *vis-a-vis* new technology they remain unemployable.

In relation with the new technology and science people find themselves in the completely different situations. The industrial type of education had deformed many of them, because their education is too narrow and insufficient for efficient further learning. They stay where they are in spite of the public animation for new knowledge, because they need first the longer process of individual development before they can accept new knowledge necessary for great technological changes and science.

Among the patterns of new knowledge transfer the third and fourth are most efficient. Of course they are suitable for the people, who can learn independently. The first two patterns show slower results and they cover up to 8-10 per cent of adults learning in our society. All other learning of adults depends upon their own search for knowledge. To find the way to the proper resource of knowledge takes approximately as much energy and time, as does the learning itself. At the same time it is necessary to have in mind, that not all attempts to get the needed knowledge are successful, many lead to dead end.

Observing these problems from an international perspective, the situation becomes even more complex. People have to continue their development (and their learning) from where they are. Not all nations are for the same distance away from the modern technology and science—their production of knowledge. The patterns of obtaining knowledge effectively develop only, when they are developed closely with the national culture and social development.

**Summary**

When the education which would bring new technology and science is discussed we touch the problem not only of knowledge (have more knowledge or have enough knowledge), but the development of new quality of man. Instead of objects man should be capable of producing ideas, innovations. He has to offer new solutions. The transition from previous stage (knowledge for serving machines in industry) to the new one (abilities for producing ideas and mastering the new technology and science giving the new face to the production and social relations) asks for deeper changes. According to the psychologists and neurologists, who are pointing out today, that men has practically no limitations for learning, when their brains are properly used. The obstacles and limitations come from the social and cultural development. Not rarely the political systems put limitations to human development and the potential natural abilities of people remain unused for ever.

The educational processes which bring about the transition from industrial stage of development to new technology, and spread out the great amount of new knowledge, can be efficient among the population only when political freedom is given for social processes, communications, and culture to brust and grow. Under the conditions of repression it is useless to expect, that the creativity, "production of new ideas", innovations which accompany new technology and science, will appear.

The popularization of new science and technology is closely related with the renaissance of spiritual values, quality of man and quality of life, the "quality of production" is the dissolution of today's world. But the expectation of new way of work and life brings to individuals and the whole nation's great fears and insecurity feelings and unrest. They may for some time in the particular social environment prevent and restrict the normal development to the new quality of man. In such socio-political conditions the transfer of knowledge, contemporary technology and science is diminished and delayed, the development of man suppressed to minimum.

The transfer of knowledge goes hand in hand with the new development of man and both with the processes of democratization which is not a luxury but necessity of economic and socio-cultural development. Complex interdependence of these processes can be discovered, when it is observed also among those societies who go in their repercussions and changes in the reverse direction, from what the development asks for.

There is also an additional factory which is to be taken into account: the discussed educational processes, new knowledge, more knowledge, and the new quality of work and life, transfer of new technology and science, cannot be any more limited to the intellectual elite, only to some individuals in each society, but it asks for mass education and mass changes. The mass approach can not be avoided in education and mass changes. The mass approach can not be avoided in education or adult education, because of the nature of new technology, which must reach certain quality of an individual, but it is interrelated and interdependent in functioning in practice. The computerized production and all what accompanies it can make only masses of people properly developed.

As much as it depends on the quality of individual and his education and development, it depends also on education and development of total population. Knowledge can not be preserved only to privileged, because when it happens, also the educated are parallized from using their knowledge. As much as the nations are dependent on each other today, so are the individuals in the society, their work are life.

**Literature**


- "L'educatione degli adulti: prospective per gli anni novanta" (Adult education: the perspectives for the nineties), Comune di Firenze, Publica istruzione, Frenze, 1987.

- Charters, A.N.; Hilton J.R.: Landmarks in International Adult Education, A Comparative Analysis, Routledge, New York, 1989.
- Titmus, C.J., edit.: "Life long education for Adults", An International Handbook, Pergamon Press, Oxford, 1989.
- Krajnc, Ana: "Yugoslavia: Trends in the development of workers education", Labour Education, No. 71-1988/1, ILO, Geneva.
- Krajnc, Ana: "New technology: Towards a knowledge-based, post-industrial society", Labour Education, No. 71-1988/1, ILO, Geneva.
- Jelenc, Zoran: "Izobrazevanje odraslih kot dejavnik nasega rezvoja" (Adult education as the factor of our development), Pedagoski institut, Ljublijana, 1989.
- Jelenc, Z.; Kodelja, J.; Mohorcic Spolar, V.; Valentincic, J.: "Odrasli v izlrazevanju v Sloveni ji do leta 2000" (Adults in education in Slovenia to the year 2000), Pedagoski institut, Lyubljana, 1989.

# 5

# Science and Technology in Public Adult Education

KLAUS PEHL

## The Volkshochschule: A Public Institution for the Provision of Adult and Continuing Education

Life-long learning must not be a purely private undertaking. The further education of adults is a fundamental community task. In the Federal Republic of Germany exist 860 public institutions for adult education which are supported by the local and regional bodies. They are called Volkshochschulen (VHS). In 1988 the VHS ran 400th courses with 12.8 mill. lessons and 5.6 mill. participants (Figure 1). Each of the VHS is relatively autonomous in planning and running its programmes. Besides the high percentage of courses which are *open for everybody* the work with special *target groups* forms an integral part of the programmes. The *contents* of the courses spread over various areas with different proportions are (Figure 2):

- socio-cultural education
- vocationally oriented further education
- learning of languages
- leisure activities
- health education
- school-leaving certificates

Science and technological courses have gained 7 per cent by 1988. Most of them are vocationally oriented or prepare participants for vocational training.

In order to match the differing expectations of adults there is a great variety in *learning objectives* and *methods*. Adults have the opportunity to

- acquire measurable knowledge and skills
- get information and orientation
- exchange experiences and options
- acquire perspectives
- receive stimulations towards social activity
- progress towards self-knowledge.

These objectives are not necessarily connected with particular areas of content. Every course can be a mix depending on the needs of the participants.

The *degree of standardization* ranges from late acquisition of school-leaving certificates to courses where participants themselves decide what and how to learn. There are different types of *involvement* for participants as

- courses of instruction
- study groups
- conversation circles
- autonomous working groups
- series of lectures.

Two-thirds of the courses take place in the evening. An increasing number of courses are

- daytime courses
- weekend seminars
- long-term full-time courses
- one week seminars within the framework of paid educational leave
- short and extended study trips

- exhibitions
- opportunities for individual studies.

According to the federal structure the VHS have formed *regional associations* in order to coordinate their programmes and to voice their interests and demands. Depending on the particular legislation of the Federal Länder the VHS are supported financially by the Länder governments. These regional VHS-associations constituted the *German Adult Education Association* (DVV) in 1953. Its main task is the representation of common interests of the 11 Länder federations of the VHS and the promotion of their pedagogical and organizational efforts. Besides an office in Bonn providing contact with the Federal administration and other associations dealing with adult education, three departments (Figure 3) are dealing with the improvement of the quality of adult education work at German VHS and with the promotion of international cooperation.

**Department for International Cooperation**

The Department of International Cooperation of the DVV supports, with the financial help of the Federal Ministry of Economic Cooperation, adult education in Africa, Asia and Latin America.

**Adolf-Grimme-Institute**

The institute carries our innovative tasks in the area of multi-media falls. The Institute is arranging and awarding the "Adolf-Grimme-Prize" for the DVV. This television prize is regarded as the most regarded television contest in the Federal Republic.

**Pedagogical Institute (PAS)**

Founded in 1957 the PAS receives institutional support from both the Federal and Länder governments by now. The institute works as a scientific service organization linking scientific research and practice of continuing education. Innovative work is financially supported by means of project-linked grants from the Federal Minister of Education and Science. It was in this context when in 1970 the PAS started its activities in the area of science and technology. As part of the *VHS-Certificate System* (Figure 4) Curricula for adults in mathematics and electronics were developed and evaluated. Manifold activities followed. As a result of these the need of pedagogical planning in this area was recognized. So persons mostly with a university degree in science were employed to adjust the programmes fit to the needs of those to whom the courses were addressed. From 1976 on the Pedagogical Institute of the DVV has organized yearly conferences to discuss innovative concepts and to exchange experiences. On the basis of these contacts and the different project-like activities in course development in cooperation with the VHS and interested teachers I will try to give a survey of the situation of science and technology in non-formal adult education in the Federal Republic of Germany. It is not my aim to present proudly on occasion of this conference the work of the German VHS, the German Adult Education Association and the Pedagogical Institute. I will try to concentrate on the problems, the difficulties and the open questions that I noticed over the years. The few solutions might be restricted to the situation of the Federal Republic of Germany, and it may be doubtful to what extent they can be transferred. In spite of the fact that the popularization of science and technology is pursued to a large extent in the context of vocational training organized by various companies my outline will be restricted on VHS as public institutions with an open access.

**Science and Technology as a Part of the Programme**

The classic natural subjects mathematics, physics, chemistry and biology have a long traditional in the general educational system for many decades. A subject called "Polytechnique" is taught only in the so-called "Hauptschule" or "Realschule", secondary school level I till age 15 or 16, not in the secondary schools level II till age 19. Informatics as an independent subject exists only in the last two years of level II.

In comparison with the programmes of VHS the main difference between formal education and adult education is easily recognizable, especially so when considering the development over the years.

The programmes of the VHS are developed according to the needs of adults. The traditional structure of subjects is therefore broken up. For adults there must be a recognizable relationship between the content of the learning programme and their perspective of life. It is the relation to their vocational qualifications which mostly makes adults participate in courses. They want to acquire new knowledge and new skills in order to

- get better paid jobs or jobs with better working conditions
- refresh their qualification profile because some of their knowledge is getting obsolete
- get a job after some time of unemployment
- get a first job after initial vocational education without success in the first step
- get a firm who accepts them for vocational initial education or because new technology is implemented in their surrounding and they do not want to loose their jobs.

So it is the applicability of the knowledge which is of great importance. The last four reasons are of an increasing importance since the beginning of the eighties when the phase of structural unemployment started in the Federal Republic of Germany.

Not every course in science and technology is strictly oriented towards the needs of vocational qualifications. There are always adults who are strongly interested in some special topic (short wave radio, astronomy). In most cases these topics are connected with a hobby they are occupied with in their spare time.

In addition to what has been said the participation is also connected with the wish to fulfil a certain social role more successfully:

- Parents learned the so-called "new math" in the seventies to be able to help their children
- Some people want to take care for relatives handicapped by special illnesses
- A lot of citizen nowadays worry about their ecological environment and want detailed information.

The needs of adults for further education derive from special situations and constellations and the structure of classic subjects is very often not able to match these.

Identifying courses for adults in the programmes of VHS by the categories of the well known classic subjects is on the other hand helpful in order to find the fitting courses in some cases (Figure 5).

So *physics* and *chemistry* are of minor importance (less than 400 courses p.a.). In some regions with a local chemical industry courses are organized which lead to an examination called VHS-Certificate. Even a VHS-Certificate in physics was developed with the deceptive hope that the fundamental role of physics in modern technology would be realized.

The development of *biology* as the third classical natural science has been very different. The amount of courses in 1986 (Chernobyl!) was already ten times higher than physics or chemistry. The reasons for the continuing increase are the following:

- The obvious ecological problems in local, national or worldwide contexts led to a more urgent need for ecological knowledge.
- The increased consciousness of a threatened health (sudden death of babies) made people more interested in biological topics.

A more detailed statistics shows that courses with *ecological topics* make up about 50 per cent of the classic category biology (Figure 6).

On the other hand a continuing decrease of courses in *mathematics* can be observed. It seems that the development stabilizes at a much lower level of 2000 courses a year since 1985. No more courses are held for parents learning "new math". As a rule nobody learns mathematics because of its applicability in his vocational environment. Many people need mathematics during a learning process leading to other goals. If they want to take the opportunity of a long-term further education mathematics may become a formally important subject again. In many cases those whose abilities leaving school are under an average level have poor mathematical skills. So there obviously will be a continuous small number of adults who have to compensate a lack of mathematical skills for various reasons.

Courses in the basics of *electronics* (Figure 7) are part of the VHS programmes since the early seventies. They were supported by VHS-Certificate Electro-Technique and Electronics since 1972 respective 1974 developed by the Pedagogical Institute. To run these courses the VHS needed more than just plain training rooms. The quality of the electronic equipment for measurement exercises has been an important factor for the applicability and practical relevance of the acquired skills. Since the beginning of the eighties courses in digital electronics for the more advanced increased as a preparation for courses in controlling by means of micro processors. Some VHS are able to run courses dealing with computer aided manufacturing (CAM), computer aided construction (CAD) or CNC. Due to the high prices of the necessary equipment these courses usually take place in regions with a high percentage of unemployed where the VHS cooperate with the supporting local working offices.

*Informatics* (Figure 7) is the discipline with the most striking development not only in the area of science and technology. In 1988 nearly 14,000 courses took place. Since the mid seventies many different types of introductory courses were offered. A VHS-Certificate Informatics was developed in 1976 aiming at problem solving by description of algorithms. As a formalism to do this Pascal was chosen. The main reason was its—to that time only theoretically—good support for structured programming. The boom started in 1982 when more and more firms began to install so-called Personal Computers. The number of courses increased with accelerate speed in two directions:

- Programming courses in two or three parts for BASIC, Pascal, FORTRAN or COBOL
- more lately courses in standard applications (text systems, spread sheet programmes, data organization programmes, graphic programmes, integrated programmes)

In the mid-seventies there were only a few VHS which were provided with a sufficient number of computers to integrate computer practice. The famous Commodore C 64 was the standard. Since some years a lot of VHS own special rooms with one Personal Computer (in most cases IBM-compatible) for every two participants. In the first years the main difficulty was to get the adequate software. In the meantime the software houses offer special prices for training institutions.

Today it is considered that the reach of courses which are oriented on special software systems is too short. It should be the task for further education organized by various companies to provide learners with the necessary skills. Public adult education should concentrate on qualifications which are less likely to get obsolete and support adults with the ability to handle coming systems. There are many suggestions how to reach these keys qualifications. But besides hope there is no hard evidence that this way will be successful.

An important topic in informatics is the question of their social implications. There have been obvious changes in everybody life, caused by the application of computers. Working conditions in some jobs got worse. Office staff was in some cases reduced. Legal problems have to be solved (right to informational self-determination). The VHS as a public institution has to consider these problems when developing didactic concepts of courses. In each special course adequate ways to do so have to be found depending on the background and the different experiences of the participants.

**The Role of Adult Education in Science and Technology**

Adult education aims at making adults able to act autonomously in vocational or social contexts. There are many incalculable factors producing unforeseeable effects. So if they are motivated to do so or if their surrounding gives them the opportunity to do so is not an easy consequence of their learning process. Adult education is not an easy control system. In many cases the reasons for supporting adult education in the area of science and technology is to make people accept new technology or even to break the resistance against it for economic reasons. This seems to be a contrast with one of the fundamental principles of adult education, i.e. to respect the interests of adult learners. The primary task for adult education should therefore be to enable these learners to handle the technological tools in respect to as human development for the society and their development. If this is accepted there are many ways to combine this aim with providing adults with adequate qualifications, required by industry.

*Figure 1*

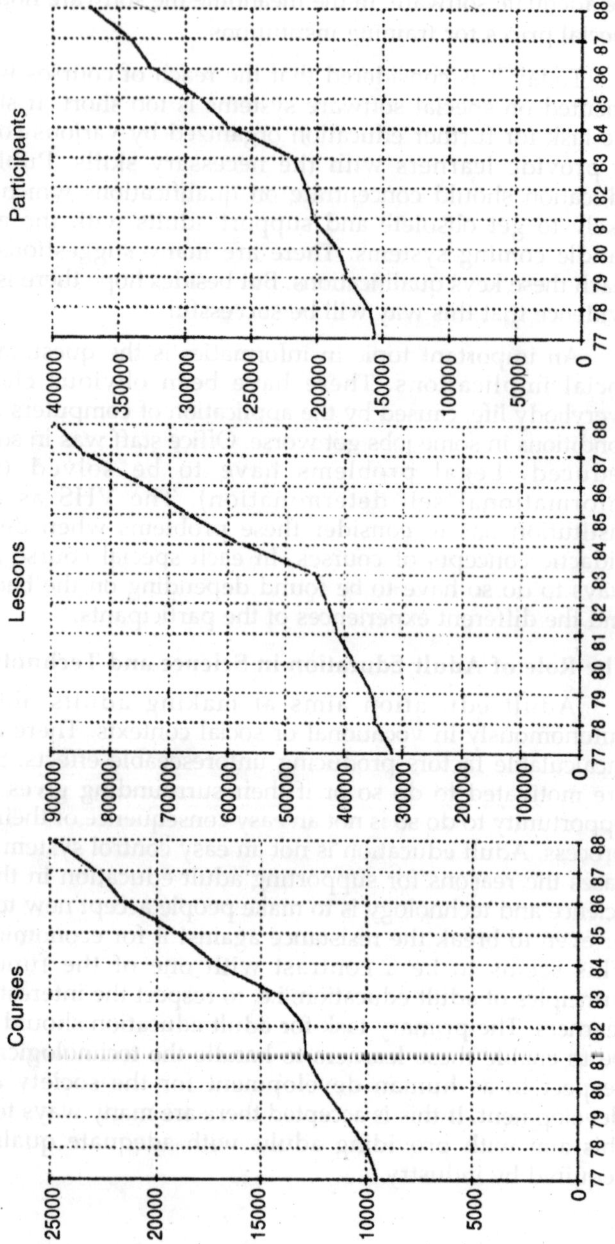
Courses
25000
20000
15000
10000
5000
0
Lessons
90000
80000
70000
60000
50000
40000
30000
20000
10000
0
Participants
400000
350000
300000
250000
200000
150000
100000
50000
0
77 78 79 80 81 82 83 84 85 86 87 88

*Figure 2*

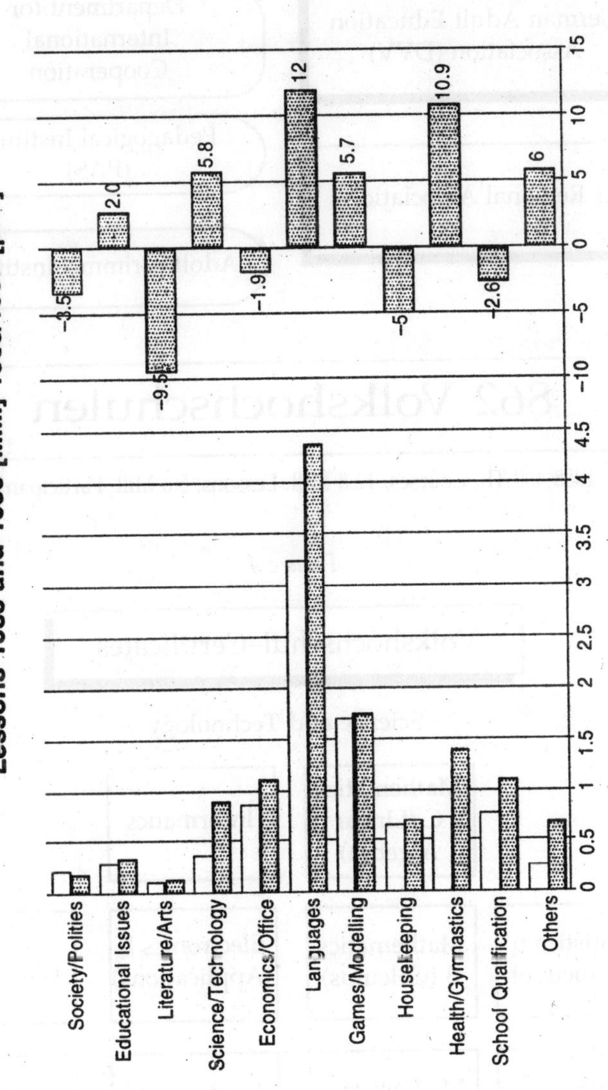
Lessons 1988 and 1980 [Mill.] 1988/1987 [p.c.]
Society/Polities
Educational Issues
Literature/Arts
Science/Technology
Economics/Office
Languages
Games/Modelling
Housekeeping
Health/Gymnastics
School Qualification
Others
0
0.5
1
1.5
2
2.5
3
3.5
4
4.5
-10
-5
0
5
10
15
-3.5
2.0
-9.5
5.8
-1.9
12
5.7
-5
10.9
-2.6
6

*Figure 3*

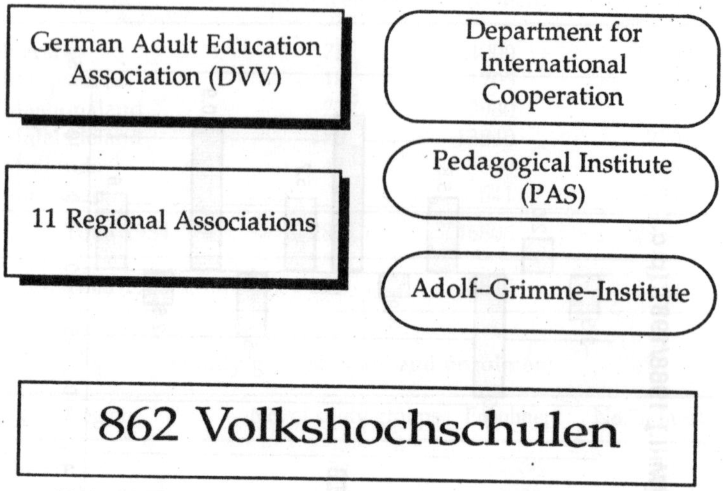

1988 400 Th. Courses, 12.8 Mill. Lessons, 5.6 Mill. Participants

*Figure 4*

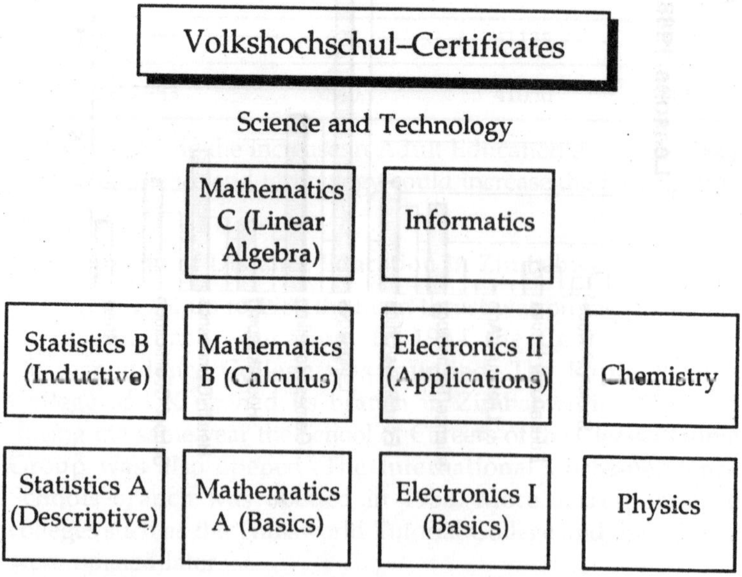

*Figure 5*

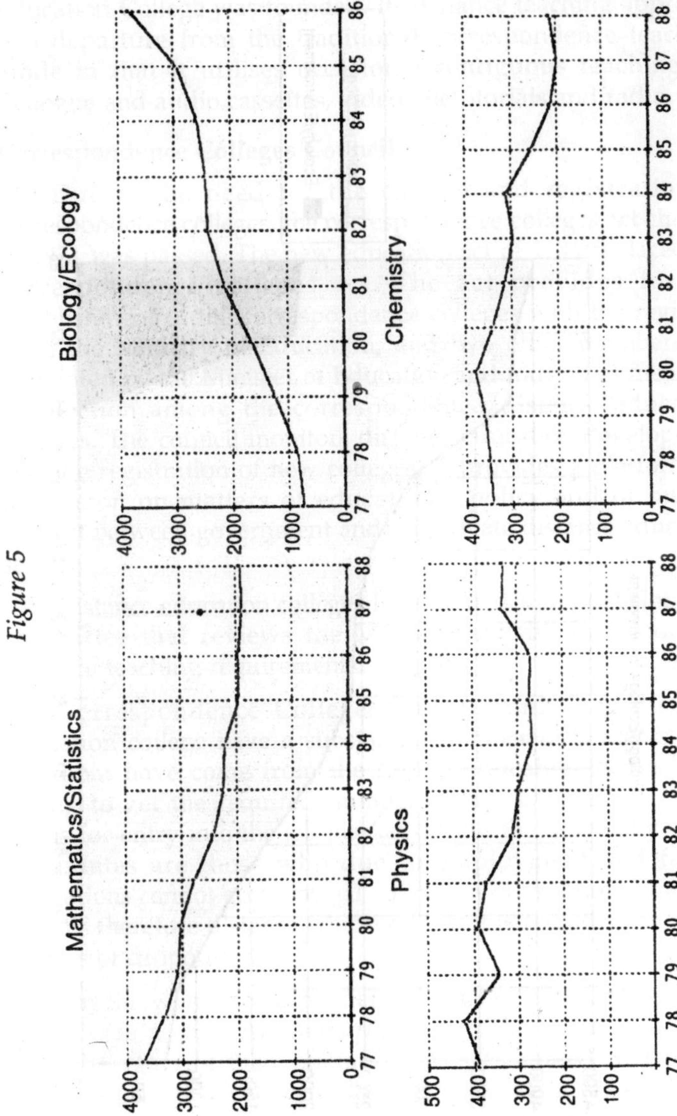
Mathematics/Statistics
4000
3000
2000
1000
0
77 78 79 80 81 82 83 84 85 86 87 88
Biology/Ecology
4000
3000
2000
1000
0
77 78 79 80 81 82 83 84 85 86
Physics
500
400
300
200
100
77 78 79 80 81 82 83 84 85 86 87 88
Chemistry
400
300
200
100
0
77 78 79 80 81 82 83 84 85 86 87 88

*Figure 6*

Biology/Ecology/Environment
4500
4000
3500
3000
2500
2000
1500
1000
500
0
77
70
79
80
81
82
83
84
85
86
87
88
Biology/Ecology
Ecology/Environment

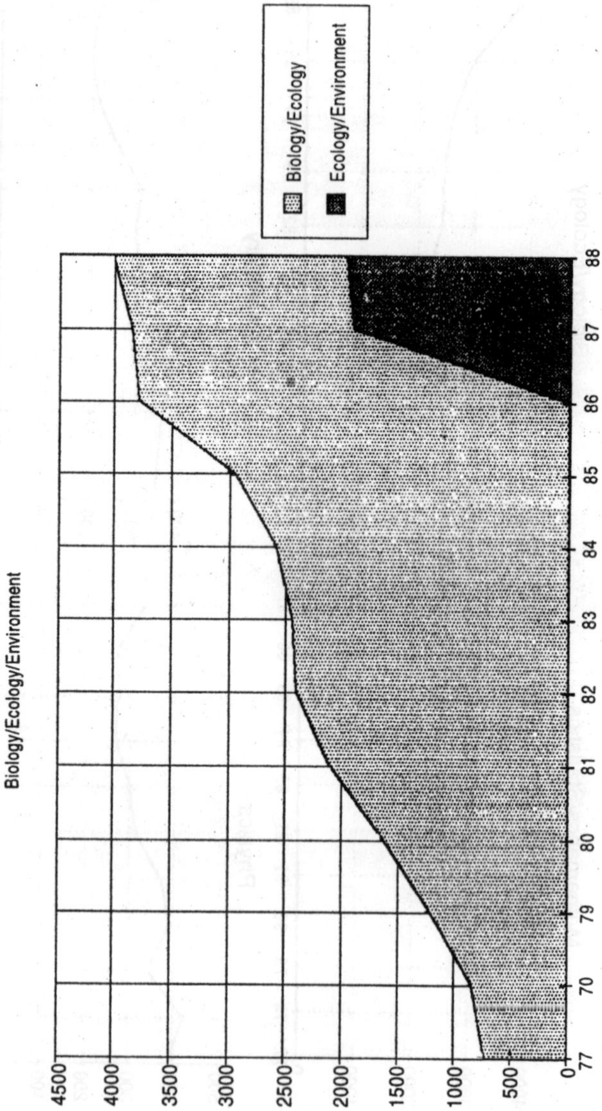

*Figure 7*

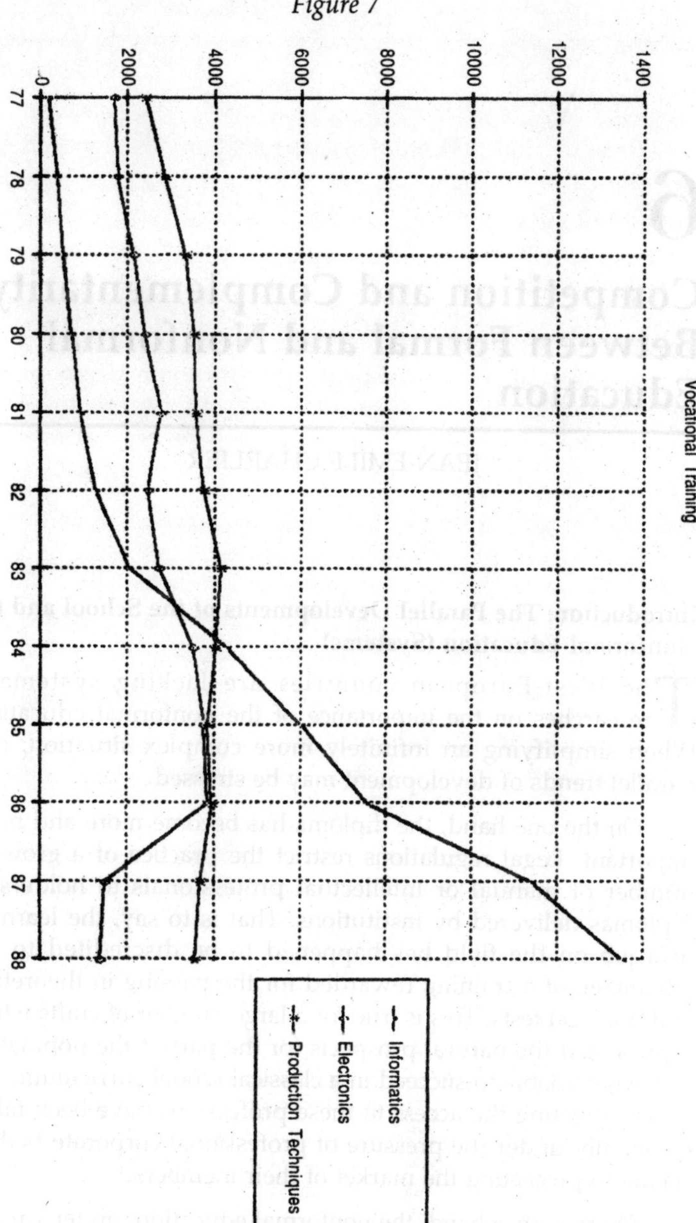
Vocational Training
0
2000
4000
6000
8000
10000
12000
1400
77
78
79
80
81
82
83
84
85
86
87
88
Informatics
Electronics
Production Techniques

# 6

# Competition and Complementarity Between Formal and Nonformal Education

JEAN-EMILE CHARLIER

## Introduction: The Parallel Developments of the School and the Nonformal Education (Systems)

The West-European countries are lacking systematic researches on the importance of the nonformal education. When simplifying an infinitely more complex situation, two parallel trends of development may be stressed.

On the one hand, the diploma has become more and more important. Legal regulations restrict the practice of a growing number of manual or intellectual professionals to holders of diplomas delivered by institutions. That is to say, the learning of a job on the field has happened to be discredited to the advantage of a training rewarded for the passing in theoretical and practical tests. This is true for a large number of crafts which represented the natural prospects for the part of the population relatively unable to succeed in a classical school curriculum. The laws protecting the access to these professions have been taken essentially under the pressure of professional corporate bodies, seeing to protecting the market of their members.[1]

On the other hand, the nonformal education, under various forms, has been developing very quickly for less than fifteen years. Two reasons at least may explain its success. First of all, the speeding evolution of the production and work methods in the secondary and tertiary industries has required the setting up of systems of permanent education similar to the nonformal education ones. Secondly, the restructuring of the north European economies has excluded the least qualified workers from the employment market. The trainings offered to them are also closer to the patterns of the nonformal education than to the ones of the school system.

School education and nonformal education are not independent from each other. The school institutions also organize short trainings, not awarding a diploma, on the fringe of their main activities. One of their aims is to win one part of the financial resources given by the individuals, the enterprises or the authorities to the permanent or further education. Moreover, the social movements are attempting to have the value of spontaneous skills acquiring processes by individuals in their places of work acknowledged. So some colleges of social and economic sciences allow workers with a few years of professional activity to enroll directly as senior students, recognizing that way the equivalence between the work experience and the curriculum of two academic years at university. Lastly, the recent law on the raising of the school-leaving age to 18 in Belgium has explicitly started that 15 to 18 years old young people can only follow a half-time education if the other half-time is to be dedicated to training periods in firms. In this respect, the formal education recognizes the worth of the nonformal education and makes use of it to fill its deficiencies and to motivate young people not very interested in a theoretical training. The model of alternation, of German origin, has been strongly backed and encouraged by the CEDEEFOP.[2] In Belgium, it has enabled various corporate bodies of craftsmen, employers federation, social movements to set up training sessions in which the main part of the training occurs on the field and in which the young people are given first a few theoretical courses in direct connection with their own work experience.

For these last decades, we have thus witnessed a pendulum motion. In the first phase, the school forms strengthened their monopoly in awarding a diploma and tried to obtain the monopoly in education by denying the validity of non school trainings/or trainings not provided by school. In a second phase, school appeared more and more clearly not to be the most efficient place to provide particular forms of knowledge and to train certain audiences. The nonformal education developed then firstly by concerning itself with what the school did not take charge of or badly took charge of and secondly by broadening its scope of concern.

Nowadays, if the two systems appear to be complementary, they also appear to be competitors, in particular as far as the further adult education is concerned. Power struggles arise in as much as the school is the only institutionalized body to be entitled to award legal diplomas and would like to plan and organize the whole of the training systems according to its criteria. The three examples of the nonformal education come within the framework of this institutional context.

### The Professional Training in the Tertiary Industry

After having changed drastically the industrial production methods the new technologies deeply modify the whole industry in full development. The most spectacular adaptation efforts are observed nowadays in the banking sector where very elaborated further education curricula have taken place and aim at maximizing the efficiency of the nonformal education. Every institution has acquired equipment of self-learning (computer aided teaching CAT, library, videotapes library,. . .) where all the employees can train themselves. The technological environment of the banks is moreover very modern and the popularization with these everybody technological instruments occurs naturally. Many sessions for internal purpose are furthermore organized for the employees who wish them. They do not adopt the form of school education but articulate with the conference or discussion patterns. Any individual having acquired experience in his work may be invited by the direction to talk about it, either to his peers or to subordinates wishing to progress in the hierarchy. The all of the accumulated knowledge in the organization is thus systematically redistributed, everyone being required to be trained or to train according to the themes dealt with. Trainings are also organized outside or are led by external experts but they belong less to the logic of nonformal education.

The case of the training courses organized by the banks is particularly interesting because organizations have endeavoured to systematize the methods of the nonformal education. Presently, some of the most competent terms in the field of adult further education work in the banks and they have acquired a remarkable experience. The efficiency of the system stems at least from three factors:

- The education budgets in the banks are very high. The means at the disposals of the persons in charge of the training are clearly more important than the ones available in the schools.
- Everyone is stimulated to follow a training on his own. Possessing the command of new techniques results in pay-raise and ascent in the hierarchy. All the culture of the organization drives the individuals to follow a training even if they had in the past negative experiences in their school curriculum.
- All the employees have a basic training of which the level tends to rise. They thus show a positive attitude towards the acquirement of a new knowledge.

**The Professional Training of the Indemnified Unemployed**

Since 1974 and the dramatical increase in unemployment, the Belgian State Secretary for Employment and Work has taken various steps to improve the professional qualifications of the unemployed. Many of these measures concern the popularization with the new technologies and belong to the field of the nonformal education. Nevertheless, one must notice that the Belgian State Secretary, faced with the number of the unemployed, has progressively focused his efforts on the most trained individuals as well as on the most likely among them to gain immediately from a complementary training. The goal of getting the least qualified popularized with the new technologies has been almost totally given up.[3] Among the most efficient measures, we may quote:

- the training periods in firms.
  A lot of measures allow unemployed to work in firms to get a training in the most modern technical equipment. Strictly speaking, there are no training courses as such but much more a real familiarization process with the instrument. The training periods are all the more efficient so since the unemployed have a basic training.
- the fast technical training.
  These training sessions which do not belong to the school training types are basically practical and aim at giving quickly the workers the ability to use new technical devices. Agreements are sometimes taken with firms which undertake to recruit unemployed workers trained by the State department. We must underline that most of the training sessions organized find their equivalent in the school system. The only differences are the pedagogical method, here exclusively based on the concrete aspect, and the duration of training, which is considerably shortened.

## The Vocational Training of Young People without any Qualification and Training •

In spite of the extension of compulsory school-attendance to the age of 18, a portion of young people keeps appearing on the employment market without any diploma and professional qualification required by the employers. The majority of these young people come from cultural environment favouring the concrete aspect; they do not manage to carry out a school curriculum awarding a diploma. It does not mean that they do not have any skills. They may possess the physical strength, the assiduity to the task, an immediate and concrete comprehension of the object. All these qualities, that would have been sufficient a few decades ago to turn them into appreciated workers, do not permit them any more to find a job. Their situation is all the more difficult that their qualities are valorized by their own cultural environments but depreciated by the professional milieux.

Among the initiatives taken in enabling them to get a qualification, we may mention "Less Enterprises d'Apprentissage

Professional". These small-scale outfits (between 20 and 60 young aged from 18 to 25) use only non-traditional methods. The training includes a very limited theoretical part and a two-sided practical part. On the one hand, a training in workshop, inside the Enterprises d'Apprentissage Professional, on the other hand, traineeships in firms. Less Enterprises d'Apprentissage Professional are subsidized by the European Social Fund, provided that they comply with a certain number of provisions; among them we find the obligation to provide their trainees a training in the new technologies. They can not afford to acquire expensive equipment. Therefore they do their best to send their young people for a training in enterprises equipped with modern devices. Unfortunately, these firms are very reluctant to accept that hardly trained young people work on top equipment. In other words, young people whose culture is the most remote from the Sciences and the new Technologies, find themselves prevented from concretely approaching them. As a result, they are even more removed from them. A functional illiteracy develops among those who have not succeeded in a basic school curriculum. The illiteracy breaks up on its own for the persons who manage to find a job in spite of their lack of qualifications.[4]

**Conclusion**

The analysis of the experiences in the nonformal education proves very systematically that they are much more beneficial to those who have a good basic school curriculum. This could indicate that the school remains the place par excellence "to learn-to-learn" and to take advantage of the later opportunities for training. It must be added that the supply of the nonformal education is clearly more important for trained employed individuals than for unqualified unemployed workers. The nonformal education makes up a market; the costs of access to it are generally too high to bear for isolated individuals. Only the authorities or enterprises can afford to offer training in the field of Sciences and Technologies to selected people.

The field of the formal and nonformal education is going through a rapid restructuring. The effort of school and universities to offer short trainings, which do not lead to the award of a diploma and which give a quick training in some forms of knowledge, has been mentioned earlier. Conversely, the will of private managers to set up training schemes close to the school pattern must be quoted. For instance, a steel industry organizes a one year full time advanced training course for engineers. In the same way, a bank has set up a training for managers of medium-scale enterprises, it also lasts one year full time. These training courses cost a lot more than similar ones organized by schools of higher education and universities.

Each side has its assets in the competition which opposes the school system and the profit-minded educationalists. The school has for itself the monopoly of awarding a diploma. It means that each diploma is classified in an univocal catalogue and corresponds to a given level of salary and responsibilities. Moreover, the diploma is linked to the person for all his professional life. The school is clumsily run because its curricula, the qualification of its teaching staff are controlled, but it gives on the other hand a diploma of which the value wanes only very slowly. Conversely, the private sector and the nonformal education offer immediately applicable and quickly controllable forms of knowledge. The aim is to endow the individuals with an operational ability in a specific language and with particular equipments. The efficiency of this method is high but the acquired abilities by the individuals are only recognized in the enterprise where they have been gained and where they are put into practice. Without any recognized diploma, the individual can only show practical proves of his abilities. No legal measures can protect him.[6]

One of the key problems between school education and nonformal education lies in the democratization of the education. For several decades, the occidental countries have been willing to put the access to school within the reach of everyone by instituting free education, by granting scholarships to students. Nevertheless, the State has a hold only over the education structures it organizes and subsidizes. It can not provide a free access to training set afoot by profit-minded educationalists, training which proves to be the most profitable on the employment market especially when it coexists with a bright school curriculum.

In that case, we could wonder how to carry on the effort on the way to the democratization of profitable forms of knowledge mainly conceived and imparted out of the school structures. The only solution to this question could consist in giving every citizen "courses-vouchers" entitling him to follow out of the school context the training he wishes.

Finally, the last problem I would like to tackle at deals with the transfer of financial resources from the school system to the independent profit-mined educationalists. The market of the nonformal education draws important amounts of money which would perhaps enable the formal education to take in charge the trainings of "dropouts" and the permanent further adult education if these financial flows were reinjected in the school system. If the formal education misses the most profitable training undertakings, it is obvious that it will be weakened and more and more compelled to impart only static forms of knowledge which are the least profitable.

This will once again present us with problems of democracy. When the school functions well, it not only teaches the operative methods but also offers a thorough comprehension of the mechanisms involved. It makes the individuals self-sufficient when faced with knowledge, it gives them the possibilities to become makers of knowledge. The profit-minded educationalists only provide ways of using the techniques. They put this way the individuals in a situation of dependence. It is not obvious that this evolution is positive when we analyze it from a democratic point of view.

**NOTES**

1. "Le temps du labeur" *Alaluf M.*, Editions de I'U.L.B., 1986.
2. "La formation en alternance des jeunes: Principes pour I'action" *Jallade J.P.*, *Cedefop*, Berlin, 1982.
3. "Formation professinelle et professionnels de la formation "*Moaroy* Ch. Doctorat en Sociologie, Louvian-la-Neuve, 1989.
4. "L'autre jeunesse, Jeunes stagiaires sans dipôlme", P.U.L., 1987.
5. "Less Enterprises d'Apprentissage Professionnel, des entreprises et des formations pas comme less autres?" *Boddson D., Charlier J.E* et Alii, Louvain-la-Neuve, 1987.
6. "Nouvelles concurrences sur le marché des formation et des savoirs" Charlier *J.E., I.S.T.*, Louvian-la-Neuve, 1988.

# 7

# Indigenous Cultural Tradition and the Popularization of Science and Technology

BERNARD H.K. LUK

It is a fact of modern life that science and technology develop very rapidly, that new knowledge is being discovered, and new inventions made, by researchers every day, only to become outmoded in a few years' time. Modern science has provided extermely vigorous and powerful explanations for natural phenomena, and has also lent its theories to innumerable applications which enable humankind to control some of the forces of nature to an unprecedented degree.

While such control has brought forth both benefits and dangers, especially such frightening dangers as the industrial importance of scientific knowledge in twentieth-century life. Technological successes have vindicated science not least among those who know very little about science and has given it a mysterious, quasi-magical aura. No wonder, then that one of the major trends in twentieth-century education has been the increasing emphasis on science education.

Science education at all levels, and in rich as well as poor countries, is needed and desired both for spreading "scientific literacy" among the members of society to improve their participation in modern life, and for training the scientific and technological personnel which a society needs for the economic and social functions of today and tomorrow. In the less developed countries, especially where both the general "scientific literacy" and the available pool of native technological personnel tend to be rather limited, the perceived need of science education is all the greater. This is well attested by UNESCO statements during the past few decades, which stress the importance of science education in helping these societies to take off from the mass misery of poverty and disease, and make good speed on the way to economic development.

But the popularization of science and technology should aim at not only the spreading of basic knowledge among the general population of scientific and technological topics, but also at de-mystification and de-dogmatization of science and technology. Since science and technology develop very quickly, a recognition of the changeability of science and technology should be a basic part of the attitude that popular as well as professional education in science attempt to cultivate. Change implies history; the history is the continuous view of things. This paper attempts to argue for the need for history of science and technology as a component in the training of science educators—not only for formal schooling, but also for informal and non-formal education, to cultivate a sense of changeability and relativism which these educators could then transmit to the learners, to enable them to rise above awe and mystification and to make the best use of science and technology in their social and economic life.

**Scientific Revolutions and Science Education**

In promoting science education, the structure of scientific knowledge should be carefully borne in mind, otherwise the investment of human and material resources might not bear the desired fruits. This writer holds a dynamic view, shared by many scientists and historians of science, that there is no permanent truth, and no permanent approach to truth, in science. Scientists observe natural phenomena, and formulate theories and paradigms to explain as many phenomena as possible. The greater the scope and rigour of an explanation, and the simpler its formulation, the stronger would be the theory. Theories derive from, and in turn constitute paradigms, which are overall views of a facet of nature. Each paradigm is necessarily imperfect, but enjoys the adherence of scientists because it provides satisfying explanations to those puzzles of nature most intriguing to the scientific community of the time. The history of science consists of the jolts and shocks of the falls and rises of paradigms, rather than just the gradual and progressive accumulation of facts and figures.

The displacement of one paradigm by another as the guiding principle of research in the scientific community is known as a "paradigm shift" or a "scientific revolution". Examples are the revolutions of Newton, Boyle, Mendel, Einstein, and so on. Each paradigm recognizes as valid and relevant a particular set of facts, theories, and methodologies, some of which the next paradigm might repudiate.

The long periods between "scientific revolutions", when scientists accept the prevailing paradigm as the guiding framework for their research, and seek only to refine or extend the theoretical applications of that paradigm, or to search for practical, technological applications of it in economic life, are considered to be periods of "natural science". During such periods, knowledge does grow by the accumulation of small bits and pieces, and when the outmoding of particular theoretical of practical applications of the paradigm by newer, more sophisticated applications serves to reinforce rather than reduce the acceptance by the scientific community of the basic paradigm itself.

This framework for the history of science, first put forward in the 1960's by Thomas Kuhn of MIT, enjoys much support among historians and philosophers of science, and is gaining ground too in the social sciences.

When in everyday conversation we talk about scientific advances and the outdating of older knowledge, we might be referring to the development of technological applications, or to theoretical refinements of extensions, or to paradigm shifts—or we might be confusing the three levels. And it is this confusing that often contributes towards a mystification of science as something so elusive yet so mighty, so inaccessible to the uninitiated yet so powerful in the hands of the scientific elite—by the individuals of nations. In fact, popularization of science and technology that succeeds only in imparting a little knowledge and not much else would likely increase the learner's sense of awe about science, scientists, and scientifically advanced countries, and the sense of powerlessness about oneself and one's own society.

Given the paradigmatic structure of scientific knowledge and the relativism inherent in scientific advances, science education, whether in school or in formal or non-formal settings, should aim not only at the transfer of specific facts and theories recognized as scientific under the prevailing paradigm, but also at the cultivation of scientific attitudes mind to accept challenges to the currently held scientific explanations of natural phenomena. But science education as it is practised in the world today all to often entails, at best, little more than training in the concepts and principles of existing "normal science"; and, and worst, simply passing on bits of scientific or technological information. This is not infrequently results in dogmatic beliefs in such explanations or information as permanently proven and ultimately established, sanctified truths.

This is a static view of contemporary science which underlies such science education, and it assumes the scientific status quo as the heroic endpoint of an arduous but no longer relevant progress in the past. Such a close-ended view of science was derived from the almost religious faith optimism of the ascendant West of the nineteenth century—faith in the "ultimate triumph" of Western civilization of Science and Technology. This doctrinnaire attitude is not only unscientific, but also counter-productive. The analogy could be drawn with the Second Law of Thermodynamics, that every closed system tends to run down and become less and less organized.

## Scientific Revolutions and Indigenous Cultural Traditions

Furthermore, the Triumphs of Science and Technology school of thought also tends of equate modernism with Western civilization, and to identify the successes of the prevailing scientific paradigms as proving the superiority of that civilization over the backwardness of the rest of the world. While there is no denying that the rise of the West in recent centuries has given shape to the modern world, and has brought many benefits as well as problems to all parts of the world, thoughtful and informed persons in the West itself are beginning to rise above the old prejudices. However, much of the Third World still live under, and suffer from the derogation, or self-derogation, derived from the old Western prejudices. While this kind of Western ethnocentrism pervades through many aspects of life and thought, it is in science education that it enjoys the most unspoken (and therefore) unchallenged entrenchment. The prevailing scientific paradigms are known to have grown out of Western civilization; they are also assumed to be the heroic endpoint of scientific progress by science teachers and textbooks in Western and non-Western societies alike. Thus in the Third World, to the dogmatism of "normal science" are added the humiliation of the learner's community and cultural tradition, a tradition that is considered, at least by implication, as backward, unscientific, and irrelevant to the future world of science and technology. Dogmatism and humiliation are not positive factors for education.

The science teachers and textbooks, whether in formal schooling or in informal/nonformal education, often imply that the native tradition had no science worth the name, and made no contribution whatever to modern science. This might be true to a large extent, if "science" is equated with the prevailing paradigms, and "technology" with "cutting edge technology" derived from such paradigms. But if a more ecumenical and dynamic view is taken of science and of scientific progress, it would be found that each indigenous civilization had its own paradigms to explain observed natural phenomena, which are more or less sophisticated and accurate descriptions and explanations of Nature. These paradigms were derived from the particular perceptiveness and wisdom of each cultural tradition, and cannot fail to be interesting and valuable in themselves, as anthropologists would know. They may yet have important contributions to make to the formulation of more powerful paradigms which scientists of a more ecumenical generation in the future might accept in place of the contemporary ones. This is not an advocacy of indigenous obscurantism against Western-derived science and technology, but rather a suggestion to look towards the future by looking also at the past, instead of focussing exclusively one the present.

The work of Joseph Needham, an English scientists and historian of science, has done much to elucidate the story of the development of science and technology in the Chinese past. It is significant that this pioneering work was done by a foreign scholar, because in China, as in so much of the Third World, it was assumed that the indigenous cultural tradition was scientifically backward and contained no history of science worthy of attention. For science education in the Third World to dismiss the scientific past of native cultures as nothing but pretty myths or despicable superstitions would be not only unhistorical, but also a disservice to the future development of worldwide science and to the cultural identity of the learner. What is needed is not to glory blindly in a native past, but to give science education in all countries an injection of relativism and ecumenism, which should come with the recognition of the paradigmatic structure of science and of scientific progress.

**Paradigms and Science Pedagogy**

In recent years, science educators in Britain, Australia, Hong Kong, and elsewhere, have been exploring the "naive" notions of children's explanation of natural phenomena, in the belief that a teacher's understanding of these "naive" notions could help improve the pedagogy to be used in teaching science to the children.

In fact, when children, or adult learners, who are uninitiated in modern science, grope about for explanations for natural phenomena, or to try to relate what they learn in science lessons to their own previous convictions about the world, they are humbly and unsophisticatedly trying to formulate their own paradigms. These paradigms are likely to be derived, in some way, from aspects of the learner's native cultural tradition. The teacher, unlike the learner, is more firmly entrenched in the prevailing paradigms. Unless previously sensitized to the value of such naive paradigm-making, he or she would fail to see the learner's gropings around as a worthwhile scientific activity from which all concerned would learn more about nature, science, themselves, and their cultural tradition, but would rather tend to perceive such efforts as an undesirable falling away from the task at hand at inculcating contemporary science, and hence discourage the learners from their own formulations.

The bulk of science education in any setting should of course be the prevailing science accepted by the scientific community as such. But that should not be the exclusive content of that education, lest it excludes even the avenues for its own future growth. What is needed is a strong dosage of the history of science, a la Thomas Kuhn and Joseph Needham, to sensitize science teachers to the relativism and ecumenism which should be the art of the underlying assumptions of science education. Thus informed, science teachers may be able to teach science in a more open-ended style, and contribute more towards the scientific, technological, and cultural development of their societies.

# 8

# Popularization of Science and Technology: The Cultural Dimension

CHENG KAI MING

The theme of this short paper is to identify the cultural elements which may contributes to the popularization of science and technology in the East Asian region. The theme has been made elsewhere in international conferences (Cheng, 1988a, 1988b, 1988c) but in another context.

## Does Culture Matter?

What may be identified as characteristic of the East Asian confucian societies—Japan, Mainland China, Taiwan, Korea, Hong Kong and to a large extent Singapore—is the low visibility of *technological unemployment and computer phobia* which, elsewhere, can easily become the major setbacks for the dissemination of modern science and new technologies.

There could be all kinds of economic, social or political reasons, internal to these societies, to explain the lack of such phenomena in these societies. However, it remains to be explained why these societies, with extremely different economic statuses and systems and of rival political ideologies, should share such common characteristics when they come to the acquisition of science and technology.

One possible answer to this question is that these societies share the same culture—the "Confucian culture" as is known—which favours competition and adaptation. It is not the job of this paper to probe the substance of "Confucian culture" in general, but it is sufficient for the purpose of this paper to identify that the societies mentioned were all once influenced by Confucius.

**A Culture of Adaptation**

A famous China sociologist, Fei Hsiao-tung (1974) made a distinction between the Chinese society and the "Western" society by identifying the Chinese society as a *configuration of hierarchy* contrasting the Western societies which are "configuration of groups".

In the former, every member of the community is very conscious of his or her position in the hierarchy and tend to act according to the role expectations of the society with respect to his or her position. This is identified by Fei, quite justifiably, as the basic interpersonal relations in typical Chinese societies. Whereas in the West, people exist as individuals and they link to each other in groups according to expedient necessities.

Fei's assertion may be used to explain a number of phenomena which are common to Chinese societies. It helps explain the way resources are allocated in Chinese societies. It helps explain the strong family tie and the strong sense of seniority in such societies. It may hence support the findings that Chinese work ethics disfavours individualism (Hofstede, 1984) and the absence of the notion of self in traditional Chinese thinking (Hsu, 1985). It may even help explain political and ideological struggles in modern Chinese history.

Among others, the *configuration of hierarchy* provides a sociological explanation to a "culture of adaptation". In such a configuration, individuals are expected to act according to what the system experts.

In Chinese societies, however, it is also well recognized that there is a built-in mechanism of social mobility (e.g. Solomon, 1971). It is not a static hierarchy; it is a strict but dynamic hierarchy. It respects efforts to change one's position in the hierarchy, and the major incentive system which facilitates such upward mobility is education.

**Education for Trainability**

Education is ever the major ladder, and almost the only ladder, for social mobility. But such a mobility can be achieved only if one works according to a uniform set of social expectations.

Hence, there is early socialization of pre-school children to adult values. There is what is seen as "rote-learning" by the Westerners, but is viewed just normal in East Asia. There is largely uniform curriculum which seldom cater for individual needs. There is the mere attention to job-market information at the expense of personal suitability in career orientations. And so on (See details in Cheng, 1988b).

The education system is so much respected by the society that it has become an instrument independent of the societal context in which it works. In other words, relevance is not an important issue in education. In ancient China, where the imperial civil examination prevails as the only education programme, scholars spent decades to study "the Four Books and Five Classics" and are appraised not on the merits of ideas, but on the styles of writing. Even in recent years, comparative studies have exhibited that in Japan, for example, contrary to all modern theories, students achieve well in science despite a rather traditional curriculum (Lynn, 1988).

In other words, the relevance of education is reflected not in the content of education—the curriculum and the applicability of the knowledge in actual life—but in the training for conforming oneself to the system. It is under this motive of conformation that students compete and work hard. Psychologists may also find that in such a society, the line between extrinsic and intrinsic motivations begin to blue (Ibid.).

The concept here is that individuals should try hard to adapt themselves to the system. Whereas in the West, the system should try hard to cater for individual needs.

Such an intensive training for adaptability, incidentally, creates the general climate in the society which favours rapid acquisition of modern science and technology, which in turn creates favourable conditions for international competition.

In essense, it is the formal education system in the Confucian societies which does the job of *informal education*—creating a culture of adaptation and "flexibility".

**The Social Costs**

Such a concept infiltrates through all walks of life and is reciprocally reinforced by the social system: lack of social security, great disparity in rewards for education, high pressure for upward mobility, and so forth, quite apart from the hard-grinding examinations in schools and the monotonous styles of teaching and learning.

These are harkly tolerable in a Western society. Seen in this light, the ideologies of equality and democracy, which are taken as axioms in the West, were, until recently, not felt as a necessity in Chinese communities.

There is therefore a dilemma, perhaps not so much in Japan, but certainly in other Confucian societies, between maintaining the original culture which favours international competition but neglects equality and democracy (which are Western, but has become international) and an enhancement of individualism which will eventually reform the social structure, but may meanwhile eliminate the privileges in international competition.

**REFERENCE**


Cheng, K.M. (1986). "Traditional values and Western ideas: Hong Kong's dilemma in education". *Asian Journal of Public Administration*, December—1986.

Cheng, K.M. (1987). "Where are the trainees? —Trainers' plans versus students' aspirations". In E.D. Fortuinjn, W. Hoppers, M.Morgan (eds) *Paving pathways to work*. The Hague: CESO, 1987a, 59-64.

Cheng, K.M. (1988a). "Preparation for work: the two cultures" Paper presented at the 13th Conference of the Comparative Society of Comparative Education, June 29-July 1, 1988, Budapest. In proceedings.

Cheng, K.M. (1988b). "From education to work: the cultural dimension". Paper prepared for the Conference on "Culture, Education and Productive Life" celebrating the 25th Anniversary of CESO, November 9-21, 1988. The Hague.

Cheng K.M. (1988c). "Graduate unemployment: absent or late-coming?" Paper presented at the Asian Productivity Organization conference on "Educated Unemployment", November 14-18, 1988, Seoul.

Fan, H.C.P. (1985) "Job Satisfaction versus Job Satisfactoriness". Paper presented at the CESO Conference on "Youth Programme and the Transition from School to Work", December 16-21, 1985 in Wageningen, The Netherlands.

Fei, H.T. (1947). *Earth-bound China*, Hong Kong: Joint Publisher, (Reprint, 1985, in Chinese).

Hofstede, G. (1984). *Culture's consequences: international differences in work-related values*. Beverly Hills: Stage.

Hsu, F.L.K. (1985). "The self in cross-cultural perspective". In A.J. Marsella, et al. *Cultuer and self*. New York: Tavistock.

Solomon, R.H. (1971). *Mao's revolution and the Chinese political culture*. Berkeley: University of California Press.

# 9

# The Role of Science Teacher Associations in Promoting the Popularization of Science through Nonformal Means

JACK B. HOLBROOK

## Introduction

The position paper (Cheng Kai Ming, 1989) for this conference suggests that science and technology have never played such an essential and influential role in our lives.

Certainly changes are rapid and have placed new demands on society. The debate over the use of nuclear power, the concerns about the depletion of the ozone layer, especially by CFC's and the ethical issues related to genetic engineering all point to a need for today's society to be more literate in science and technology.

## Science Literacy Standards

Yet the recent results from an International science study in Hong Kong at the form 2 (grade 8) level (Holbrook, 1989) show that about 6 per cent of students in Hong Kong are barely scientific literate achieving little above chance level and the overall average for all students at this level by international standards. After only one further year of study many of these students will have completed their formal scientific level of understanding of such students will remain low and any gains in the realm of science and technology, as such students progress into adult life, will fall solely on non-formal and informal means.

Evidence of the lack of awareness of science and technology can be easily observed using Hong Kong as an example. Two illustrations that can be cited are the lack of care of the environment, particularly by dumping rubbish on the streets, in the country parks and in the sea; and unsafe practices leading to industrial disasters such as the serious fur factory fire which occurred fairly recently through a lack of education on appropriate procedures to be employed when handling benzene (petroleum ether).

The popularity of science subjects at school is currently high at the senior secondary level in many Asian countries although this is far from being the case in many Western countries. Yet this science is only for a minority and is very much school orientated and lacks serious concern for technology. The curriculum is based on building up fundamentals leading to conceptual development rather than relating the science to the technology in the society. Without transference skills students can complete a school course in science and still be illiterate towards the technological problems in society. There are moves today to introduce more relevant and technologically orientated science curricula e.g. Chemcom by the chemical society. *Satis* by the British Association of Science Education and Salter's Science by the Science Education Group of the University of York, UK, but their impact has yet to be clearly observed even though early signs are encouraging.

**Non-formal Science Education**

All this points to an obvious need for more than formal science education. This need is for both students and adults if the level of technological awareness is to be raised and citizens are to be better able to grasp issues confronting society. This education has the unenviable task of overcoming the poor image science and scientist have acquired and to popularize science as a first step to increasing scientific awareness and scientific literacy.

May be unwittingly the task of popularizing science has been made more difficult by the mass media, particularly television. Science television as such does not receive high audience preference ratings and thus such programmes are rare and often confined to specialist channels (Public Broadcasting Service (PBS) in the US) or aired late in the evening. Entertaining television, especially cartoon, tend to put forward a stereotyped image of science as magical, dangerous and conducted by "mad" scientists who are old, white haired men in white labcoats. Science is thus portrayed as being in a world of its own and too obscure for the average man in the street.

Science magazine or newspaper writers have a difficult job making the science comprehensible to the majority of its readers and tend to gear stories to topical happenings, glorified by striking headlines. Such headlines are all too often disasters e.g. Chernobyl, impending doom e.g. flooding resulting from the greenhouse effect, or fantasies that would enhance the image of science if only they would come true e.g. cold fusion. Little wonder that the population is not clambering to become more scientifically literate and may well be perceiving science as obscure, dangerous and irrelevant to their lives.

**Non-formal Education at the School Level**

Yet there are channels of non-formal education at the school level that can play a positive role in the popularization of science. Such examples are well known e.g. science clubs run after school, inter-school competitions such as exhibitions, young inventor, story writing, fairs and olympiads and regional and international competitions of a similar nature. It is suggested that greater efforts in these areas provide a good platform for encouraging the study of science and in bringing science to link with concerns in the society.

Hong Kong has a very good example of an exhibition which is open to the general public and provides an excellent platform for the popularization of science and technology. This is the Joint Schools Science Exhibition (JSSE). Every year Hong Kong plays host to a science exhibition in which students exhibit their projects and are judged on its merit and their ability to explain the project to members of the public. The exhibition, usually organized in late July or August, is open to members of the public free of charge and held in the exhibition centre for about 1 week. This year marked the 22nd joint schools science exhibition and it has truly established itself as a major function in Hong Kong in this area.

An unusual feature of this science exhibition is that it is completely organized by students. This does not simply mean that students develop the projects by themselves, but that the whole planning, fund raising, timing, judging are carried out by the joint schools science exhibition preparation committee which is composed entirely of students from different school with officials elected to their positions entirely by the students.

All member schools hand in a description of their project to the Project Inspection Group before the exhibition, the deadline being set by the Project Inspection Group. A member from the Project Inspection Group checks that the project in each school is progressing well and is completed in time for the exhibition. All individual projects are under the responsibility of a student from a member school. The school is responsible for all financing of the project. Joint projects between member schools are permitted.

The exhibition was initiated from a concern that science in senior secondary schools was too academic and too narrow and there was a wish to encourage students to gain wider experiences. It was shown to the general public to give greater awareness to science and to link schools a little more closely with the community. The first event was such a success that the JSSE became an annual event.

The exhibition is given a theme each year. For 1989 this was Dreams Come True. Living in the modern world, everything around us such as buildings, vehicles, clothes and even foodstuffs are products of technology. All increase the quality of life. Just as man would never have flown had he not first dreamed of flying, so man's dreams for the future can shape the technology for tomorrow. Dreams come true is thus an opportunity for students to consider how technology of the future is evolved from the scientific world of today.

**The Role of Science Teacher Associations**

This year for the first time, thanks to contacts with the Hong Kong Association of Science and Mathematics Education, the committee made contact with the China Association for Science and Technology and had arranged for a winning exhibition to be shown in the Hong Kong exhibition. Unfortunately visa difficulties made the realization of this not possible.

Thanks to contacts with the International Council of Associations for Association for Science Education which runs the Brunei science week in December each year. The committee has secured funds for the Hong Kong winning entry to be exhibited in Brunei in December 1989.

For the event in Hong Kong to become larger and to have the potential to involve all schools, there is a need to offer help to the committee and to assist in the promotion of the event from one year to the next. Further, to coordinate projects and perhaps arrange for regional miniexhibitions prior to the main event, there is a need for help from a body with expertise in this field. In Hong Kong this role could be filled by the Hong Kong Association for Science and Mathematics Education, a teacher organization that has already offered support to the Joint School science exhibition preparation team and has organized many events of its own, sometimes with the general public in mind. Such a development may well be a future trend, further enhancing the ability of the exhibition to popularize science and technology by making a greater impact on the public, the media and linking with organizations overseas. The role of science teacher associations is thus seen as being very important in promoting the pursuit of non-formal science and in the popularization of science to the general public.

This can be more understood when it is realized that additional events links with the exhibition. For example the organisers arrange a poster competition among students during the Easter holidays with the winning poster chosen to publicize the exhibition. This year over 100 entries were received and were judged by a team of 4 invited judges from the Government Education Department and persons from tertiary institutions and the Hong Kong Association for Science and Mathematics Education.

In July a seminar on astronomy was organized for about 300 students to publicize the Joint Schools Science Exhibition to be opened on the 29th July. The speaker invited was Mr. Leung Kam Cheung, President of the Hong Kong Amateur Astronomical Society and arrangements were again made with the help of the Hong Kong Association for Science and Mathematics Education.

Further publicity for the Exhibition is organized through the publication of a series of articles in the local newspaper, each article written by a group form the Joint School Science Exhibition Preparative Committee Publicity team. By keeping the themes topical and readable to members of the general public, the publicity team wished to draw attention the exhibition and popularize science amongst adults.

Many events of this and a similar nature which have great potential to popularize science amongst the general public do however go unnoticed. Publicity and coordination are a problem. This has been recognized in some countries and out-of-school activities have been carefully coordinated and propagated by a separate body e.g. the Out-of-School Department of CAST (China Association for Science and Technology).

Many countries do not possess such an umbrella organization as CAST and even then there are between country contacts to consider which can sometimes benefit from the informality when not solely dependent on governmental controlled organizations e.g. UNESCO.

Many countries however do possess Science Teacher Associations. These are non-profit making professional organizations with the aim of promoting education by (HKASME prospectus) improving the quality of Science and Mathematics education; affording a means of communication amongst people concerned with the teaching of Science and Mathematics in particular and with education in general; providing a responsible medium through which opinions of those in Science and Mathematics education matters may be expressed; and extending the professionalism of Science and Mathematics teachers.

Science bodies are in a very good position to coordinate efforts between organizations be it students, the teachers or other bodies such as Chemical societies, Physics societies etc. and provide the necessary infrastructure to ensure participation in a friendly and voluntary manner (the teachers being the level of communication) and being a recognized body, having communication channels with Ministries of Education, the press and the public at large, to encourage the popularization of science and technology.

Science Teacher Associations are linked internationally by ICASE (International Council of Associations for Science Education). The International Council of Associations for Science Education was established in 1973 to extend and improve education in science for all children and youth throughout the world by assisting member associations. It is particularly concerned to provide a means of communication among individual science teachers' associations and to foster cooperative efforts to improve science education. Its beginning stemmed from a realization at a conference at the University of Maryland that UNESCO could not be expected to fulfil such a role, but could be supportive of a body created specifically for communicating amongst science teacher associations and other organizations interested in science education. To date ICASE has communicated to its members by means of a newsletter, a yearbook, occasional teacher resource publications and by the organizing of symposia usually on a regional basis.

ICASE has the infrastructure to coordinate efforts by member associations around the world and promote regional and even international cooporation that bring science and technology to the attention of the public and in so doing further popularize science. This role is only limited by financial constraints such an organization inevitably suffers where it is not governmentally controlled. Its publications such as a newsletter and yearbook ensure sharing of developments and suggestions on how to organize non-formal events among teachers and through them further promoting such events.

The potential role for science teacher associations in the popularization of science and technology is thus great. Unfortunately the enthusiasm of such persons is not sufficient to create extra working hours in a day and there is a limit to which voluntary labour can cope with the enormity of the task.

Yet their potential to arouse the interest of teachers and through them of the students and to sustain efforts at a local and informal level, makes them indispensable in any real attempt at the popularization of science amongst the general public. After all a good scientist or for that matter a good administrator is not necessarily a good presenter of science and technology to students or the general public; the popularization of science depends on its image and what better than that from teachers and students? The role of Science Teacher Associations is worthy of greater consideration and better support.

## REFERENCES

1. Cheng Kai Ming, position paper for the conference on the popularization of science and technology through nonformal and informal means, 1989.
2. HKASME (Hong Kong Association for Science and Mathematics Education).
3. Holbrook J.B. Science Education in Hong Kong, vol. 1, Hong Kong IEA Centre, University of Hong Kong, 1989.
4. ICASE (International Council of Associations for Science Education) prospectus.

# 10

# Popularizing Educational Technology: The INNOTECH Model

JOSE B. SOCRATES

A major obstacle to the popularization of science and technology—especially products of educational research—is the lack of even absence of a systematic dissemination programme. The difficulty is compounded if the educational technology, or innovation is to be applied in the nonformal and informal sectors. It is a common disappointment and discouragement of researchers, after going through a time-consuming, expensive, and generally demanding research, to find that their study is just one more statistic in research archives.

The fact is, any innovation, a new technology, if it is the result of a research process, is known only to the developer or researcher. For it be applied on a wider scale, it must be known to those who will apply it. It goes without saying, therefore, that a remedy, the solution, is a deliberate, resolute and sustained programme to disseminate the technology. Indeed, the so-called R and D (Research and Development) process, is more properly called the RD and D process, or Research, Development and Dissemination process, or Research, Development, Diffusion and Adoptation (RDD and A).

The question, therefore, arises—how to properly disseminate an educational technology that is a product of a research activity, and which is a process, a series of processes, with attendant assumptions and principles; and which moreover, has definite and specific objectives.

This is a problem which INNOTECH, the Regional Center for Educational Innovation and Technology of the Southest Asian Ministers of Education Organization (SEAMED), confronts every time it undertakes research. The problem is endemic to INNOTECH, because the Center is not an implementing institution. Its mandate requires INNOTECH to conduct research only for the purpose of finding solutions to problems of education faced by the member countries. It leaves to the Ministries of Education the prerogative to implement or not to implement the results or products of its research activities.

In view of this peculiar problem situation INNOTECH deliberately plans out a dissemination or popularization process for all the outputs of its research. It is this experience, which I refer to as the INNOTECH model of dissemination, which I would like not to describe and share with you. In the process I will be citing two INNOTECH research outputs as examples of educational technology.

Let me assure you, however, that INNOTECH has not always been successful in disseminating its research outputs. As in fact this model for dissemination had not been used for all its research products. Indeed, it must be admitted that it was refined and made operational by Project DELSIFLIFE, the latest of INNOFTECH'S R and D researches completed only in 1989.

Toward the end of this paper I will be referring to the actual process of dissemination or popularization—following the development of the technology—as a really simple and straightforward process. However, as model, the process is based on, and is greatly dependent, on a number of pre-conditions or prerequisites, for it to be successful or effective, as follows:

**1. Relevance**

An initial precondition is the relevance or timeliness of the research. Relevance, of course, is relative. To assure itself of relevance of its research, INNOTECH has, so far, undertaken mainly developmental research and has avoided pure or experimental research.

This Project IMPACT, which resulted in the development of the IMPACT system, an educational intervention system for mass primary education, was conducted in response to prevailing adverse conditions surrounding primary education in the SEAMED Region characterized by poor quality, high drop out rates, lack of qualified teachers, and generally expensive operation. These conditions, observed in the 1970s when Project IMPACT was conducted, persist to a great extent in the 1980s and perhaps even beyond.

Project DELSIFIFE, out of which came the DELSIFLFE system—another educational system but unlike IMPACT, applied in the nonformal sector—aimed at improving the quality of life of the rural poor through self-reliance. Like project IMPACT, Project DELSILIFE was undertaken in the light of the failure of development programmes and projects to reach the greater majority who need them most—the rural poor.

**2. User as Researcher**

One other factor which adds a great measure of guarantee that a technology will eventually, be disseminated and used, is the involvement of the user in the research. This is perhaps an aspect of other models, just like relevance. However, in the case of INNOTECH research, the user is, in fact, the researcher.

For developmental projects, such as Project IMPACT and DELSILIFE (there are other examples) whose eventual user is the Ministry of Education, the studies are actually undertaken in field conditions, and it is the participating Ministry which identifies the researchers or research teams. In which case INNOTECH'S role is more of guidance and monitoring, or technical assistance. (As in fact the trips of INNOTECH staff to the project sites are called Technical Assistance Visits).

Aside from the research team, INNOTECH always sees to it—insist, in fact—that a Ministry official, with decision-making prerogative, is identified as a member of the research team, if only in an advisory position. This official or his representative is always expected to participate in crucial meetings, especially a Consultative Meeting (CM).

A Consultative Meeting is a mechanism used by INNOTECH to bring together key participants to a research project for the purpose of sharing information, discussing and generally learning from each other significant development concerning a project. A CM is a monitoring devise called at crucial points of a project and is an occasion to recall common guidelines previously agreed upon and to make necessary modifications.

Incidentally, a second monitoring mechanism is the Technical Assistance Visit.

**3. Finance Agency as Research Colleague**

INNOTECH has had the good fortune of having its two major research projects financed by funding agencies, which are themselves research institutions, or which collaborate with a research body.

The experience of INNOTECH in this regard are of two kinds, one formal, the other, informal. In the case of Project IMPACT, which was given financial support by the International Development and Research Center of Canada (IDRC), the then Head of the Social Science Division took it upon himself to monitor the project. In the end he even published a book on the project and the IMPACT system.

In the case of Project DELSILIFE, funded by the Dutch Government, the participation of the Center for the Study of Education in Developing Countries (CESO) was formally built-in into the Memorandum of Agreement with INNOTECH.

INNOTECH, therefore, was given, not only financial support by institutions that were convinced of the relevance of the research, but equally important the time and energies of its own staff of competent and concerned experts. As a model for other similar researchers, it may not be easy to replicate the congenial and professional relationship between financier and researcher. Yet, it is inevitable that we suggest that for research outputs to be effectively and efficiently disseminated, a collaborative working relationship between financier and researcher be an a prior condition even if the financier modestly refers to its staff only as (is the case of DELSILIFE) "Consulted Colleagues."

Needless to say, the researcher has the tendency (as INNOTECH did) to exploit this relationship to ensure itself of continued funding. The truth is that both parties (and here I refer only to INNOTECH and CESO) from the start, had objective which both pursued with sincerity, trust and understanding.

**4. A Disssemination Instrument**

It is decidedly a deterrent to effective dissemination of an educational technology, if it is popularized in the absence of the proper adequate dissemination instrument. Hence, the marketing of a technology is usually done with the use of brochures, videos, film, slide-tapes, books, pamphlets and others.

In many cases, however, these are produced mainly to afford the researcher, especially an institution, a convenient vehicle to describe a product to visitors and other interested parties and researchers.

Thus, in the case IMPACT, INNOTECH and with IDRC, a book was also edited by INNOTECH of which only 1,000 copies were printed are, in fact, for sale. There is also a slide-tape presentation for our visitors: and a brochure. A monograph and a module were also prepared, but used mainly by the trainees of INNOTECH Training Programmes. The final report on Project IMPACT contains a replication manual which remains only in the few copies of final report on the project.

In addition, the last year of Project IMPACT was declared a "demonstration year". But then those who took advantage of it were mostly foreigners, academicians who visited the sites for only one day each. At that time all the materials mentioned above had not been produced.

What I am saying is that these instruments, which may be perfect as dissemination materials, (are) were not really used in a systematically dissemination programmes.

The same is true with DELSILIFE. There is a brochure, a module, a slide-tape and a monograph. Unlike the cast of

IMPACT, however, but because of the lessons learned from the IMPACT experience, INNOTECH took the cue from the business community—DELSILIFE was "packaged."

**The DELSILIFE Package[1]**

The DELSILIFE package is a set of multi-media (print and non-print) materials which describe in specific details the intervention process and provide directions and guidelines to the different persons, groups, actors and performers who participate or who have responsibilities to undertake. Each component of the package is addressed to and is expected to be utilized by specific users and performers.

Each country which participated in Project DELSILIFE produced its own package, in the local language. The use of simple language is especially crucial since parts of the package are to be read and utilized by villagers who are assumed to be, at best, semi-literate—who are in fact, the object of nonformal education programmes. INNOTECH, however, produced its own package, borrowing from the country packages, in the English language for wider use in and outside the Region.

On closer examination, it appears that each country packages is of two parts. One part is a general information on DELSILIFE as a system, how it operates, its components, principles and features; what it attempts to achieve. This part is addressed to decision makers, to administrators, to entities and institutions concerned with developing and improving the lives and living conditions of peoples and communities. Physically this is made up of videos and cassette tapes and printed pamphlets or booklet.

The second part, made up of a number of booklets compose the set of manuals which provide the necessary guidelines to those I referred to as the actors or performers in the living drama that is DELSILIFE.

Generally, the booklets or pockets have the following contents:

**Booklet number 1. The Delsilife Intervention System**

The booklet is meant to explain the principles of the Delsilife system to Promoters and Initiators of the Delsilife Community Council, the Group and Area Leaders of the Village and Resource Persons.

**Booklet number 2. Manual for the Initiator**

The booklet explains to, specifically the initiators who will introduce Delsilife system in the villages, what her functions are and how he/she can perform these functions.

**Booklet number 3. Manual for Training**

The manual is aimed at all those who are expected to have leadership roles in the implementation of Delsilife. The booklet describes who will need to be trained, who will train, and in what the training will be.

**Booklet number 4. Manual for the Delsilife Community Council (DCC)**

The booklet addressed to the leaders of communities. It tells how the DCC is formed, what the functions of the DCC are and how the DCC can perform its functions.

**Booklet number 5. Manual for the Group Leader**

The manual describes in some detail the conduct of Learning Programmes, which is the core of the Delsilife system; the role of the Group Leader, how he/she is chosen, what his/her functions are and how he/she can function.

**Booklet number 6. Basic Life Skills**

This booklet describes what, and how some Basic Life Skills are obtained or developed in the Delsilife system.

The DELSILIFE Package is an attempt on the part of the developer of the DELSILIFE system—INNOTECH to transfer the technology to the implementors in the field. Theoretically, DELSILIFE was known only to INNOTECH and the few participating research staffs of Indonesia, Malaysia, the Philippines and Thailand. For the technology to be known and utilized by others, it was decided to "capture" the system into a "package".

There are certainly other ways of transferring technology, such as through seminars and workshops. It was thought, however, that through the package, the essence of DELSILIFE can be capsulized in as pure a form as possible; assuring therefore, a minimum of dilution of its concept, principles, processes and even objectives.

Thus, it is not so much a question of whether or not the concept can be transferred in its true form—since the package has assured that—but whether the user, the one who opens the package, will want the whole package, or simply pick those part that suits his fancy or which appeals to him most because of his circumstances or working environment.

Moreover, it was also the hope that if the package can be made as complete and comprehensive enough, that it will be self-sufficient and that it need not entail additional verbal explanation, or intermediation by the original developer.

In other words, the package takes the place of the developer of the technology. If the package is placed in the hands of a person in authority such as an education regional officer, this officer, after studying and understanding the system, may cause the package to reach all concerned personnel under him. In turn, each will study and understand his part and role and perform this accordingly. In the bureaucracy of the Department of Education, Culture and Sports of the Philippines, for example, the last person to receive the package will be the District Nonformal Coordinator, or the school NFE teacher—who will have direct responsibility to motivate a village to adopt DELSILIFE.

**5. Official Endorsement and Encouragement**

It goes without saying that the best package, and the presence of all the favourable pre-conditions, would be inutil and ineffectual without the accompanying support in the form of endorsement by the appropriate official or person in authority. This is especially crucial in a bureaucratic set up, such as the Ministry of Education, Happily for DELSILIFE the Ministry of Education of Indonesia, the Philippines and Thailand gave official sanction for DELSILIFE to be adopted as one more approach to their nonformal education programme.

The effect of this endorsement, or its absence, is demonstrated quite will in both project—IMPACT and DELSILIFE.

IMPACT was favourably endorsed by the Indonesian[2] Ministry, hence there was an extended experimentation and more extensive implementation of the system. On the other hand the Philippine Minister of Education simply "encouraged further experimentation by schools." Only the Philippines has more than one school applying the IMPACT system.

In the case of DELSILIFE, the Ministry of Education of Malaysia, since it does not have a nonformal education aim, did not participate in Phase C of Project DELSILIFE—which is an implementation phase.

**6. Effectiveness**

Underlying all these pre-conditions, however, is the primary assurance that the product being disseminated works—that the technology can effectively attain its objective. And this assurance must be shared by both the financier and the researcher.

**The Process of Disseminastion**

Admittedly all these preconditions, individually and collectively may not guarantee success in disseminating a product. The assumption that by itself alone a package would be self-sufficient may be unfounded, or at least its basis weak.

Happily, again, the Ministries of Education went one big step further. They utilized their training mechanisms.

The example of the Philippines in disseminating or popularizing Delsilife, is a case in point. On the strength of a Department Order, encouraging the adoption of DELSILIFE, the Bureau of Nonformal Education conducted four regional seminar workshops on DELSILIFE which eventually included all Regional and Division level action officers in nonformal education. Following these seminars, all regions conducted Division level "echo" workshops to which Division and District Nonformal education supervisors and coordinators participated.

The net result of this is that it is now virtually impossible to make an accurate count of the number of villages in the Philippines in which DELSILIFE in its pure form, or aspects of it, has been introduced.

In other words, given all the aforecited pre-conditions, the actual process of dissemination or popularization of the DELSILIFE technology was really a simple thing.

The "echo" seminars conducted at the Division level was in fact a training workshop for the promoters and initiators. The DELSILIFE package identifies two levels of personnel who perform quite crucial roles, in popularizing and implementing DELSILIFE.

The promoter (in the instance of the Philippines) is a nonformal education supervisor with jurisdiction over a number of schools. An initiator, is likewise a school personnel also in charge of nonformal education whose responsibilities require of him/her to take or introduce a nonformal education programme in a specific district or village.

The two terms are interchangeable, but the concept requires one of them—the promoter to cause the technology to be accepted by other entities involved in development, including personnel under him/her; the other—the initiator—is expected to directly motivate a village to adopt DELSILIFE. The initiator performs a very crucial role in the popularizing (and implementation) of the technology that is DELSILIFE; as seen in the list of his/her functions after convincing a community to adopt the Delsilife System.

1. Helps the Community Council in coordinating and monitoring Learning Programmes.
2. Helps the Community Council in motivating potential target clientele to participate in the Learning Programmes/organize learning groups.
3. Helps in the development, evaluation of Learning Programmes.
4. Assists in securing human and material resources for learning programmes.
5. Assists in the training and development of group leaders.
6. Helps keep records of DELSILIFE data and facilitates their optimal use.
7. Facilitates the diffusion and adoption of the DELSILIFE system.

In summary, dissemination, or popularization of a technology as experienced by INNOTECH (with Delsilife example) goes through four stages:

1. adoption by a national body
2. production of a package as the dissemination instrument
3. orientation of high level officials; training of promoters and initiators
4. motivation of the community; Implementation
   - Creation of the Support System (Steering bodies; Organization of the DCC)
   - Formation of Learning Groups
   - Conduct of Learning Programmes

**Problem of Research, Dissemination and Implementation**

Although INNOTECH utilizes various ways by which to disseminate information about its research projects and other activities, there are many problems and constraints which militate against more effective and efficient dissemination of information.

These are general problems but they may apply to popularization programmes in the informal sector; hence shared in this seminar.

1. The apparent lack of a more positive interest on the part of some of the MOEs are to implement, or at least try out more extensively the results of INNOTECH research.

Perhaps MOEs are immersed in their own problems or planned which any preclude their adoption or adaptation of finding of research studies and other technologies. Perhaps too, the technologies do not appeal to the MOEs.

2. Limited circulation of the Journal.

Only 1,000 copies are printed, some of which must have to remain on file.

3. Language poses a problem in a number of ways.

A case in point is Project RIT, the outputs of which include learning materials all written Thai. Assuming there may be a desire on the part of another member country to adapt RIT, the need to translate the materials poses a big problem.

4. The creation of Steering Committees for project do not ensure implementation or even dissemination.

There is secant evidence that the Committees have actively worked toward implementation of the research findings.

5. Finally, one obvious factor which a center like INNOTECH would inevitably be confronted with, is the composite of differences in policies, socio-economic and educational conditions of the member countries.

At first glance, these differences would be immediately considered as stumbling blocks to a unified, concerted or efficient conduct of a research activity. And this is true to some extend. For example, not all countries have participated in all INNOTECH researchers because of differences in the socio-economic conditions. As a result too of variations in the educational climate, field staffs have been of wide diversity in their qualifications. Because of policies, not all research methodologies and procedures could be followed in certain countries. More seriously, the differences in policies have prevented greater implementation of research products.

The happy part of it, however, is that this same factor—the variance in policies and socio-economic and educational conditions—has also been a positive factor to INNOTECH.

For one thing INNOTECH has been able to achieve its mandate of assisting member countries by serving each country more directly and specifically through the conduct of a research. All methodologies and processes of a research project must adjust to country policies and conditions. In so doing the resulting product, such as a model, is directly relevant to the country.

Secondly, as a result of adjusting to national policies, INNOTECH researchers have resulted, not only in regional models, but also in a variety of national models. From a professional point of view, there is great satisfaction in achieving more than just one stated goal through one activity.

At a more macro level, the difference in policies have also resulted in different products and by-products which are otherwise not anticipated. Again, this has been a source of satisfaction on the part of the researcher, INNOTECH.

Project IMPACT is a good example. In Indonesia, they developed the Learning Post. In the Philippines, the staff produced an integrated set of modules as against the subject modules of Indonesia. The concept of the "itinerant teacher" is quite different for the two countries.

Project DELSILIFE is another. Two types of the DELSILIFE Community Councils have been developed. Various versions and parts of the package are anticipated. Different criteria are used in the organization of Learning groups. A wide variety of Learning Programmes have been undertaken—giving INNOTECH an almost unlimited lost of possibilities open to rural communities which would want to implement DELSILIFE in order to improve their quality of life.

This is, of course, saying that INNOTECH manipulates apparent hindrances and impediments and turns them around into facilitators to its advantage.

INNOTECH, in other words views these problems as opportunities for perfecting its R and D approach to product development. As new products are developed, new insights are gained and the R and D approach is fine-tuned further.

## NOTES

1. "Package" is used for want of a better, more appropriate term.
2. In Indonesia the project was known as Proyek Pamong, for Pandidikan Anak Oleh Masyarakat Orang Tua Dan Guru.

# 11

# Out-of-School Activities: The Road to Success

CHENG DONGHONG

In the contemporary world, science and technology are playing an important role in every country's social development and economic progress. Successful competition in science and technology is directly related to the success of failure in the field of economy, military and politics. Many facts have proved that to increase the national awareness of science and technology and train a large number of specialists and scientists at various levels is an essential task for our country to accomplish if we are to keep up with the rapid development in science and technology and meet the challenge in the fierce competition in the world market. Therefore, it is our important basic construction to engage in the popularization of science and technology in the whole society using various means and media. And the popularization of science and technology among youngsters, who represent the future of the country, is of strategic significance to us.

It is true the formal education, which is education in science at school, plays the leading role in the popularization of science and technology among youngsters. But facts have shown that in China it is far from enough to depend on school education in science to popularize science and technology among young people. The reasons are as follows: First of all, formal education contains materials that is relatively fixed which is unable to reflect the latest development in science and technology. Secondly, as China's formal education is not well-developed, it can not shoulder the whole younger generation as the objects of education. In China's rural areas, only 70 per cent of the primary school children enter middle school and 30 per cent of the middle school students continue their study in senior-middle school, consequently the few middle school graduates who are able to receive college education takes up only a very small percentage of the younger population. Under these circumstances, non-formal education in science and technology becomes an indispensable supplementary to education in science at school.

In the recent ten years, non-formal education in science and technology among Chinese youngsters has mainly been conducted in the form of out-of-school activities in science and technology. It has been proved that out-of-school activities in science and technology is indeed an effective means to popularize science/technology among young people.

One of the characteristics of China's out-of-school science education is that governments of all levels, various unofficial organizations and science associations and societies are all sponsors or supporters in various forms of such activities. The following is a brief introduction to the youngsters' science and technology work of China Association for Science and Technology (CAST).

**1. Organizer**

The top organizer for the whole nation's youngsters' science activities is the Leading Group of All China Children's Science and Technology Activities which is established in 1981 by the chief officials from China Association for Science and Technology (CAST), the State Education Commission, the Central Committee of the Chinese Communist Youth League, the All-China Federation of Women and the State Physical Culture and Sports Commission. The Group coordinates the different departments in their work of science and technology activities, works out the major regulations and policies, organizes demonstrative nationwide activities and commends outstanding science instructors. The office of the Group is located in the Department of Children and Youth's Affairs of CAST.

CAST, which has 153 natural scientific and technological societies, associations and research institutions, is a society of scientists and engineers. To express scientists' concern on nurturing science reserves, CAST takes it as one of its major tasks to carry out the youngsters' science and technology activities and set up the Department of Children and Youth's Affairs which is in charge of organizing youngsters' science and technology activities among the affiliating organizations of the CAST. Among the 153 natural scientific and technological societies, associations and research institutes, I want to mention the China Association for Youngsters' Science Instructors. It has 130,000 members, through whom the Association keeps contact with the vast science instructors and science teachers. Science instructors and the grass-root directors and organizers of various science and technology activities, mostly volunteers doing the work in their sparetime, with only a small number as full-time instructors.

Besides the institutions and organizations mentioned above, there are more than 8,000 youngsters' palaces, activity centres, science centres and such institutions in China. The number of county level and above youngsters' palaces has been increased from 92 in 1979 to over 700. There are sizable youngsters' palaces, activity centres or sciences centres each of the 30 provinces, autonomous regions and municipalities. In cities like Beijing, Shanghai, Xi'an and Wuhan and in Liaoning Province, out-of-school activity stations are set up in most of their neighbourhoods thus forming a complete network with the municipal, district and neighbourhood levels for out-of-school education. Many enterprises and institutions also have founded centres or stations in their residential areas. Some well-off rural villages are beginning to set up such places for their children. These out-of-school activity centres do not only provide needed sites for the young people, but also they are the supporters for various activities. CAST established its Children's Science and

Technology Centre in 1980's and has set up more than 20 children's science and technology centres in different provinces throughout the country, which are actively involved in various activities in science and technology.

**2. Multi-level Activities, Multi-subject**

China started its organized out-of-school activities in science and technology for children and youngsters in the 1950s. It organized its first national exhibition on science and technology in 1955. In the 1980's, when China's modernization campaign found itself in needs for a large number of scientists and millions of people armed with advanced knowledge of science and technology, the popularization of science and technology in the society became an urgent and important issue. As a result, activities in science and technology for children and youth met with an unprecedented development along with the increasing educational programmes in science. Science activities for children and youth have been organized at different scales by organizations and societies at various levels. They are:

(a) Multi-subject Comprehensive Activities

- National Contests for Inventions and Seminars on Science and Technology Development by Children and Youth, in the field of mathematics, physics, chemistry, astronomy, geology, biology, . . . Since 1982, these contests and seminars have been co-sponsored every other year by the Leading Group of All China Children's Science and Technology Activities and the National Natural Science Foundation of China. Candidates with outstanding essays and inventions for the contests are selected from the corresponding activities organized by various countries, prefectures and provinces, thus forming a relatively comprehensive selective system that presents nearly three million children and youth for each session.
- "Science-loving Month" has been started in many places. During that month, every children and teenagers is called on to get to a popular science talk or a science

(c) They provide chances for outstanding youth display their talent. On the one hand, talent can only be displayed in and identified through its application; on the other, only by constant use can talent be developed. The opportunity provided by classroom education is quite limited while out-of-school activities create a much greater opportunity because they are more active, more flexible, more practical, more adaptable and more interesting. The recent decade of science and technology activities have brought into full play the potential and talent of a large group of young people who won the prize of competition with their achievements and were recommended to further their education in colleges and universities. Now we are glad to see that a large number of active participants in the out-of-school science activities have made their serious commitment to the country's development of science and technology and the cause of popularizing science and training the qualifies citizens for this country.

**4. Future Perspective**

Great efforts have been made to engage in science and technology activities through non-formal channels. However, China, as a developing country with an unbalanced economy, has shown a serious need for balance in education and science activities among young people. It is almost impossible for those rural grade schools and high schools to provide enough money for the simple need of the instructors for after-class activities when their classroom threaten to cave in at any moment.

This author believed that greater efforts should be made in the following three areas if China's science and technology activities and youth are to make further progress:

(a) To expand the scale of these activities so that more schools, children and youth will be involved in these activities;

(b) To increase the number of science instructors and make sure their knowledge in the subjects is continuously renewed;

(c) Strengthen the theoretical research work for the out-of-school science and technology activities to find out the innate regulations in this form on non-formal education;

(d) To open up other new possibilities for new forms of such activities that will effectively reflect the latest development in science and technology.

**Conclusion**

Practice in the past thirty years have indicated that out-of-school activities in science and technology is an effective means to popularize science and technology among children and youth and complement the formal school education. They have made great contributions to speed up the country's development in science and development in the modern area.

# 12

# Education and Technology Transfer in Shenzhen Special Economic Zone

GERARD POSTIGLIONE

## 1. The Special Economic Zones (SEZs) and Technology Transfer

In 1979, China decided to establish four foreign investment enclaves in southern China. Five years later, Chinese leader Deng Xiaoping toured the four SEZs, proclaimed them a success, and called upon the nation "to learn from Shenzhen," the largest of the SEZs (Da Gong Bao, 1984:1). Since that time, at least 21 coastal cities have been declared open as preferred cities for foreign investment. More recently, Hainan island, formerly a part of Guangdong province, was designated a special economic region with its status being upgraded to that of a province. Also, China has opened the coastal regions of Fujian and Guangdong provinces, the Liaodong peninsula in the northeast, the Shandong peninsula, and the Yangtze delta area to attract foreign investors (SCMP, 1988:7). A large number of regions will follow this pattern, including Zhong Guan Village, an area of Beijing with a concentration of high technology work units, often referred to as Beijing's Silicon Valley.

Among the stated goals of the SEZs are to generate foreign exchange, to create employment, to attract foreign investment, and to facilitate the transfer of technology (Xu Dixin, 1984). Of the four SEZs, only Shenzhen was mandated to establish a large comprehensive zone involving across the board development of industrial, commercial, property and tourist undertakings. The other zones were, to varying degrees, hedged in by policy directives which called for limiting zone size and for gearing zone objectives to local resources (Falkenheim, 1986).

The major vehicle for development of these zones is the joint venture. This is an agreement in which the foreign side provides the foreign exchange and technology, while the Chinese side provides buildings, site, equipment, and renminbi (local exchange). The joint venture company is managed jointly, and profits and losses are distributed in proportion to the participants' equity shares in the venture. Aside from the chance to learn the new technologies and management techniques from the foreign partner, the Chinese partner enjoys other advantages as well, including flexibility in hiring personnel, pay scales for personnel, import and export control, management of the firm's investment, purchasing, and sales policies.

Although a number for impediments, many relating to foreign investment, have inhibited the attraction to China of foreign technology, there are equally important non-investment related problems. Even when high technology transfer to China does occur, there are serious difficulties in the assimilation, innovation, and dispersion of that technology. To relieve the investment related problem, new regulations grant a privileged position to export oriented and high technology foreign enterprises (United States Congress, 1986). Solutions to the non-investment related problems rest almost totally with education. It is these that will be a major concern of this paper.

**2. The Shenzhen SEZ**

The Shenzhen SEZ is the most ambitious of all the zones. In 1980s, Shenzhen was designated a special economic region of China by the Central Committee of the Communist Party and China's State Council. In 1979, its population was 23,000 in what was then the rural Baoan county. The new zone was to be the largest special economic zone in the world, 327.5 square kilometres in area, stretching 49 miles in along the border of Hong Kong's New Territories, and incorporating one-third of the area of the newly designated Shenzhen municipality. The population of the zone is 400,000 of whom almost half are temporary workers (Shenzhen TEQU, 1985). In the draft ten year development plan, technology intensive industrial development is stressed (Wen Wei Bao, 1983:2). The average annual rate of projected economic growth through the year 2000 is 31 per cent. By the year 2000 the population growth is expected to reach one million.

The number of specialized personnel transferred to Shenzhen up until 1985 was 10,000. Also, as many as 100,000 construction workers have come from other parts of China. The total work force is over 154,400, which does not include over 118,000 temporary construction workers. By the end of 1984, there were 3,495 contracts with foreign businesses and direct investment exceeded US$2,200 million. In 1984 alone, 1,183 contracts were signed exceeding US$600 million in direct investment. However, only a minor portion of the investment (10.3 per cent) is foreign, with the largest portion (89.8 per cent) coming from Hong Kong and Macau. In 1984, the output of joint ventures, cooperative enterprises, and wholly owned foreign enterprises in Shenzhen accounted for 53 per cent of the total output. Moreover, overseas investment, equipment, and technology imported to Shenzhen are mostly used in technology-intensive and knowledge-intensive products, i.e., electronics, light industry, petrochemicals, precision machinery, and building materials.

After Shenzhen was declared a special economic zone, many Hong Kong industrialists who found themselves hard pressed by labour shortages and rising wages in 1979 and 1980, saw the SEZ as a way to cut costs through the decentralization of low-skill, labour-intensive processes in Shenzhen. However, Shenzhen industrialists are clearly not interested in attracting only simple and assembly types of industry. Instead, Shenzhen wants more sophisticated industries (Sit, 1986). One investor's handbook, in referring to types of industries, stated that the zone did not want "those involved in assembly and processing activities".

The Shenzhen SEZ Development Company, one of the three major promotion agents of the SEZ, listed nine high-priority promotion items for 1984, all of which belong to the high technology electronics industry. Another agent, the Shenzhen Municipal Electronics Company, listed 31 items in the handbook for promotion. All except two required an ultimate investment of over US$10 million, one even of US$200 million. The size of the capital and preference for high technology production (Sit, 1986:240). In 1978, there was only one electronics assembly factory in Shenzhen employing about 300 workers. By 1983, there were 60 establishments employing over 15,000 workers.

In principle and practice, the Shenzhen SEZ is socialist. Socialism and high technology have combined to influence the nature of work and labour markets, expansion of the educational system, and the content of education. Unlike Hong Kong where workers had much manufacturing experience, Shenzhen has had to condition a new work force.

**3. Education and Technology Transfer in Shenzhen**

China's major problem has been tied less to acquiring technology, than it has been with assimilating, innovation, and effectively diffusing that technology (United States Congress, Office of Technology Assessment, 1987). The problem of assimilation is linked to the issue of technology. In the past, merely purchasing technology has avoided much of the foreign dependence, but it has fostered a kind of self-reliance that has stifled solutions to the problems of assimilation and diffusion. Ironically, in the case of China, "the risk of dependency increases as the problems of assimilation remain unsolved" (Zhang, 1985:62). The problem of assimilation of technology may be looked at as composed of three areas: production (using the imported technology); manufacturing (replicating the import); and, design (capability of redesigning the technology). It is in the last of these that China is the weakest. Although other parts of the problem are structural, i.e. choosing the right technology to buy, balancing the purchase of expertise and software with hardware, getting managers to focus on absorption rather than production quotas and output, etc., it is the capability of redesigning the technology that is most important at present. Its major solution rests with providing the most appropriate education.

With few exceptions, the Shenzhen education system follows the nation-wide policy of expanding vocational-technical education at the secondary school level (Postiglione 1988, 1988a, 1989). Aside from ensuring a good investment climate, the greatest need of Shenzhen's high technology environment is to raise the level of the technical qualifications of its people. It has made clear its direction toward high technology production by such things as the establishment of a massive Science and Industrial Park project. If the Shenzhen SEZ continues to insist on only allowing high technology projects and discouraging assembly industrial processes, then it will have to show that it is able to support such operations with a highly skilled work force. Although it is making a strong effort, mainly through the use of adult education and continuing education to supply trained personnel, this could not possibly provide the type, level, and quality of training needed. Shenzhen will only be able to maintain the supply of highly skilled personnel, as it has in the past, through the movement of individuals from other parts of the country. For example, it has already imported over 10,000 professionals from other parts of China. However, this is not nearly enough to deal with the problems of assimilation, innovation, and diffusion of technology. According to Wang (1987):

> . . . 29.8 per cent of the administrators and staff from all walks of life had an education of junior college or above; 23.3 per cent had a vocational education; 20.7 per cent had a senior high school education; and 28.7 per cent had an education below junior high school level in 1985 . . . among the province's 120,000 in-service workers, 42 per cent had a senior high school education or higher level education, and 58 per cent had an education below the junior high school level in 1985 (1987:8).

Predictions by the Audit Education Bureau of Shenzhen are that before 1990, the regular higher education institutions and vocational schools can only train enough people to meet about 10 per cent of the total development need. In addition to the 20 per cent professionally trained people that Shenzhen now has, it will still need about 70 per cent more by 1990 (Shenzhen Adult Education Bureau, 1987).

The Shenzhen education authorities view an increase in the provision of vocational-technical education as one of the most important parts of their education development plans. However, a shortage of resources has kept the pace slow. In 1985, there were only 9 vocational-technical middle schools, offering 11 specialization, with 1,086 students. The ratio of vocational-technical school students to upper middle secondary students is 1:3. Post-secondary specialized colleges receive graduates from the vocational-technical middle schools in ratio 2:3 to the academic upper secondary schools (Chen, 1985:217). At the policy level these vocational and technical schools are seen as preparing people for work in a special economy, and at the same time providing continuing education. Conditions in the schools need to be improved, and the "fenpei" system, whereby students are assigned to work unit, needs continued deemphasis to allow for more choice on the part of graduates seeking employment.

Although Shenzhen follows the main policies espoused by the Central Government, its special conditions differ from those in other parts of the country and, therefore, the Shenzhen education authorities have identified ways that their vocational-technical secondary education must align itself with the special conditions of the zone. For example, a rapidly expanding economy calls for a number of new specializations. Every year there is an increase of a hundred factories, and therefore, at least a thousand technicians and managers are needed each year. In recent years, the practice has been to appoint someone to work and train them later. The problem exists in all of the vocational work areas. Because of the nature of the special economics zone, unlike other parts of China where less intense competition exists, the vocational-technical schools in Shenzhen must be competitive.

Skills change quickly and need to be constantly updated. Student aspirations in the rest of China only also differ from those in Shenzhen. Thirty to forty per cent of students graduate from lower secondary schools in the country as a whole. However, in Shenzhen the figure is 85 per cent. Very few students want to go to vocational-technical schools. There are other problems as well, many of them shared with other parts of China, such as a lack of trained teachers and a shortage of school resources (Chen,.1985:218).

The Shenzhen education bureau contends that half of the work force are engaged in some kind of continuing education. These courses are run by a variety of institutions, including the work units themselves. The level of training may not be very high. Nevertheless, according to the city's Bureau of Adult Education, 149,223 people were enrolled in 186 specializations at the higher education level and secondary adult education level in 1986. In 1985, more than half of the total number of workers and staff were enrolled in some kind of adult education (Ren Min Ri Bao, 1986). By 1990, the Shenzhen Bureau of Adult Education plans to have all leaders of large and medium sized enterprises and community authorities trained with at least a junior college education. The reason for the heavy reliance on adult education are obvious. Without a large educational infrastructure, it would take too long to run great numbers of students through the system in time to meet the needs of the rapidly expanding economy.

## Conclusion

Shenzhen is a potentially interesting region for the study of the Informal and Non-formal education and the popularization of science and technology. The following five features combine to form a set of circumstances supporting further study of this region:

1. Unlike other SEZs, Shenzhen is not hedged in by policy directives which call for limiting zone size and for gearing zone objectives to local resources;
2. expressed intent to develop high technology rather than processing operations;
3. proximity of Hong Kong;
4. the importation of large numbers of skilled and unskilled workers from other parts of China;
5. the establishment of a large scale science park; and,
6. the extensive amount of adult education.

## REFERENCES

Chen, Xian Hong (1985). "The Characteristics and New Measures of Technical-Vocational Education in Special Economic Zone," in *Educational in Special Economic Zones,* edited by The Shenzhen Institute of Educational Research, Wuhan; Wuhan: University Press. (In Chinese)

De Gong Bao (1984). Hong Kong, April 7, p. 1.

Falkenheim, V. (1986). "China's Special Economic Zones," in *China's Economy Looks Toward the Year 2000*, Volume 2, *Economics Openness in Modernizing China*, Washington, D.C.: Congress of the United States, pp. 348-369.

Postiglione, Gerard (1989). "Education and Technology Transfer in Shenzhen: Human Capital or Screening?" A Research Proposal Funded by the Center of Urban Studies and Urban Planning, The University of Hong Kong, February 13.

- (1988). "Education in Special Economic Zones and Open Cities," in *Chinese Education*, Armonk, New York: M.E. Sharpe Publishers, Volume 21, Number 3, Fall, 1988.

- (1988a). "Education, Technology Transfer, and the Convergence of Special Zones in South China," International Education Association Meeting, Atlanta, Georiga, March 19-24, 1988.

Ren Min Ri Bao. (1986) Beijing, People's Republic of China, January 26, p. 4 S.C.M.P. (1988) South China Morning Post. March 11.

Shenzhen Adult Education Bureau and Shenzhen Adult Education Association. (1986) *Adult Education in the Shenzhen Special Economic Zone*, Shenzhen: Adult Education Bureau.

*Shenzhen Tequ* Xin Mao (1985). *The New Look of the Shenzhen Special Economic Zone*, China Urban Reform Series, Beijing: Red Flag Publications (In Chinese).

Sit, V. (1986). "Industries in Shenzhen: An Attempt at Open Door Industrialization," in Y.C Jao and C.K.Leung, eds., *China's Special Economic Zones*, Hong Kong: Oxford University Press, pp. 226-246.

United States Congress, Joint Economic Commission (1986). *China's Economy Looks Toward the Year 2000*, Volume 2, Washington D.C. Government Printer.

United States Congress, Office of Technology Assessment (1987). *Technology Transfer to China*, Washington D.C.: Government Printer.

Wang Jian (1987) "Educational Development in Shenzhen" The Comparative and International Education Association Western Division Meeting, University of Southern California, November 12. Wen Hui Bao (1983) Hong Kong, February 1, p. 1.

Xu Din Xin (1986). *China's Open Cities and Special Economic Zones*, Beijing: Economy and Science Publishers.

Zhang Shi Hong (1985). "A Noteworthy Issue: Digestion, Absorption, and Renewal in Technology Importation as Viewed from Shanghai" *Ren Min Ri Bao*, May 3.

# 13

# Popularization of Science and Technology

KURT PROKOP

Popularization of science and technology is an important task for the society depends, how we judge and understand science and technology, either as the tool of human development or as a dominant factor of the human life. This basic precondition reflects itself on our education systems in all three areas of education policy: in the formal education, in the nonformal and informal education. Therefore the introduction and popularization of science and technology is not a neutral process, it is a very hot political issue. Personally, I see this question through the eyes of a worker educator, who dedicated his whole working life to workers and adult education. Therefore the introduction and popularization of science and technology in the formal and nonformal education system demand an overall concensus amongst the economic pressure groups of our societies. Because of this precondition the rate of adaption and change of educational structures in societies is rather slow. We have to be aware that structures, especially in the formal sector, are on the whole not able to cope immediately with the progress of technology and science.

In the nonformal sector the rate of innovations is relatively higher, because nonformal education has not so tight structures as the formal education system.

The existing gap and the growing knowledge in science and technology is one of the fundamental problems of our societies, especially of the underdeveloped regions on our earth. It is a fact, that the breakthrough of the so-called "key technologies" has totally changed our leisure and working life.

Popularization of science and technology could help to bridge the growing gap between the progress of science and technology and the needs of societies. In the process, we observe a steadily rising demand for higher qualified and skilled people, who are able to operate and manage new technologies and science.

Especially the developing countries suffering under illiteracy and therefore on a great waste of human talents and abilities. The popularization of science and technology must therefore have differentiate character in the developing countries than in developed countries. For these problems a separate item on the agenda of this conference would be necessary.

**Science and Technology—A Challenge for Education**

We are observing the global breakthrough of the so-called "key technologies", which are the driving force behind change. Our historical experience shows, that if the technology and science are changing, also the instrument of society to control and to manage technological and scientific development must change. The important "key technologies", who are the driving forces amongst others, are as follows: microelectornics, electronic, media, satellite technology, bio and gen-technology.

All these "key technologies" are changing and revolutionizing our society and are influencing our educational, social and cultural structures in a very serious way.

Especially the microelectronics, the computers, the electronic communication and the satellite technology has developed consequences for our leisure and working life.

Three tendencies are challenging us in a serious way:

1. The typical process character of new technologies, which demands extensive integration, flexibility and adaptation from our education system.

2. The system character of work and production. The new technologies and the increasing application of science do not change individual working places alone; they are changing the total system.

3. By application of new technologies and science, we are able to use them in a universal way, in all areas of production, in communication, in services, in agriculture, in the development of science and technology itself, and even in our daily life.

These three tendencies demand a radical new approach in formal and non-formal education. The informal education is especially affected by means of new communications (electronics media). The new approach means a new type of learning and the application of interdisciplinary thinking and learning to control and to work with the new process and system character in work and leisure.

We need a breakdown of the faculty system and interdisciplinary thinking in all areas in education of society. Therefore we need, for example school students with a sound polytechnic knowledge. We are needing doctors with technical and sociological knowledge, we need engineers with knowledge on medicine and human relations, we need lawyers with knowledge on human, electronic and technical management, we need economists with a sound knowledge on human resources and we need teachers, who are motivating are not demotivating for life long learning.

**The New "Learning"**

Traditional learning was the key of success of our past. Traditional learning was directed to get or to teach defined issue, method and rules to manage situations, which repeatedly took place for centuries. This learning guaranteed the survival of the existing systems and our way of life.

This traditional learning was basically interrupted by unforeseen shocks with all their social and cultural consequences. Learning by shocks and events like Chernobyl, environment hazards, hunger in the third world and other catastrophes are far too dangerous for us in our time and could lead in chaotic situations with the danger of a total collapse of our societies.

At present in spite of billions of investments in education, we have to admit that we know very little about other people's technological, science, social, cultural and religious situations and development, their human values, beliefs and their religious and cultural practices.

In spite of undoubtedly better, higher and far more widespread education, hate and racial discrimination is not decreasing, it is increasing. We have to take in account that our education system worldwide has more or less failed, a possible global and fundamental questions is far. A head inspite we are dealing with global technology and science.

**What Do We Need?**

We need urgently a way out of this human dilemma.

We need innovative learning processes, which integrate anticipative and participative learning. Participation means more discussion, more orientation and learning in alternatives.

Participation means also dialogue, communication and co-operation. Popularization of science and technology in formal, non-formal and informal education will be a helpless beginning, if we are not able to change and adapt the learning processes for the youth and adults.

**Popularization of New Technologies—An Austrian Case Study**

Austria is a small, but highly industrialized country. It was heavily destroyed after Second World War and has now reached roughly the seventh place in the social and industrial ladder of Europe.

Besides a well developed parliamentary system, the social-economic partners of Austria (Trade Union and Employers Associations) has contributed a lot to the Austrian economic, social and educational development. They are permanently involved in all major economic, social and educational discussions and decisions.

Popularization of science and technology outside of the working world is not very difficult, because commercial interest has made computer games, electronic and video technology to an everyday instrument, for instance, the home computers are at present a dominant factor of our leisure time.

In industry, in production and services as well as in the formal and nonformal education the introduction of computers was more complicated. Traditional behaviour and structures were endangered and challenged by new technology and science.

Many workers lost their jobs and qualifications. In the formal and nonformal education system new technologies were for years not seriously discussed. An overall campaign for new technologies at schools, universities, as well as in the non-formal education system was urgently needed.

**Attitude of Workers Organizations Towards New Technologies in Formal Education**

The approach of workers organizations *vis-a-vis* technologies is rather simple. If founded its expression in a simple sentences: we are for the introduction of new technologies and science in all areas of education, but under negotiated conditions. This basic position was also accepted by the social partners in Austria.

By consensus the Austria ministry of education and science was asked to introduce new technologies in the formal education system following pre-conditions where for this step necessary on education.

A commission to reform the formal education system decided, together with the minister of education that within the curricula a subject "preparation for the world of working has to be introduced".

Secondly factory visits and an extensive professional orientation has been introduced in the curricula.

A consensus between employeers and trade organizations to support the ministry to install computers and other technologies was negotiated and agreed.

A computer center in a teacher training college was built up for the study of all computer system available on the market.

The next step was an extensive training of teacher in this area. We know that teacher has only little knowledge in science and technology and their practical applications. At last 20 per cent of teaching was dedicated to discuss the social and economic consequences of new technologies and science.

For this demand trade unions and employees organizations prepared materials, videos and other written material for schools and universities. In addition they nominated their own experts for discussions and lectures on school university level and in the broad area of nonformal education.

The trade unions of Austria offered a large scale of teacher training seminars at their own cost. The trade unions trained in these programmes in the last year more than 1000 teachers in Austria.

New technologies are now accepted part of the formal education and workers organizations are pressing permanently for a test installation of new technologies in secondary and especially in apprentice schools. The universities are inviting trade unions and employers organizations to participate in seminars for technology orientation.

**The Nonformal Education**

The formal and nonformal education system has to be linked in popularization of science and technology. It is a fact that all what we miss in the formal education. We have to educate in the non-formal area with heavy investment. We know that the formal education system will never meet the requirement of changing technology and science.

Therefore adult and workers education gets more and more important. The demand of long life education reflects also in the rapid change of science and technology and their application. In Austria there are different programmes of adult and workers education in operation. Mainly they are qualification programmes for retraining and further training.

The financial burden for these education and training programmes which include also elements of workers education are partly borne by private institution, the employees organizations and trade unions running big professicnal training centres for adults.

These institutions are mainly financed by "active manpower policy" funds of the state budget or by other subsidies. These institutions are equipped with all modern machinery and technologies and co-operates very strongly with universities and other educational bodies. The main contents of these training courses are mainly qualification seminars, which are planned together with job demands of the economy. The courses, where education and training are combined with job creation, are coming more and more in the forefront, because training and education isolated from job creation and development could be a great failure. The demand for high qualifications is a strong issue for popularizing schemes of new technologies and science.

**The Growing Informal Education**

The informal education structures are growing because of new electronic media, which are offering science and technology programmes.

An interesting features is the growing interest of the population on science and technology programmes in radio and television. In Austria the social partners started so-called combined media programmes, on science and technology questions. They consisted of 10-12 minutes TV-programmes, printed material to these TV-programmes and organized study circles, which were organized by adult and workers education associations.

Similar programmes were also distributed in the radio system. For such a development it is important that adult and workers education associations have access to the electronic media and a certain influence on their programme.

A great extent of informal education programmes take place in the cultural field, whereby animation and participating by doing things in the general line of educating people. Informal education provides normally programmes which offering the chance to activate people in the educational and cultural field.

Finally may I underline that popularizing of technology and science has the following preconditions:

1. The status and financing of education especially nonformal in society has to be improved.

2. Technology and science in informal and nonformal education have to be adapted to the economic and social demands and needs of the society. The education system has to orient itself not purely on economic interests, but also on the social and cultural consequences of our technological environment.
3. Popularization of science and technology means also to challenge educational structure, learning processes and the development of interdisciplinary thinking and approaches.
4. Innovative learning is needed instead of pure traditional learning.
5. Participation and anticipation in learning processes.
6. Teacher training has to be radically improved and changed.
7. Popularization of new technologies and science must be developed in an atmosphere of political consensus to safeguard a balance economic and social interest in society.

# 14

# Country Paper: China

PAN ZHONGMING

China is at present making great efforts in developing socialist construction and fulfilling the magnificant modernization programme. The realization of modernization programme cannot do without the development of science and technology. Accordingly, much efforts must be made in primary and secondary schools to popularize the knowledge of science and technology among young students for laying a solid foundation for improving the citizens quality of science and technology and training a large number of qualified personnel in science, technology and management.

Over the past a dozen of years or more, science and technology have been enjoying a rapid development. As a result, the new science and technology in microelectronics, biological engineering, optical-fibre communication and new materials have entered various fields of social production and daily life. Education is confronted with the challenge of new technology. Ever since the implementation of the policy of reform and opening to the outside world, the long-existing closed-door situation has been changed and the waves of various kinds of new science and technology have been surging into China. Meanwhile, along with the prosperity of economy and culture, science and technology are now being popularized on a even more extensive scale. The new development and popularization of science and technology are now challenging the primary and secondary education in China.

In the Decision of the Central Committee of CPC on the Reform of Educational Structure issued in May of 1985, it is pointed out that education must serve socialist construction, which in turn must rely on education. The Decision has not only made clear the important strategic position of education in the socialist modernization programme, but also put forward that the reform of educational structure must adapt itself to the economic structural reform and that the structural reforms of economy, education and science and technology should be interrelated and interpromoted. The following points are also pointed out in the Decision of CPC: (1) the fundamental aim of restructuring education is to improve the quality of the whole nation and produce as many skilled personnel as possible; (2) the responsibility for developing basic education should be entrusted to local authorities and the nine-year compulsory education should be implemented in a planned way; and (3) the secondary education should be restructured by vigorously developing vocational and technical education. In July of 1986, the Chinese government formally issued the "Law of Compulsory Education of the People's Republic of China", requiring that the nine-year compulsory education should be gradually popularized in varied paces from place to place throughout the country.

For the past decade, on the basis of restoring the teaching-learning order in schools, a series of reforms have been undertaken for meeting the needs of social progress and scientific and technological development.

Under the above-mentioned circumstances, the education of science and technology in primary and secondary schools has been paid extreme attention by educationists and people from other circles, and has been consequently developed in the wave of reform.

## 1. The Situation of Education of Science and Technology in Primary and Secondary Schools in China

China is now implementing the school system of 5-year or 6-year primary education, 3-year junior secondary education and

3-year senior secondary education. For each academic year, 40 to 42 weeks are spent on teaching and learning in two semesters.

The education of science and technology is offered to primary and secondary students mainly in the form of class teaching with extra-curricular and after-school activities as its supplement.

In the draft of the teaching plan for 6-year full-time primary schools in urban areas, the offered courses of general knowledge of science are as follows:

| class hours per week / grade / subject | 1 | 2 | 3 | 4 | 5 | 6 | total class hours | percentage of total |
|---|---|---|---|---|---|---|---|---|
| general knowledge of the nature | | | 2 | 2 | 1 | 1 | 204 | 4.1 |
| general knowledge of geography | | | | | 2 | | 68 | 1.4 |
| reading on science and technology and recreational activities | 3 | 3 | 3 | 3 | 3 | 3 | | |

The following is the draft of the teaching plan of general knowledge courses offered in 6-year full-time primary schools in rural areas:

| class hours per week / grade / subject | 1 | 2 | 3 | 4 | 5 | 6 | total class hours | percentage of total |
|---|---|---|---|---|---|---|---|---|
| general knowledge of the nature | | | 2 | 2 | 2 | | 204 | 4.1 |
| general knowledge of agriculture | | | | | | 2 | 68 | 1.4 |
| general knowledge of geography | | | | | 2 | | 68 | 1.4 |

In secondary schools, physics, chemistry, biology, physiological hygiene, and geography (including the contents of both natural science and humanities) are offered as independent courses and called as science courses. The task of these courses is to impart the knowledge of science and technology to students and to develop their competence and the relevant skills. Moreover, the offered course of labour techniques can enable the students to master some basic techniques. In the following table, the concrete information of these courses is shown:

| subject | junior secondary grades | | | senior secondary grades | | | total class hours |
|---|---|---|---|---|---|---|---|
| | I | II | III | I | II | III | |
| physics | | 2 | 3 | 4 | 3 | 4 | 500 |
| chemistry | | | 3 | 3 | 3 | 3 | 372 |
| biology | 2 | 2 | | | | 2 | 192 |
| physio-logical hygiene | | | 2 | | | | 64 |
| geography | 3 | 2 | | | 2 | | 234 |
| labour skills | 2 weeks | | | 4 weeks | | | |

The practices of imparting basic knowledge in the form of independent courses and developing students' basic skills in light of the subject system have been followed for the past decades and are still being followed at present.

## 2. Developing and Reforming Education of Science and Technology in Primary and Secondary Schools

As to the present reform on education of science and technology in primary and secondary schools, the focal point lies in the restructuring of curriculum. It is known that the curriculam is the means for realizing the training objective of schools. Most of the primary and secondary students learn the systematic basic knowledge and skills and have all-round development of body and mind through class teaching under the guidance of teachers. To keep abreast of the social progress and scientific and technological development, a series of measures have been adopted for the reform and development of curriculum in China.

(1) Renewing the content of curriculum. When working out the teaching programme of science and courses for 10-year schools in 1977, the following principle was determined: The teaching content of primary and secondary education should be enriched by introducing the knowledge of advanced science and technology in light of students' comprehension ability, while cutting out the outmoded knowledge. Consequently, the content of basic knowledge and skills imparted in primary and secondary schools has been gradually renewed along with the development of science, technology and production, and the new and advanced science knowledge has been introduced into each subject.

In order to keep abreast of the social requirements for the knowledge of physics and take the social requirements as important basis for determining the teaching content of Physics in secondary schools. China physics Teaching Society has made surveys among 16 occupations and found out the social demand for 132 items of physics knowledge. On the basis of the surveys, a plan for restructuring the courses of physics in secondary schools has been accordingly formulated. The survey results showed: of the 47 items of physics knowledge which had not been compiled into textbooks or given enough class explanation, 28 items were about electricity making up 59.9 per cent of the total, while 10 items were about electrotechnics and electronic technology accounting for 35.7 per cent of the total items about electricity. The above survey results have reflected the demand of scientific and technological development in China for the knowledge of electricity.

(2) Adding new courses. According to the incomplete statistics, by the end of 1986, there were in China about

50,000 sets of micro-computers in 4,000 secondary schools and 8,000 full-time and part-time teachers in charge of teaching 800,000 students on computer science at different levels. Therefore, the following measures have been adopted: (a) to offer elective courses in regular senior secondary schools; (b) to provide preliminary computer education in junior secondary schools; and (c) to implement computer-aided teaching in some schools with good conditions.

Since the population education in a newly-emerging integral discipline which is of special importance for Chinese people, lectures of population education have been offered in school since 1981.

Moreover, the course of labour skills has also been popular in schools for the past years.

(3) Trying out various kinds of elective courses on the basis of reducing the number of required courses. For example, the Attached Secondary School to Nanjing Normal University offered the senior secondary students in 1987 with 28 elective courses including a third of courses on science and technology as follows:

| subject | number of student | class hours per week | total class hours | target grades | sources of teacher |
|---|---|---|---|---|---|
| experimental chemistry | 46 | 2 | 30 | 2nd semester of senior I | from this school |
| computer science (I) | 136 | 2 | 30 | " | " |
| electrotech-nics & radio | 161 | 2 | 30 | 1st semester | " |
| physics | 46 | 2 | 60 | 2nd semester of senior II<br>1st semester of senior III | " |
| astronomy | 30 | 2 | 30 | 1st semester of senior II | " |

| | | | | | |
|---|---|---|---|---|---|
| geography | 9 | 2 | 30 | 2nd semester of senior II | " |
| biology | 25 | 2 | 30 | " | " |
| method of science | 84 | 2 | 30 | " | invited |
| computer science (2) | 57 | 2 | 30 | " | from this school |

For another example, the Attached Secondary School to Beijing Normal University has offered the elective courses such as "Science, Technology and Society (STS)", "Human Beings and Environment", "Physics in Daily Life" and "Contemporary Physics".

Facts show that the extensive knowledge, strong synthesis and new viewpoints of the elective courses provide a favourable environment for improving students' knowledge structure, opening up their mind and developing their individuality.

(4) Renewing educational concepts, restructuring curriculum system and improving teaching methods. Although the titles of some courses have not been changed, their content and structure as well as the teaching methods have been undergoing changes as a result of the renewal of educational concepts. For example, according to the traditional concepts, the course of General Knowledge of the Nature in primary schools is the main subject for pupils to learn the knowledge of natural science and the task of this course is to teach pupils some simple knowledge about natural science. For this reason, this course was usually offered in grade III after finishing reading primer, and class teaching was the main way for imparting knowledge of natural science. Consequently, this originally interesting course was made dull and dry. After curriculum reform, it is stipulated that the course of General Knowledge of the Nature is an important basic discipline for providing pupils with enlightenment education of science. Accordingly, the course is

determined as educational subject instead of formerly-determined knowledge subject. The pupils should not only be taught with knowledge of natural science, but also be cultivated to love our motherland, the nature and natural science, to develop the ability to learn and apply science knowledge, and to have a scientific attitude towards the nature. The teaching method of inquiry—discussion should be employed in guiding the pupils to seek knowledge direct from the natural world. This course should be taught from grade I so as to stimulate pupils' strong interest in learning.

In recent years, the research activities on strengthening the education of science and technology in primary and secondary schools have been very brisk in China. Only referring the Unesco-assisted national workshops, we have organized for four times. China Central Institute of Educational Research conducted the Workshop on the Competence of Teachers for Science Subjects in 1984, the Workshop on Integral Science Subjects in 1986, and the Workshop on Curriculum Reform of Science Education in Secondary Schools in April this year. Moreover, the Research Institute of Curriculum and Teaching Materials organized in 1986 the Workshop on Development of Science Courses in Secondary Schools in China. This Programme of Education for Development and the Principle of Science for All have attracted the extensive attention and influenced the active considerations of reforming the education of science and technology in China.

(5) Planning to offer integral science course in junior secondary schools. As to the necessity of offering integral science course, there are three different opinions in the ongoing heated debate.

Those who are in favour of the integral science course believe that the separated academic science courses should be changed into practical integral courses for training qualified citizens. This change is also necessary for training students to enter social life instead of merely seeking the chance of entering higher-level schools. Considering that students are in the period of changing from imaginary thinking to logical thinking, the courses should not be offered in the same way as to adults. Viewing from the tendency of integration of science, it is appropriate to offer integral science courses.

As to the supporters of separated science courses, they hold that each subject has its own characters and different characters reflect the different science methods. The separated science courses are advantageous for the junior secondary students to lay a comprehensive foundation and have all-round scientific training.

Those people for the third opinion maintain that separated science courses have the drawbacks while integral science courses have their strong points. The integral science courses should neither be popularized blindly nor denied rashly.

It is evident that the debate on this issue will influence the curriculum development.

Viewing from the development tendency of curriculum reform, the following conclusion can probably be reached: in formal schools, not only the static knowledge should be imparted to students but also the basic knowledge of science and technology with the value for extensive application should be introduced into curriculum step by step. Among the disciplines are environmental science, energy source science, population theory, information technology and etc. Otherwise, the schools will be blamed by the society for training useless people. Naturally, so the training aim of schools is not to fill in the student's head with all the new science and technology but to teach students to master the methods for learning and solving new problems. Although the teachers and students sometimes go to the society for popularizing new science and technology, the promotion role of formal education to the progress and development of society should be displayed by its qualified "product"—skilled people adapting to the social needs. It is impossible to solve all the problems through formal education. Since the relative stability of curriculum makes it impossible to avoid the stagnation of curriculum content, some problems can only be solved through non-formal education and informal education.

### 3. The Second Channel for the Education of Science and Technology in Primary and Secondary Schools

For a long time, extra-curricular and after school activities have been emphasized in primary and secondary education. The recreational activities, activities of science and technology, and social public labour have been the indispensable conditions for the all-round, vivid and healthy development. In 1984, a well-known educator wrote an article advocating that an educational system including the second channel (also called second classroom) should be established for changing the practice of relying merely of formal class teaching. Here, the second channel is different from extra-curriculum education. The aim of the former is to use all the educational conditions in the society such as factories, rural areas, research institutes, museums and the stations of science and technology for setting up an extensive social classroom and for creating favourable conditions for the development and creation of students interest and intelligence. In so doing, the qualified modern personnel with real ability and intelligence. Taking extra-curricular activities as another channel inside the educational system is an exact evaluation of the role of these extra-curricular activities.

Along with the present prosperity of science and technology, the activities of science and technology in primary and secondary schools are getting richer and richer in content and more and more lively in form. In this regard, Miss Cheng Donghong from China Association of Science and Technology has provided a very good report. Now, please allow me to introduce other efforts made by the mass media for the education of science and technology in primary and secondary schools.

(1) Broadcast of popular science is an important channel for disseminating the knowledge of science and technology to young people. In the early days of the People's Republic of China, the Central People's Broadcasting Station began the Programme of "Lectures on Natural Science", introducing the knowledge of the nature and of new science and technology. The main contents are

as follows: (a) the general knowledge of some basic disciplines such as mathematics, physics, chemistry, astronomy, geography and biology which contribute to the enhancement of people's quality in science and culture; (b) the knowledge of applied science and technology for serving the economic construction; (c) new techniques, new materials, new product, and new technology; (d) the knowledge having close relevance to the daily life of audience; (e) the new development and tendency of both domestic and foreign science and technology; and (f) history and figures of science and technology. Although the title of this programme has been changed for times, it has been having a strong appeal to the audience. Many famous scholars such as Zhu Kezhen, Zhou Beiyuan, Hua Luogeng, Qian Xuesen, Qian Sanqiang, Bei Shizhang, Jin Zhanbao, Wu Zhonghua and Yan Jici have been writing articles for this programme or making live speeches. Nowadays, new science and technology have entered the society and economy for promoting the civilization of modern human beings. To adapt to this tendency, the above-mentioned broadcasting programme is now called "Scientific Technology and Society" and new content is unceasingly added into this programme.

The knowledge of medical science and hygiene is introduced in the broad-casting programme called "Attention to Hygiene". Dr. Lin Qiaozhi, a famous expert of gynaecology, has written a special article entitled "Puberty Hygiene" for the programme. Other programme such as "Cross the Land", "Touring the World" and etc. have been introducing extensive knowledge about the geography, history, construction, economy, natural resources, culture and custom of other countries.

The programmes of popular science which account for 7 per cent-8 per cent of the total broadcasting hours of the Central People's Broadcasting Station, are transmitted two times a day and each lasts for ten minutes. The young people are the main audience of these programmes and they can listen can listen to them both in the morning and in the evening.

With the new development of science and technology, the Station has transmitted the programme called "Automation and Information Times" which gives a detailed explanation of the application of computers in all trades and professions. At present, the programme entitled "Game Theory" is being transmitted for popularizing the knowledge of systematic management.

(2) TV undertakings are enjoying a rapid development in China. Among the TV programmes transmitted by CCTV are "Science and Technology", "Second Classroom", "Try to Do it", "Computer Science for Children" and etc. The newly-produced programme entitled "Times of Science and Technology" (including 155 kinds of items) will be transmitted in October this year. The main contents for this programme include spaceflight, navigation petroleum, electronics, energy-saving stove, superconduction, microfilm, energy sources, and environmental pollution. This Hong Kong made TV programme called "Secondary Students Learn Science" has been transmitted four times.

At the approval of the State Council in 1986, a set of satellite TV relay equipment was given to the relevant sector of education and a number of ground-based TV programme relay stations were also built up. The Ministry of Broadcasting and Television decided to arrange a special TV channel for transmitting educational programmes for the whole day. At present, the main content of this special channel is the programmes of primary and secondary teacher training and adult education. Some of the programmes are suitable for primary and secondary school pupils and students to watch.

(3) A large amount of reading materials concerning science and technology have been published by many publishing houses for young people. From the following list of new books, we can have a broad outline about the contents and characters.

People's Education Press has published a series of Contemporary Science and Technology and the list is as follows (First Volume):

"Triangle with Equal Angle-dividing Line",

"Strategy for Controlling Population",

"Theory, Application and Development of Computer",

Immortal Member of the Family of Particles",

Theory of Relativity is not mysterious",

"Space Flighting and Carrier Rocket",

"Theory, History, Today and Future and Nuclear Energy",

"Laser in the Future Chemistry",

"The Mystery between Order and Disorder",

"Strange Liquid Crystal",

"Genetic Engineering", and

"Compass and Modern Geomagnetics".

The following is the list of the series published by Jilin Education Press:

"Modern Science and Thinking Mode",

"The Grand System and Function of Modern Science",

"An Introduction to Information Culture",

"Computer and Social Development",

"Artificial Intelligence and Social Progress",

"The Competence of Modern Skilled People of Science and Technology",

"System Science and Social System",

"Progress of Science and Technology and Modern Education".

Fujian Education Press has published the "Modern Secondary Students Series" with the contents as follows:

"Fifty Questions for Secondary Students",

"Sports and Body Building",

"Occupation Guide",

"Newly-rising Science and High Technology",

"The Future of Human Beings",

"A Full Reflection of New Stage Literature",

"The History of Books in China",

"Appreciation of Four Famous Classical Novels",

"Stars in World of Sports",

"The Track of Explorer".

(4) Exhibitions are often displayed and lectures on science and technology are often organized by museums, hall of science and technology, libraries, exhibition halls, institutions of higher learning, and mass academic organizations.

All the above-introduced programmes and books have some common features: (a) having wide range of knowledge; (b) reflecting new tendency, new knowledge and new concepts of science and technology; (c) having interdisciplinary contents and strong synthesis; (d) having close relevance to social realities and individual life of young people; (e) being participated by experts and suitable for self-learners; and (f) being loved by young people for the interest, artistry and popularity. All the above characteristics are exactly the objectives which are found difficult to be achieved in the reforms on teaching and curriculum.

The reforms in schools should be tried out before extensive popularization. For the reform of curriculum, teaching materials should be well compiled, the needed teachers should be trained and necessary teaching equipment should be added. Compared with extra-curriculum education and after-school education, school education lacks flexibility and adaptability. Therefore, the roles of extra-curriculum and after-school education should be brought into full play and they should be interacted each other.

The international environment, domestic needs of modernization programme, the development of science and technology, and educational structural reform will all influence the education of science and technology in primary and secondary schools. The education of science and technology in schools should be unceasingly reformed, and the extra-curriculum and after-school education should be developed vigorously. The three aspects should supplement and promote each other to form an organic whole. Only by doing so can we provide the young people with a satisfactory environment for the education of science and technology, so that they can receive comparatively overall cultivation and training for becoming a new generation with high level quality of science and culture.

# 15

# Country Paper: Ghana

ERIC MENSAH

## The Utility of Science and Technology

Scientific knowledge and modern technology like any other type of knowledge constitute power. The kind of power exemplified by the two phenomena is, however, perhaps more critical because of its concern with our very survival. Science and modern technology empower us to adjust satisfactorily to our harsh physical and social environment. And they have been used to improve upon the quality of life on several dimensions: to promote industrial and agricultural growth and to improve upon health.

The contribution of science and technology to Ghana's agriculture and health programmes, for example, is very instructive. Ghana is an agricultural country and approximately 80 per cent of the population live in the rural area where agricultural activities are dominant. But less than 13 per cent of the country's total arable land is under cultivation and the average farmer cultivates five acres or less. One half of the country's 92,373 sq. miles of land lies within the coastal and interior Savannah. The interior Savannah which is our focus of our attention covers some 50 per cent of the total area of Ghana with 20 per cent of the country's total population. But only a small proportion of the area is cultivated by peasants who operate less than six months a year. It would appear the Ghana's potential in food production lies in this area and irrigation is gradually facilitating the realization of this potential.

The health problems facing Ghana are also associated with a very rapid population growth of about 3.1 per cent per annum. The other factors are a very ineffective system of controlling disease and an unsatisfactory and poor sanitation. Life expectancy in Ghana is estimated 55 for males and 57 for females. The answer to some of these health problems is rooted in science and modern technology. As a young nation child survival activities have been very crucial in the solution of health problems. They include programmes of immunization and oral rehydration for diarrheal diseases. Science has also confirmed some long standing traditions of spacing births through prolonged breast-feeding. Modern technology in the health service also emphasizes Primary Health Care which is aimed at prevention rather than cure.

**A Critical Missing Link**

There is a need for continuous research to make life less burdensome, less difficult, rewarding and less boring. The exodus of persons from the rural to urban areas provides a vivid demonstration of this need. There is no doubt that a great deal of research is being conducted by organizations of one kind or another into these matters. The organizations include the Council for Scientific and Industrial Research (CSIR), and the three Universities of Ghana. It seems, however, that the people who need the research findings most are not aware of outcome of such results. There appears to be a critical missing link between the people who need the research findings and the task that needs to be accomplished to translate research results into application and adoption.

In 1972 a workshop was organized at the University of Ghana on "The Pooling of Resources Among the Universities and Scientific Research Institutions in Ghana" to address itself to some of the problems created by this yawning gap between research and application. One of the outcomes of the workshop's deliberations was the appointment of an Advisory Committee on the "Dissemination of Scientific Information to the General Public". The Committee was charged with the task of studying and making recommendations on how to "organize an effective form of disseminating useful scientific results obtained from the Universities, the Research Institutions and any other creditable source to the population so that they not only benefit but get to know what is happening in our scientific institutions".

The Committee was sceptical about a follow-up on its proposals and therefore recommended what is described as an "Action Group" or "Striking Force" to bring its work into fruition. The joint action expected of the Universities and the CSIR indeed failed to materialize. The popularization of science and technology through the dissemination of scientific information to the general public remained a Cinderella.

The efforts of the three Universities of Ghana and the CSIR in the popularization of scientific information illustrate what is currently being in these directions. It will be argued that these efforts need to be augmented by other informal and non-formal educational activities to enhance the application of research findings to societal problems.

**The Council for Scientific and Industrial Research (CSIR)**

The CSIR was established in its present form in 1986 to organize and coordinate research in all aspects in Ghana. It is expected "to undertake or collaborate in the collection, publication and dissemination" among other statutory functions. Its research institutes are as follows:

(1) Animal Research Institute;

(2) Building and Road Research Institute;

(3) Crops Research Institute;

(4) Ghana National Atlas Project;

(5) Herbs of Ghana Project;

(6) Industrial Research Institute;

(7) Institute of Aquatic Biology;

(8) Oil Palm Research Centre;

(9) Scientific Industrial Centre;

(10) Soil Research Institute; and

(11) Natural Resources Research Institute.

The technical services and assistance that these institutions offer include consultancy advice and extension work. For example, the Animal Research Institute provides advice and consultancy on subjects such as feed formulation, pasture establishment, poultry breeding and farm management. The Institute's extension service also covers activities such as the training of farmers and individuals in animal management animal of suitable types as a source of food. The Food Research Institute is one of the Institutes whose services have been directly related to national development. It helped to reactivate the Bolgatanga Neat Factory through the improvement of the Volta Corned Beef. It also assisted the Tema Food Complex Corporation (TFCC) to set up production lines for fish canning, smoking, cold storage and fish meal plants, and flour packaging in small units.

Information dissemination by the Institutes is varied. Annual and technical reports are published. Symposia, seminars, open day and exhibitions are organized. Lastly, research results are communicated to user-agencies.

**The Universities of Ghana**

The three Universities in the country, namely, the University of Ghana, the University of Science and Technology, and the University of Cape Coast are actively engaged in research of one kind or another. The mode for the dissemination of research results does not differ so much from the format used by the CSIR. There are, however, some unique features of their research institutions which are instructive.

The University of Ghana, for example, maintains two Agricultural Research Stations. The Faculty of Agriculture which overseas these research stations also publishes the Legon Extension Bulletin which is designed to provide technical information on a variety of themes. The following examples of publications provide some information on the Faculty's efforts in these directions: "Hot Pepper Production" (1984); "Garden Eggs/Egg Plant Production in Ghana" (1986); and "Hints on Poultry Farming in Ghana" (1987).

### Alternative Modes of Education

The efforts of the resarch institutions and Universities notwithstanding, it is generally recognized that the target population of research findings is very limited. In a country with a 60-70 per cent illiteracy rate, annual and technical reports in professional jargon, workshops, seminars and symposia as well as other such sophisticated modes of transmission scientific information is clearly unsatisfactory.

It would appear that a conscious attempt would have to be made to promote a scientific culture by emphasizing alternative forms of education, namely, informal and non-formal education which maximizes learning resources in and out of school for both children and adults. The rationale behind this assertion is the failure of the school system to have the desired impact on the promotion of a scientific culture in Ghana. It is estimated, for example, that even in the field of literacy, although 70 per cent of Ghanaian children are enrolled in school, adult literacy rates remain stagnant around 60-70. This suggests that attendance in school does not necessarily promote permanent literacy for a majority of Ghanaians.

### Objectives and Target Groups

It would appear important to clarify the objectives of this educational effort to facilitate the determination of appropriate strategies for the popularization of science and technology. The following objectives are suggested:

(1) to inform the general public and other agencies of what is happening in the scientific world;

(2) to help user agencies and persons needing specific information or to identify the sources through which help could be obtained;

(3) to organize scientific educational programmes for the general public as and when necessary;

(4) to promote a scientific culture that may enable Ghanaians to understand the technological world in which they live to become science conscious and develop a scientific attitude towards problems;

(5) to enable various categories of scientists to keep abreast with scientific development in the country.

The target groups would have to be categorized, given the foregoing objectives, to enhance the process of dissemination. The majority of the people who need to be informed are illiterate and this suggests a linkage with the planned Functional Literacy Campaign which is due to be launched in Ghana towards the end of this year. The next target group would be persons with some education who can read and understand material in both English and Ghanaian languages. After this group would be those whose educational background is the General Certificate of Education and above and who can understand the language of elementary science. Scientists or young persons in Secondary Schools who are taught science and are interested in applying their knowledge to particular scientific situations would constitute the next groups. It is also important to aim at government, public and private agencies such as regional development corporations and private manufacturers. It is vital to pass on scientific information to this group because it is through these agencies that such information could be most effectively used to make an impact on national development. Lastly, a programme for the popularization of scientific information would necessarily have to include scientists who need to broaden their own scientific knowledge with information outside their own field of specialization which may be of interest and relevance to their work. Problems for other agencies may also be brought to the attention of the scientists.

**The Channels and Media for Reaching Target Groups**

(1) *The use of Ghanaian languages*—As indicated earlier, the dissemination of scientific information may be accomplished as part of the projected Functional Literacy Campaign through the production of post-literacy material. Moreover, Ghanaians have their own expression for some scientific concepts and the medium for the dissemination of scientific information need not be exclusively English. Borrowing will earth the language instead of attempts to force vernacular

translations of well-known scientific concepts where much can be achieved with a word with the same euphony but spelt differently. Perhaps this would be one of the ways by which Ghana could evolve a purposeful scientific vocabulary, and the publication of scientific material in some Ghanaian languages appears to be worthy of consideration.

(2) *Publications*—There is a need for the population of a wide variety of publications in English and Ghanaian languages for the dissemination of scientific information. Bulletins, journals, pamphlets, newsletters, teach-yourself material, broadsheets, and columns or pull-outs in daily newspapers may be considered. Areas of immediate importance are animal production, crop production, fishing, food preservation, health and intermediate technology including cottage industries.

(3) *Do-it-Yourself materials*—These may be produced in fields such as gardening, animal production and intermediate technology.

(4) *Audio-visual aids*—The production of educational films could be used to supplement programmes organized for the dissemination of scientific information.

(5) *Radio and T.V.*—The Ghana Broadcasting Corporation has a major role to play in the popularization of science and technology. The content of its science programmes is, however, geared towards the General Science syllabus of the West African Examinations Council. There is a need for the Corporation to broaden the content of its science programmes to cater for the general public as a whole.

**Adult Education Agencies**

(1) *Organizations*—It is proposed that the various adult education agencies in Ghana should be fed with scientific information, pamphlets and other publications for use through their normal channels to various targets. A promising strategy for the popularization of scientific

information is the Adult Education Networks established by the Ghana National Council for Adult Education. The utility of a network lies in "the strength or weak ties" and is symbolized by the looseness of ties in a network. The networks would therefore enhance the popularization of scientific information because a network is also a system of communication channels which promotes the sharing of experiences, knowledge and skills.

(2) *Cultural centres or science museums*—Ghanaians have a scientific heritage. The establishment of cultural centres or science museums where science could be practised in the traditional setting would therefore go a long way in popularizing and inculcating a scientific culture among the general public. An attempt to bring science closer to the people through the establishment of more science museums and cultural centres preferably in the regional capitals would also help to allay some of the superstitious beliefs prevalent in Ghana society.

A conscious attempt to popularize science and technology through informal and non-formal education would help promote a scientific culture in Ghana. This would in turn facilitate an understanding of the contemporary technological world and the creation of a scientific attitude towards societal problems. The Non-Formal Education Division of the Ministry of Education would appear to be the appropriate governmental machinery with the necessary administrative and political clout to implement such a programme to popularize science and technology in Ghana.

## REFERENCES

1. "The Dissemination of Scientific Information to the General Public" (1974). A Report of an Ad-hoc Advisory Committee Set Up by the Legon Workshop on the Dissemination of Scientific Information to the General Public. Accra.

2. Book, John C. The Institutionalization of Non-Formal Education. A Response to Conflicting Needs in *Comparative Education Review* Vol. 20, No. 3, October 1976.

3. Coombs, P.S. and Ahmed, M. (1974). *Attacking Rural Poverty: How Non-Formal Education Can Help*. London: John Hopkins University Press.

4. Evans, D. (1981). *The Planning of Non-Formal Education*, Paris. Unesco.

5. Goody, Jack (1971). *Technology Traditional and the State in Africa*. London: Oxford University Press.

6. Institute of Adult Education, University of Ghana (1980). Report on 1980 Northern Easter School.

7. Mensah, E. and Okunor, V. (Eds) (1989). *Adult Education Networks in Ghana*. Accra: GNCAE.

8. Oletcia, T.O. and Adewole, A. (1985). *Sociology: An Introductory African Text*. Hong Kong: MacMillan.

# 16

# Country Paper: Keyna

DAUDI N. NTURIBI

## Introduction

Like the proverbial traveller to strange and distant lands, who inspires wonder and curiosity, the expert who can manipulate modern gadgetry and is seen to control the laws of nature through his ability to use scientific knowledge leaves fellows villagers shaking their heads at his wizardry. At best they will be suspicious of attempts to woo them to try their hand. Their reservation is compounded further by the incomprehensible language and the know-it-all attitude of those who introduce such innovations.

For those lucky to be initiated into the new technology "cults" through formal education and industrial training the mysticism of science is soon replaced with confidence, so adoption and use of gadgetry is easy. But for the unlettered the mystery remains and adoption is fraught with hesitancy and mistakes, sometimes fatal and at best ludicrous as to make them a laughing stock.

A case in point is that of a traditional herdsman who wiped out his whole herd when he failed to understand how to administer a pesticide he had purchased. Such discomfort does not auger well for the rapid advancement that is necessary to increase production, survival and self-sufficiency in the developing countries.

This paper will examine the issues involved in assessing the needs and problems that make the popularization of science and technology in these countries such an urgent issue. An attempt will be made to examine how this process has evolved in Kenya in respect to non-formal education practice. The issues of relevance of science and technology will be examined in relation to the society's level of readiness and perceptions.

## Issues in Promotion of Science & Technology

We can safely start with the observation that people will use knowledge or a technique which they understand, feel comfortable with and that is likely to meet a need they have. For those trying to promote a new idea or way of doing things it is therefore important that they understand the psycho-social realities of the people they want to influence. Thus they need to know:

- the prevailing knowledge, beliefs, attitudes and experiences of peoples as they are related to the issue
- the people's level of awareness and readiness to change
- the need for change and how pressing it is—who feels this need
- traditional of past way of coping with perceived problems and ways of doing things.

In this respect it is pertinent to note the cultural lag and inertia that has slowed down adoption of new medical, agricultural and architectural techniques. Many of our societies prefer to use traditional healers and mid-wives, to eat traditional foods and build like their fore-fathers. This is what they feel confident to do.

The introduction of new ways will therefore not get very far unless it is grounded and builds on what people know, and are comfortable with. Strange, gleaming, modern gadgets and complicated sequences just make people feel clumsy and lose face before their peers and followers. No one likes to look stupid.

What is then likely to be "appropriate" science and technology as recent wisdom has counselled? The introduction of new ideas must start from development of existing knowledge and skills. This techniques must be simplified and must also be introduced with sensitivity. We must know and think seriously about how the people will see the change or new ideas and techniques and how they will feel in their new roles—are the shoes likely to cause corns or the dress appear clownish? We need to go about the task slowly and patiently, correct mistakes during the initial faltering steps and uncertainty. We cannot afford to push people too hard to change their practices. Heavy handed condemnation of people for their ignorance or "foolish" past ways will only alienate potential adapters.

**Approaching the Task**

Non-formal and informal techniques of promotion of adoption behaviour call for intensive association and involvement by change agents or animators with community members. We have already noted the need to respect and listen to "clients" in order to understand where they are and their perceptions of the issue. Once rapport has been established it is easy to move with an individual or a group systematically through steps of:

- need or problem identification
- analysis of the need or problem to understand its effects and dimensions
- proposals for solutions that might work and be less painful or expensive
- planning of how to proceed in implementation of decisions
- periodic evaluation of success, assessment of subsequent difficulties and problems.

Groups have been found to be a viable approach because of the way in which members influence one another by sharing knowledge and pressurizing each other by example. As early adaptors demonstrate how to go about it and dispel fears, others will be more willing to follow their footsteps.

Careful development of relevant messages for awareness and in-depth instruction suitable for each client group is called for. This can be done best if the group or individuals involved take part in all the above stages and develop the messages themselves.

**Examples of Popularization**

It has been extremely enlightening to work with women group leaders in developing leadership and group management manuals for groups involved in pig keeping, poultry and livestock rearing, tailoring and bread making at the cost in Kenya. The groups trained under the Tototo project umbrella have grasped these concepts and techniques quickly to the amazement of their facilitators. They have gone further to develop guidelines for health, nuritition and child care based on the needs of members and their families.

The John Snow Inc. Family Planning Programme in Kenya has also involved workers in enterprises, women groups, youth groups, school children and out-of-school youth in popularizing family planning through such traditional entertainment as song, dance, poetry, drama and story telling. The groups' rich wealth of knowledge and enthusiasm once guided by skillful facilitators, has popularized and opened to public discussion issues of contraception and family health that were once only whispered to friends. In health, the simplified approach by UNICEF to promote child survival technologies has caught the people's imagination and increased the use of Oral Rehydration Salts, immunization coverage, re-emphasized breast-feeding and clinic attendance for growth monitoring. These practices have brought about a drop in infant mortality, to a point where Kenya is experiencing a resultant spiralling population growth rate.

In food and agriculture the widespread adoption of new varieties of hybrid maize, the rearing of improved breeds of dairy cattle and poultry, the widespread use of new ways of planting and use of fertilizers have been brought about by extension staff able to work at the village level, to train and visit farmers individually. There is also a growing demand for new technologies in industry and energy. Energy saving "jikos" or cooking stoves have taken off very well especially as they are promoted through women groups. Efficient but simple adaptations of traditional technology that can be done by village craftsmen are easily done cheaply using locally available materials. Adoption of "weaving" looms and cloth dyeing has also shown a lot of progress in impoverished urban slum communities where women groups have organized themselves into income generating projects.

**Conclusion**

There seems to be no lack of enthusiasm in communities for new ideas and skills as long as they fit into their perception of what will improve their welfare, but will not bring tears. They eagerly seek knowledge and are prepared to learn new ideas and to improve their skills.

The knowledge and techniques advanced by change agents must be seen to enhance the adaptors' image and status in their communities. The promoters must also be seen as friends and fellow travellers along the rough road to modernization. Those extension workers who are close to their communities will achieve the best results.

# 17

# Country Paper: Republic of Korea

CHAE KWANG-PYO

## Introduction

The recent movement on popularization of science and technology started since 1970's by government in Korea. For example, the 'Sea-Ma-Ul' movement has greatly changed life style in rural areas.

The social change of Korea for the last 30 years has been tremendous. In the process of industrialization, it has been arisen as an urgent need to prepare suitably qualified and skilled manpower. Science and technological education at college level has been forced to fulfil this need.

The movement on popularization of science and technology has been carried out at formal and non-formal education level. It is said the development of country is resulted from education, but little analysis is performed to show how such development is related to education. It is generally agreed that the popularization of science and technology also has great effect on the modernization of country.

## Programmes for the Popularization of Science and Technology

Various types of programmes and activities have been presented by public and private organizations in Korea such as provide the information and knowledge about modern science and technology, the influence of science and technology in the future, what is the scientific way of life, etc.

These programmes could be classified as follows:

**1. National Science Museum and Provincial Students' Science Museums**

Korea has a 'National Science Museum' (NSM) in Seoul and 10 students' science museums in provinces. The NSM devotes itself to collecting, preserving, and exhibiting materials in the fields of science, technology, industry and history of science and technology. The functions of the museum are:

- to diffuse scientific and technical knowledge
- to promote a scientific way of living for all.

The NSM operaters exhibition halls all around the year. The number of visitors were about 351,000 in 1987. The NSM has summer and winter Science Classroom for scientific experiments, and computer study for the students during vacations. Usually about 210,000 students yearly join in this programme. Sometimes the museum provides the public with special lectures and science film service for the topics such as genetic engineering, food production, travelling universe, underwater science, etc.

The students' science museums not only display prototypes and models of science equipment and various instructional materials related to science and science learning but also provide actual learning activities to students and teachers regarding their school science. Sometimes the museums exhibit aquariums and rare plants, etc.

**2. Science Exhibitions and Science Fairs**

Various kinds of science and technology exhibitions are opened several times a year by private and public level to enhance the interests in science and technology and to promote the creativity in those fields.

A students' science fair has been operated by the National Science Museum and the Ministry of Science and Technology since the early 1960s. The subjects were about 4,500 in the 34th Science Fair (1988) and about 6,000 in the 10th Student Science Invention Contest (1988). The purposes of the science fair are to stimulate students' scientific creativity and to cultivate their interest in science and science learning. The winners have been awarded with flight-benefits, such as scholarships and overseas study tours. Other industrial fairs and contests are also held to show the new industrial products.

Other scientific contests are held in various organizations: airplane model contest, making the radio, personal computer contest, science experiments contest, drawing and composition contests about science, etc. About 1.3 million persons have participated in national programmes during 1988.

### 3. Various Magazine for Science and Technology

There are various kinds of magazine concerning science and technology for students as well as the public. They are published monthly, bimonthly, quarterly, and so on.

The most popular science magazine for students are 'Student's Science', 'Student's Electronics', and 'Electric Wave Science for Students'. They are published monthly and carry various types of workshops, project, products and information which are fascinating enough to stimulate students' imaginations and creative minds.

Some magazines for adults are published weekly as well as monthly, and provide recently developed information on modern science and technology. The most popular ones are 'Weekly Science' and 'Monthly Industry' which carry the most up-to-date information about industry and technology developed in the world.

### 4. Mass Media Communication System

In the Republic of Korea, daily newspaper, radio and television have contributed to enhancing the understanding of science and technology.

Daily newspaper carries various kinds of information on science and technology in everyday science and technology. It also carries the summaries of scientific research papers, which plays an important role in immediately conveying some ideas and information about the development of modern science and technology to the public.

Broadcasting systems such as KBS and MBC, and KEDI's own programme provide the public audience with special topics about science and technology.

## Concluding Remarks

There are various types of programmes and activities in Korea for the popularization of science and technology. It is generally agreed that these programmes and activities attributed greatly to the industrialization of the nation but we have some problems. For example, the main groups of the participants in scientific exhibitions and science fairs are students and teachers. The publications of science magazine are still low level, and the portion of the science programme in TV and newspaper is small.

I want to close my paper by introducing the new science curriculum view of the popularization of science and technology education.

The elementary, middle and high school science curricula have been revised in Korea in 1987-88. Computer, as a learning task has been firstly introduced in the subject, industry art, at the 4th grade of elementary school.

The revision of science curricula was undertaken under the guidelines as follows:

- The science curricula should be revised for the purpose of preparing the future society which are supposed to be oriented to high science and technology.
- It should be incorporated with interaction and interfacing of science and technology, and with relationship between science/technology and society.
- It must emphasize more creative works and activities linking to real life situations of students.
- The science programmes should be more flexible and diversified for alternatives.
- The up-to-date information and knowledge such as genetic engineering, computer science, etc. should be incorporated in the school science curricula under the above guidelines.

The situation of non-formal education for the popularization of science and technology in the Republic has been roughly introduced. More detailed one will be discussed in subsequent meetings.

# 18

# Country Paper: New Zealand

CYNTHIA M. ROBERTS

*Section 1*

**New Zealand—Key Facts**

*Population:* 3,307,084 (Census '86) 3,356,200 (Est. 31 Dec '88)

| *Ethnic composition:* | Maori population | 404,775 | 12.4% |
|---|---|---|---|
| | European mix | 2,732,652 | 83.7% |
| | Pacific Island/Polynesian | 125,853 | 3.9% |

*Key exports:*

Meat, Dairy Produce, Wool, Wood/Pulp/Timber, Fresh Fruit, Casein and Caseinates, Raw Hides, Skins and Leather, Aluminium and Articles of Aluminium.

*Deficit: $M1583 (May '89)*

*Labour:*

Registered unemployed (A): 148,667 (June '89) 11.09%

Number on Department of Labour Access training for unemployed (B): 15,295 (June '89)

Number of Job Opportunities Scheme and other subsidized work schemes (C): 9,633

Total of A+B+C: 173,595

As a percentage of the total workforce: 12.95%

*Labour budget:*

Employment and Training (D): $M355 (1988)

*Social welfare:*

Unemployment Benefit (E): $M780 (1988)

Total D+E: $M1135

*Education:*

The total expenditure on Education: $M3118.2 (31.3.89) as a percentage of government spending: 5.3% GDP and 13.5% net government spending.

*Retention rate to Form 7 (final year of secondary schooling)*

| | 1987 | 1988 |
|---|---|---|
| Males (including Maori): | 23.5% | 27.1% |
| Females (including Maori): | 23.5% | 27.3% |
| Maori: | 6.9% | 8.5% |
| Non-Maori: | 26.8% | 30.9% |

Percentage of students taking Maths/Science combination in Form 5, 6 and 7.

Girls: 63.6%
Boys: 74.4%

(A breakdown of these figures reveals further difference with more boys taking 2 maths subjects and 26 per cent girls taking physics and 45 per cent chemistry in Form 6.)

**Definitions**

For the purpose of this paper the definitions of informal and non-formal educational will be based on those as set out in APEID/UNESCO publication "Formal and Non-formal Education Coordination and Complimentary".[1]

"Informal education, which is sometimes called 'incidental' education, refers to unorganized education acquired during the entire life span of an individual through interaction with parents and siblings and with other members of the society, or through engaging in work and exposure to social events and movements and through mass media such as newspapers, radio, television, etc.

Non-formal education differs from formal education in the sense that it takes place outside the traditional framework of the formal system. This characteristic is also shared by informal education. However, like formal education, non-formal education is organized and has pre-determined objectives. It also has sequential learning structures, which are not necessarily graded. While formal education is rigid and is characterized by uniformity to a large extent, the hallmark of non-formal education is its flexibility in terms of time and the education of learning, age group of learners, content, methodology of instruction and evaluation procedures."

*Section 2*

***What is the current state of science and technology education and why are these skills and knowledge important for New Zealand?***

A number of recently published reports [Beattie, CERTECH, Royal Society[2]] all highlight the concern in New Zealand over the shortage of skilled and qualified people in science and technology. These reports sound warnings that unless something is done soon the economic viability of New Zealand is under threat. Other writers have been predicting that although economic prosperity is around the corner this will be stunted without the skilled workforce to back it.[3]

The major focus of concern has centred on the number of young people (33 per cent) who are leaving school with no formal qualifications and the additional problem that 65 per cent of these school leavers receive no further formal education and vocational training.

In New Zealand the percentage of 18-year-old enrolled in full or part-time education in 1984 was 32.6 per cent compared with 73.1 per cent in Switzerland, 71.9 per cent in West Germany and 54.75 per cent in the United States.

The CERTECH report[5] in their analysis of the destination of fifth formers shows that out of every 1000 students only 9 gain some technology related qualification.

In a discussion document put out by the New Zealand Vocational Training Council, August 1986, based on a major survey of developed industrialized countries, they state from their respondents:

"The unmistakable conclusion that must be drawn in their overwhelming recognition of the importance of education and training in economic performance. This is in keeping with a major overseas research study of West Germany, the United States and Japan in which . . . 'Every single body of opinion believed that their economic success would be impossible without a strongly sustained effort in vocational education and training.'"

New Zealand's chief export earnings remain those of a primary producing country namely meat, dairy, produce, wool, and wood/pulp/timber.

CERTECH[6] in their report believe that 10 per cent of those currently in our labour force need to be doing something different from what they are doing now. Whatever that something turns out to be it assuredly will need mathematical and technological skills in quantities not currently being generated. They contend that:

- there is a shift from industries primarily labour intensive to industries primarily knowledge intensive
- major markets like Europe, India, China, South Korea, Indonesia will become net exporters of food rather than net importers
- world demand for non-farm commodities is in decline owing to changed relationship between materials and knowledge
- capital movements rather than trade in goods and services is now the driving force of the world economy.

In their latest report CERTECH[7] predict, if present trends of the destination of school leavers continue, the output of technological skills will have decreased 21 per cent by the year 2000.

The outlook for New Zealand could be an inability to compete on the international market with resulting increase in foreign ownership and control of our existing resources and a lower standard of living.

Research investigating the deficit of New Zealand-trained scientists and technologists have largely focused on formal education and the shortcomings.

Clark and Vere-Jones[8] in their report on science education in schools found that science education was operating under major handicaps of teacher shortage education and inadequate financial and material resources. This was compounded by the low level of science knowledge on the part of primary school trainees and the low priority given generally to science education. The outcome they assert has been a lack of interest in science subjects, especially amongst girls in the upper secondary school; the poor performance of New Zealand children, particularly at 3rd form level, in the recent IEA survey on mathematics education; and the inadequate numbers of students enrolling for science and technology courses in the tertiary institutions.

Compared to what is happening in other countries technology education has hardly begun in New Zealand. It is a core subject in Britain, Europe, Scandinavia, Russia and Eastern Bloc countries, in the most states in the USA and in most provinces in Canada. In these countries technology education programmes are generally activity based and concerned with the development of and awareness of a range of technologies and the ability to select appropriate technologies. It includes an understanding that technology has an impact on society and the environment and an ability to solve technological problem through investigation, design and construction.

Adult education has an important contribution to make in addressing these issues in New Zealand. Adults play a key role in influencing children in their subject and career choices. As citizens and voters they can exert public pressure to bring about change in educational offerings.

The importance of simultaneously educating both adult and child has been well documented and researched by bodies concerned with adult education such as UNESCO but it is seen to be of secondary importance in NZ and often overlooked in the budget allocations.

"Never before have so few of us understood the devices and systems surrounding us. Yet we are faced with controlling this tremendous power. People need to understand the limitations, as well as the capabilities of emerging technologies. The technologically literate person should have a sense of what technology cannot do or be."[9]

For adults such knowledge and skills are in fact life skills, in that they enable a person to function effectively with matters, scientific and technical, as they arise in everyday life.

The acquisition of these skills enables the person to become an effective citizen able to be a participant in political debate on important issues such as the environment, the arms race, energy use, nuclear matters, health, the funding of research and the interpretation of statistical data. As areas that are far too important and far reaching in their consequences to be left to scientists alone.

As already discussed it is not just in the role of citizen that adults need to be scientifically and technically literate. An informed citizen is an informed worker able to contribute innovative suggestions or lead organizations to provide excellence in service or produce through the application of appropriate technology.

These skills and knowledge are vital for New Zealand's future prosperity and growth.

*Section 3*

***Science and technology education: What is currently happening?***

Before a discussion on what informal and non-formal education can do to assist with this crisis it is necessary to take a look at what attempts have already been made to address these concerns. Below are listed just some of the many activities going on in this area.

There has been a problem in selecting which material to include for much of what is going on in the formal area spills over into the informal area. In fact many activities in the formal area such as science fairs and science badges in schools inevitably involve parents in assisting children to complete projects.

As the focus of this paper is non-formal and informal education, comment on the formal area has been restricted to a mention of some special efforts to promote education in science and technology.

**Universities**

Science in Learning, Waikato University. The aim of this project has been to research how children learn science. The research findings set the underlying philosophy for the review of the Form 1-5 science syllabus. The Learning in Science Projects have shown that students make sense of their world by building on their own experiences and prior knowledge.

There are two other projects still in the formative stages, worth noting, with which the universities have been associated. The first is "Heritage New Zealand", a project that aims to involve thousands of New Zealanders in the creation of a desktop, national mixed-media database about NZ past and present. (An improved version of UK's "Doomsday").

The second is a science centre to be based in Christchurch similar to science museums in other countries aiming to give people "hands on" experience of scientific and technological models.

**School**

*Curriculum Review*

Review of the Form 1-5 science syllabus. The approach of the new syllabus is student centred, encouraging students to take an active part in their own learning. The student is central to the learning process while the teacher is the facilitator providing the optimum opportunities for the student to learn. An exciting aspect of the new syllabus (as yet not officially in place) is the recognition of different learning needs of both girls and Maori.

*Science fairs* which are for students to exhibit investigative, technological or display projects are now a feature of science education in New Zealand. Eighteen fairs are conducted on an annual basis throughout New Zealand inviting both school children and the public to view the exhibits.

*Special weeks, science extravaganzas and travelling road shows:* Conservation Week, Technology Week and Travelling Road Shows are other activities aimed to encourage interest of both parent and pupil in the field of science and technology.

**Polytechnics**

*Link* Courses are designed to introduce secondary students to polytechnic education by exposure to workshop activities unable to be offered within the secondary schools curriculum. A review of the effectiveness of the LINK programme in encouraging students to undertake further training is currently being conducted.

*Try-a-trade-day* is aimed to bring girls into the polytechnic to have some "hands on" experience in occupations that have been seen as traditionally male.

*Bridging* courses are offered by most polytechnics, a few schools who take adult students and the extension studies department of some universities to encourage students to "catch-up" on maths and science that are pre-requisite subjects for entry to certain courses.

*Foundation and pre-apprentice training courses* have been introduced recently to provide training in areas normally only open to school leavers who have an apprenticeship.

**Community and Non-formal Education**

*Community Education and Evening Classes*

This covers a vast array of classes offered through government funded institutions such as schools, polytechnics, university extension studies as well as non-governmental organizations. For many these classes are an introduction to skills and knowledge missed out in schooling. It has been a key place for adults to access the new technology, particularly computers.

*Radio New Zealand:* Continuing Education Section has a popular following and is respected for the variety, depth and quality of its programmes.

*Television* provides a number of science programmes each week. "First Forward", a New Zealand production, introduces new developments in science and technology. "Our World", "Life on Earth" and "Nature Watch" are examples of international nature programmes offered, and specifically for children there is "Scientific Eye" (Yorkshire).

*Cable television* is shortly to be introduced into NZ. There is some fear that the introduction of this new technology will affect the quality of programmes provided by the National Broadcasting Service. It has been suggested that only those who can afford the new technology will have the option of quality programmes while the National Broadcasting Service, through economic necessity will serve up a diet of second rate overseas programme.

*Access radio* is people making their own programmes, learning to use the equipment themselves and cutting out the middle person who often acts as a "gatekeeper". There are a number operating in NZ, of special note are the two Maori Access Radio stations, one in Auckland (promoting Maori views and concerns on issues in both Maori and English) and one in Wellington (using only Maori language).

The Christchurch Polytechnic, through their Media Studies Department, is training students for broadcasting and have set up an Access Radio as part of their training programme. Many interest groups, clubs and organizations have taken the opportunity to learn the technology associated with producing a radio programme and regularly have a slot on air.

*Access TV* is soon to be available in NZ. It will be a far more expensive operation. It remains to be seen if this is as empowering to the users as Access Radio has proved to be.

**Scientific Journals, Newsletters, Associations, Networking and Support Groups**

There are a wide variety of these. Some geared to specific professions, others to a wider audience. Here are a few that are directed to the lay person.

Computer users clubs to share information and to support in the application of computers to work or home use.

"Forest and Bird" magazine of the Royal Forest and Bird Protection Society. New Zealand Technology Advancement Trust, a non-profit organization dedicated to the development of scientific and technological skills in NZ.

Science and Technology Advisory Committee (STAC), a government advisory committee.

**Environmental Groups**

The three prominent groups in NZ with a large national membership are Forest and Bird, Maruia Society and Greenpeace. Through newsletters and public meetings these environmental groups do much to keep their membership and the public informed by debating environmental issues of concern to the country.

**Affirmative Action Groups**

With research and the sharing of women's experiences in the sciences it became increasingly obvious that some affirmative action was needed if any change to improve the participation of women was going to take place.

The Department of Education currently has three women officers working in each of the tertiary, secondary, and Maori and Polynesian spheres. They have been responsible for both policy and implementation. Much of their work has been directed at creating a better learning environment for women and girls as well as encouraging females into non-traditional careers. The new Ministry of Education has only provided a "watch-dog" role in policy formation. Women are concerned that the vital role of producing resources, which back up policy, will be lost.

A women's employment officer currently works in each of the main regions and is based in the NZ Employment Service. These women have the task of working to encourage women to consider non-traditional employment options.

Women working in science and technology have set up groups to be a support for each other and to promote more women into these fields.

They include DSIR women's network, equals maths/science network for teachers and WISE (Women into Science Education). One aim of WISE is to develop a "Sisters in Science" programme in which women scientists identify with particular schools. They have also been associated with the preparation of a booklet on four New Zealand pioneer women scientists in conjunction with DSIR and the Development of Education.

**Maori Studies Association**

This group and other Maori groups have been concerned with the neglect by scientists of things Maori. Traditional Maori methods of cultivation and fishing and the laws of conservation that were developed to protect and preserve precious or limited resources have largely been replaced by Pakeha methods and laws. One outcome has been the loss to NZ, through scientific breeding, of the many varieties of Kumara (a sweet potato brought to Aotearoa by the Maori). Through a dialogue with scientists interest in traditional plants, crops and their uses has been revived (recently species of Kumara, no longer present in NZ, but preserved in Japan were brought back for cultivation).

**Industry-based Training, Inservice Training, on-the-job Training, Management Training**

Most leading industries and organizations have a commitment to inservice and ongoing training. How much employers can be expected to contribute to ongoing training or upgrading of employees skills is currently the focus of discussion of one of the "Learning for Life" working parties.

Dr. Mervyn Probine[10], a prominent figure in the debate for the need to increase our output of scientific and skilled personnel, believes leadership has a vital role to play in this. He has put this into practice by recently taking a group of "captains of industry" in food technology to America to inspire them to look anew at technology and marketing for New Zealand products. Further trips with other key leaders are planned.

**Skills Training for the Unemployed**

The main government funded skills training scheme for unemployed is called Access. While some providers have been particularly successful in equipping their students with skills recent research[11] point out some of the major shortfalls of this type of training. The mixture of providers and educational/ teaching standards, the lack of any systematized qualifications and haphazard ongoing vocational guidance all raise questions as to whether this scheme and its bureaucratic administration is the most useful way to address this problem.

*Section 4*

***The Popularization of Science and Technology: Why has it failed? What are the Barriers to this Happening?***

Although New Zealand has been active in the popularization of science and technology through various avenues and activities (and there are even more than those listed above) there is a major shortfall in the number of people receiving education in this field compared with the number required. For instance girls and Maoris only participate in this form of education to a minor degree.

Why is this? Why are girls opting out of science and technology courses? Why are Maoris not only opting out of science but education generally at a greater rate than their Pakeha peers? Why if there is a critical shortage of scientists and technologists is the general population non clamouring for more money to be allocated to this area? Is it just because they are ignorant and need to be informed about the skills crisis or are there other issues needing to be addressed before action can take place.

One obvious reason is the perception these groups have of science and technology. The stereotyped view of the scientist is one of a remote figure, elitist in thinking. A person who is often environmentally insensitive and inhumane (nuclear bombs and the arms race). A person who has poor inter-personal communications, is not concerned with social issues and takes on responsibility for the abuse of the product of science.

Such a person and their profession naturally lacks appeal!

It has been well researched that women's perception and experience of science and technology has been alienating.[12] Research further indicates a strong bias in girls' choice of vocation towards occupations which are people-oriented and show a social concern. No doubt research as to who Maori students have dropped out of science could throw up some useful information also.

Although efforts have been made from many quarters to change girls' thinking about science and technology with little noticeable effect the question is now being asked is this appropriate? Who should change? Women or science and technology?

At an international conference that I attended in Denmark in 1986 entitled "Women Challenge Technology", I was interested to note how many scientists were posing this question. They gave graphic stories of the loneliness and hardship ensured by women working in non-traditional occupations.

One paper traced back to the origins of current scientific thinking through philosophers such as Plato, Aristotle, Bacon and Descrates. The impact of their thinking, which believed in the division of body and soul, is very much with us today; it associated 'body' with feminine which is unscientific and 'mind' with masculine which is scientific.

Another paper examined computers, describing them as "a masculine machine that can only work in a linear hierarchical why with data that is fed into it which is reduced and uniquely defined. The road of knowledge must pass through the computer wedge subtleties and intuition cannot be computerized".

Janet Burns in her paper "From Changing Women to Changing Science"[13] examines some of the myths surrounding the perceptions that women cannot do science. These myths include beliefs that men are logical and that women are intuitive, that men are objective and that women are subjective. Janet Burns supports the need for science and technology to change, rather than women, when she describes a "revised view of science, as suggested by scientists like Medwar and Nelson. The focus of these writers is on the importance of intuitive thought in the real process of scientific creativity, as opposed to the sterility of logic in the standard scientific method".

As Henri Poincare (1929) said ". . . it is by logic that we prove. It is by intuition that we discover."

Janet Burns goes on to quote Stephen Toulmin and his revised view of science which he calls "post-modern" science as one that recognizes the subjectivity of the observer and applies standards of fairness.

Other characteristics that can be added to post-modern science include a recognition that it is holistic, value laden and socially determined.

"Post-modern science reinterprets the process of science launched by Galileo and others 250 years ago moves on to accommodate changes that will allow scientists to address issues encountered today".

The adoption of this revised view of science (more attuned to female socialization/characteristics) would I believe make a significant impact not only in attracting more girls into science but more people generally.

With the majority of women alienated from science and the majority of Maori generally alienated from a pakeha schooling system the poor of people which can be drawn on to fill this huge gap of scientifically and technically competent people is very small. The answer has to lie in increasing this pool of students.

In spite of the government's commitment to equity, the majority of the population can still see no connection between creating a more effective learning environment for girls and Maori (this means addressing racism and sexism) and an increase in the number of students who will stay on in the formal education system or join non-formal classes, which in turn, would lead to a more educated workforce and economic prosperity. Many people are openly hostile and see the government as getting their priorities wrong. I would argue that simply throwing more money at the already privileged group is not going to get New Zealand on the way to economic prosperity or make for a better society.

Interestingly Suzanne Dillon[14] found in her research that although many girls believed women could and should take careers in maths/science they would not as they saw a conflict in the future between home and career.

All of this adds another dimension to the need for increased funding for training in not only science and technology but teacher and parent education. Inservice training is indeed to change teacher attitudes to classroom management and what creates an effective learning environment for all students. As well as this there must be a provision of resources and equipment for the teaching of a revised view of science and technology.

This cannot be achieved successfully without taking the adult population along too, as expectations that women and Maoris have of themselves shape career choice and ongoing educational initiatives. Hence the need for resources likewise to be directed to continuing education.

Although barrier, related to that discussed above, is the question asked by some but possibly thought by many more, who benefits and who loses from the introduction of new technologies? Katherine and John Peet in paper presented to the 1987 ANZUS Conference[15] make a plea for the nation to collectively plan the future and the use of new technologies so that they are used wisely to benefit all people and not just a privileged few. "The New Institutionalist"[16] has many case studies of the destruction of the fabric of communities through exploitative technology which while seemingly bringing riches is in fact creating an improverished society with profits to the wealthy few who run and control the resources.

Peter Fensham in an article entitled "Science for All"[17] poses another possibility as to why the popularization of science and technology has problems to overcome. He sees the formal education system as having gateway subjects that filter through the relatively few students who are allowed to move into professions of status, social, experience, and economic security.

Scientists, Peter Fensham contends, are "now a powerful faction with a major interest in maintaining their subject as an elite and important field".

In preparation for this paper I was surprised to find this argument put forward from other professionals who were concerned about the attitude of their colleagues perpetuating the mystique of their particular skill. After all, the slogans "Science for All" and "Technology for All" could be very threatening if a person believed their job depended on others not knowing how to do it.

Penny Carnaby, Head of Learning and Resources Centre at Christchurch Polytechnic, elaborates on this further when she expresses deep concern with New Zealand's move towards user pays and the growth of the knowledge broker. She defines knowledge brokers as those who have technological know-how and equipment to access the major data bases, such as DIALOG, and charge the users for that information. For the non-formal learner this has important ramifications in their access to knowledge and information. The conflict between those with knowledge and skills and their unconscious desire to hang on to these as their source of livelihood and status could well be one of the contributing factors in New Zealand's problems with popularization of science and technology.

*Section 5*

### *What Can Non-formal and Informal Education do?*

The most important role that non-formal and informal education can play is to work actively to bring about changes in attitudes. It is only by a shift in public opinion that our crisis in education can be overcome and that we as nation can benefit from science and technology.

Below are listed some possible strategies:

1. Support the Government's moves to equity in education. Without a changed learning environment for girls, women and Maori little progress will be made in reducing the deficit of skilled people in science and technology.
2. Lobby for inservice training for teachers and community educators in order to present "post-modern science" to students, which challenges the existing myths surrounding these subjects.
3. Consciously promote appropriate role models of scientists and technologists that fit the new image needed for science, that is of socially concerned and responsible people.

4. Promote more public discussion on science and technology, debunk some of the myths and openly discuss fears as to who benefits and who loses from more spending on science and technical education.

5. Promote courses that empower people. Such courses include assertiveness training, knowing your rights, health issues, understanding technology, computer skills. It is by empowering people to feel confident and good about themselves that they then are able to question academics and professionals. This can only work to bridge the gap that now exists between lay and academic and start the dialogue that will see the problem as a shared one.

6. Develop a public understanding of learning theories. There are many different approaches to learning. By enabling people to experience a variety of learning styles they can then identify how they best learn and begin to take control of their own learning. 'Learning how to learn' must continue to be a key aspect of adult education.

7. Develop strategies to reach those not currently being reached by non-formal and informal education process. Promote through one of the main informal medium, television, a much more interactive approach to learning.

8. Support and cultivate the "Tall Poppies", the leaders in industry, education and the community by acknowledging the importance of leadership skills and training.

9. Request that Technology Education become part of the education system in New Zealand and call for the establishment of technology centres. These would provide impartial advice on technologies available for educational and public use, provide inservice training for teachers and a place where teachers and parents could come and engage in technology tasks.

10. Promote the development of high quality career services and directories that will assist parents and children to

be aware of the wide range of career options that have now opened up with developments in science and technology.

11. Examine the current allocation of government spending on unemployed schemes with a view to a redistribution to create:
    - technology high schools
    - technology centres
    - senior colleges
    - providing more places in existing courses

12. Lobby for continued financial support for Adult and Continuing Education offered through government and non-government organizations. Our ongoing national wellbeing requires an informed and broadly educated adult population committed to life long education.

## NOTES

1. UNESCO Regional Office for Education in Asia and the Pacific Bangkok, 1986. "Formal and Non-formal Education".
2. Beattie, D. (1986). "Key to Prosperity: Science and Technology, Report of the Ministerial Working Party" Wellington Government Printer.

   CERTECH "The Supply of Technological Skills to a Changing Economy" Massey University, CTI, Industries Development Commission, 1986.

   "Science Education in NZ, Present Facts and Future Problems" by Megan Clark and David Vere-Jones. The Royal Society of NZ Miscellaneous Series.
3. "Management" NZ Journal, May 1989.
4. An analysis of the 1981 census by the Wellington Polytechnic principal Bob Bubendorfer.
5. CERTECH, ibid.
6. CERTECH, ibid.
7. CERTECH "The Secondary-Tertiary Student Flow 1979-86; And the Implications for a Changing Economy" CIT, Massey University, NZ Technology Advancement Trust.

8. Megan Clark and David Vere-Jones "Science Education in New Zealand", ibid.

9. Don Fergusson, "Technology Education—Its Importance and Growth", Curriculum Development Division, Department of Education.

10. Dr Mervyn Probine, Physicist, former Head, State Services Commission currently Director, NZ Adventure Trust.

11. Lauder, Khan, McGlinn, Education Department, University of Canterbury, Christchurch, 1988 "A report on the pilot evaluation of transition programmes in schools, polytechnics and private provider institutions in New Zealand".

12. "Jobs for the Girls, Why Not Technical?" Suzanne Dillon, Knowledge Systems Research Pty. Ltd., Melbourne, 1986.

13. Janet Burns "From Changing Women to Changing Science", Department of Education, paper presented to SCION '88.

14. Suzanne Dillon, p.183, ibid.

15. Katherine and John Peet "Turning Data into Wisdom: Who Decides?" ANZUS Conference 1987.

16. "The New Internationalist", No. 157, March 1986 "Our Throw Away World", No. 162, August 1986 "How Affluence Causes Effluence", "Patterns of Control, The Human Shape of Technology".

17. Peter Fensham, Faculty of Education, Monash University, Australia "Science For All" reprinted in "NZ Science Teacher", Autumn '89.

# 19

# Country Paper: Poland

STANISLAW KACZOR

I would like to present some problems involved in adult education in Poland in the context of the popularization of science and technology, as a task especially important in the fall of the 20th century. As far as industry and agriculture are concerned, Poland is medium developed; it is weakly developed, however, in the sphere of services. At the same time, however, it possessed great possibilities of accelerated development because of strong traditions in the field of research and relatively well-trained workforce. I mean here traditional vocations, which implies the shortage of workers for future occupations, managers included.

After the period limited share in the international division of labour, Poland is now entering the period of accelerated processes, which were characteristic of highly developed countries much earlier.

The rebuilding in Poland refers to all spheres of life, i.e. politics, economy, science, technology, culture and education. Each trend is characterized with its own peculiar processes; all spheres of social and economic life, however, undergo changes aimed at the acceleration of the development of the country. An important role in these process is played by the Polish science, connected in many ways with the world science, co-operation with UNESCO being one of the most significant fields of activity.

This contribution of the Polish science to changes occurring everywhere consists in the development of diagnostic, prognostic and monitory expertises, which are then submitted to authorities and social organizations.

In order to illustrate the contribution of the Polish science to profound changes that occur in all spheres of life, I will present the latest publication of the Forecasting Committee for the Development of the Country, called "Polska 2000" and attached to the Polish Academy of Sciences. The publication is entitled "The Modern Shape of Poland. Development Dillemas at the Threshold of the 21st Century" (Ossolineum Publishing House, 1989, pp. 605). The authors presented different variants of forecasts, stipulating for one of the suggested scenarios. They pointed to four elements of the quality of life. They are as follows:

- healthy natural environment,
- proper health protection and social welfare,
- cultural and civilizational promotion in the sense of modern education, the participation in the national and international culture, modernized working conditions, the improvement of service and living standards,
- joint participation in social and political decisions, joint management.

It has been taken for granted that human being is, and will be in the future, the originator of the rebuilding. What is thus important is the promotion of intellectual work, creative attitudes and initiatives among workers. This requires careful reconsideration of the relationship between the individual and the collective.

The researchers working for the "Polska 2000" Committee have presented in their report three scenarios of the country development that are most likely to be carried out during the forthcoming decades:

1. the scenario of raw materials and energy priority
2. the scenario of basic needs priority
3. the scenario of civilization development priority.

They have stipulated for scenario 3, which is likely to ensure the deepest changes in the economic structure by means of:

- the foundation of those industries that require advance technology,
- making our economy open to the world,
- making economic policy support the market,
- the intensification of scientific and technological development,
- the thorough rebuilding of the national education system, together with the improvement of the conditions of education.

As it appears from what has been mentioned before, all elements of the development forecasts include the problems of education. In 1987 the Experts Committee for the National Education was founded in Poland. The Committee is supposed to work out a detailed diagnosis of the state of the national education in Poland and to submit it, by the end of 1989, to the government and the society. The diagnosis will also include suggestions concerning educational reforms, which should be in agreement with social, economic and cultural demands, as well as with individual aspirations, in the perspective of the first decades of the 21st century. The Committee is of the opinion that it is impossible to carry out effectively the reform in any sphere of social or economic life without modern schooling, capable of teaching young people how to think in a new way. For many years in Poland it has been emphasized that education ought to serve the society, economy and culture. Nowadays we put the main stress on its stimulating function and, for this purpose, we try to popularize the achievements of science and technology.

The Institute of Vocational Education in Warsaw, in co-operation with the Polish National Commission for UNESCO, organized under the auspices of the UNESCO three European conferences on adult education (held in 1983, 1985 and 1987). The latest conference concerned the out-of-school forms of adult education, i.e. those forms that we call informal. A problem of great importance—and still up to date, I think—is the question about individual and social expectations as regards educational standards in the sphere of occupational life, labour market, leisure, family life.

I agree with the statement included in the introductory paper and saying that primary and secondary schools do not perform their function sufficiently as far as the popularization of science and technology is concerned. This is the case in Poland, despite permanent changes in curricula and teachers training. Curriculum changes have resulted in many negative aspects, e.g. the overloading of curricula with information. This caused subsequent changes—the reduction of the content, not always accurate, etc. This brought about the danger of formal only, not actual, teaching.

I also share the doubts that have been expressed in the introductory paper and referred to the question; can the school perform the popularizing function in agreement with social demands? The main task of the school will be, at least in the forthcoming years, to organize educational processes aimed at the development of universal, humanistic values, in order to ensure the development of the mankind. What is important is to prepare human beings to be able to control the development of civilization. It seems that if the school fulfilled this task properly, it would deserve approval.

The contemporary school has often been criticized, and proposals of descholarization have been heard and there. It seems, however, that there is something of the truth in the statement that the school ought to be conservative in a sense, at it is to guarantee universal values.

Informal education, however, is more flexible in its very nature, geared to the contemporary and the future, both in its content as well as in forms and methods, together with the whole infrastructure. I believe that it is necessary to carry out the research, international research included, into the multitude of information sources and into the functions of informal education teachers. I think, and base my opinion on the research that has partially has been carried out, that the teacher, especially in informal education, is becoming a guide in the world of science (science and technology) rather than a source of knowledge or information. It is much more difficult to perform this new function than the traditional one, when the teacher was the only source of information, or at least the most important one. In Poland, however, the teacher still plays this traditional function in many cases. It is easy to observe this at courses, where a lecture delivered by a teacher is the only source of information for participants. The investigative as well as the innovative functions of the teacher must also gain importance. As regards the investigative function, the teacher must undertake an attempt to measure the effectiveness of his work, then draw conclusions useful for self-improvement.

Because of the increasing availability of computerized data banks, and in Poland first of all libraries attached to scientific societies, occupational organizations and enterprises, of radio and television programmes (satellite broadcasts included), the ability to select information, interpret it and apply in different spheres of life is becoming more and more important.

Informal education in Poland is carried on mainly in enterprises. This is because employees ought to improve their qualifications in consequence of changes occurring in technology, work organization, etc. Unfortunately, in Poland there is relatively little demand for in-service training, for the structure of economy is science-consuming to a very limited degree. The process of restructurization, however, has already been initiated. This, in turn, has caused the danger of closing down certain factories. And this process will result in the increased occupational mobility.

Course and other forms of informal education have been conducted so far by educational units in enterprises (mostly large and medium-sized) or by organizations specialized in educational activity. They are carried on in enterprises or at schools, when there is a break in their daily activities.

Of great importance for informal education is the development of a new system of course, including introductory courses, lasting for several hours, development courses and improvement courses.

Another problem to be solved is the permanent training of teachers from the point of view of both specialization and pedagogy. Participants of the out-of-school forms of education expect both competence and authority on the part of their teachers.

In the Polish situation, of great importance is to solve the problem of educational infrastructure, starting with buildings and equipment and ending up with study materials and handbooks.

In every field of informal education it seems necessary to carry out researches into teaching effectiveness, and then to popularize the most effective solutions. International exchange of experiences may result in the acceleration of many process that have started in Poland.

# 20

# Country Paper: Sri Lanka

S.M.D. PERERA

**Brief Geographical Description**

Sri Lanka situated at the southern end of the Indian subcontinent is an Island of 65,000 sq. km. It is an independent country, a member of the non-aligned group as well as a member of the SARC group of countries. A democratic system of government prevails in the country with an elected president. An open economic policy is adopted since 1977 with many opportunities made available to all its citizens. A decentralized system of government prevails and there are 8 decentralized administrative systems for the nine provinces of the country (North and East Provinces are temporarily merged).

Historically Sri Lanka recorded past goes back to almost 2,500 years to the 6th Century BC. Buddhism was first introduced to the country from India during the reign of the Indian King Asoka in the 3rd Century BC, and through its inspiration the cultural traditions and development progressively took place over the years. In the sixteenth century the arrival of invaders from the western world (the Portuguese, the Dutch and lastly the British) influenced to a great extent the patterns of indigenous culture and economic sustanance of the country through the infusion of western culture and patterns of living. The plantation industry (Tea and Rubber) as well as a system of schooling in the English Medium were prominent introductions. Western industrial products too flowed in to strengthen the colonial administration.

In 1948 after securing independence from colonial rule which lasted approx. 400 years, Sri Lanka was again on the path of progress as a sovereign independent nation. In the 41 years since independence we have attempted to create a welfare state. Education is free from Primary Grades to the University and available to all. There are in addition free Health Services and many support services to all people whose circumstances are comparatively not so well off. There is a free text book scheme, a free midday meal programme and the new 'Janasaviya' poverty alleviation scheme (Janasaviya—to strengthen the people) where those below the poverty line are supported by the state both financially and through assistance in education/ training and employment.

## Demographic Data

The population of the country now stands at 16.5 million and early in the 21st century it is likely to touch the 20 million mark. The population statistics and trends are mainly based on the 1981 census. There has been a significant decrease in population rise, and the 0-15 age group has decreased from 39 per cent in 1971 to 36.3 per cent in 1981. The population in the productive years (15-64) has increased from 56.8 per cent in 1971 to 60 per cent in 1981. The 5-9 age group has decreased from 13.2 per cent in 1971 to 11.4 per cent in 1981. Similarly the 10-14 age group has declined from 12.7 per cent to 10.7 per cent. The total school going population now stands at close to 4 million and the annual enrolment at Grade I (90 per cent) totals almost 400,000. Sri Lanka is multiethnic and multireligious. 74 per cent are Sinhalese with 2.6 per cent Sri Lanka Tamils, 7.1 per cent Muslims and 5.6 per cent Indian Tamils. Buddhists compose 69.3 per cent, Hindus 15.5 per cent, Christians 7.5 per cent and those of Islam faith 7.6 per cent.

## The Economic Scenario

The socio-economic scenario in the country has always shown a progressive outlook even though problems that affect many nations today such as increase in violence and youth unrest would also have had their drastic impacts in the country.

British rates have declined, fertility rates have fallen and child and material morality are at very low levels (25 and 0.8 per 1000). There is a significant decrease in the 0-4 and 5-9 years old and the young women of today are better equipped to face the world ahead. A wide range of assistance schemes are available to help the low income groups in the country. The period 1977-85 witnessed one of the highest economic growth rates of 5.8 per cent on an average; unemployment fell and the real incomes for many received an increase. The GDP going into investment averaged 27 per cent. The changing economic climate of the world, however, and external factors affecting Sri Lanka's trade balance have forced her along with many developing countries of the world to apply adjustment policies which would often affect the forward steps taken for needed social process in the country (debt service ratio 22.5 per cent of exports in 1985 and estimated to be 30 per cent by 1989).

There is also a negative side in the sense that inequalities have really increased. The lower 20 per cent, which received 7.1 per cent of the total household income in 1973, received 5.7 per cent in 1982. Associated factors such as acute malnutrition also showed an upward rise. The population of the country is still rural based (78.5 per cent as per 1981 census). The present policy of decentralized government is in fact to support the development of the rural sector. Further, Government policy encourages people moving away from the cities and also from the populous Wet Zone to the Dry Zone of the country. This has resulted in the population of the Dry Zone increasing from 35.4 per cent in 1953 to 42 per cent in 1981. Governments have always invested heavily in rural infrastructure development, e.g. major invigation schemes and rural housing schemes. Throughout agriculture has been the main income earner for the country. During the period 1978-87 agriculture contributed to 28 per cent of the GDP and makes up 60 per cent of total export earnings. It generates 15 per cent of the government revenue and provides employment for about 45 per cent of the labour force. The manufacturing sector however had recorded a steady growth since 1978 due to incentives provided. From a share of only 15 per cent of export earnings in 1978 it has risen to 49 per cent in 1987.

A variety of factors affecting developing countries have their impacts on the countries' economy and progress. The recent ethnic disturbances and internal strife have forced countries like Sri Lanka to make heavy commitments on items such as defence expenditure further slowing down planned progress.

## Roles and Responsibilities of Education System

*1. The Formal System*

There is no doubt the formal education system of a country is primarily responsible for providing scientific attitude, fundamental knowledge, skills, ways of thinking and developing values on science and technology of our present and future generations. Schooling years are impressionable years and what is internalized during these periods often lasts a lifetime. Formal science education commences right from the beginning at Primary Grades (Elementary Science at Grades 4 and 5) and continues as 'science' education at secondary stages. All school pupils follow this course. At collegiate level the Science and Arts courses are separately followed with more pupils following the 'Arts' course. This is usually due to the lack of facilities (teacher/ lab facilities) in the school system. In the 11 years of schooling most of the pupils will therefore follow a course in science. In countries like Sri Lanka we have a persistent problem of a hard core non schooling group (8 per cent-10 per cent of 5-14 years old) as well as a drop outs problem (20 per cent of each cohert at grade 5, and 40 per cent grade 8).

Invariably therefore an appreciable proportion of our younger generation would miss an education as such, and therefore not be exposed to the basics of science which pupils who complete schooling would receive (15 per cent largely and approx. 40 per cent to a fair extent). These pupils would come from deprived and low income families (almost 40 per cent live below the poverty line).

In the formal area there is much work being done to make the science course more relevant to needs of the day as well as for the future. Curriculum developers consistently follow these trends and curricula are updated regularly. Science and associated technology is a subject area advancing at a rapid rate and the formal system of schooling being highly conservative and often suffering from this drawback is slow in keeping pace. School science education (like the whole to the formal system) following needs of the sixties to provide for the elite who will follow the professions (medicine, engineering, etc.) more or less continues on this track. There is a need now for interdisciplinary adjustments to meet societal needs of science and technology (for basic development programmes) as well as for science and technology more universal (considering science and technology as essential for a literate person). In this connection teacher training schemes (regular in service is needed), school facilities (lab and workshop design) as well as extra or supra school activities in the community and the outer environment, have to be rethought and redesigned to meet the real needs of pupils and their eventual life as adults.

2. *Non-Formal Areas (NFE)*

The Non-Formal Educational areas which are organized programmes outside the formal could provide a continuing as well as a complementary form to formal education. They are also in most instances an alternative to formal systems when recipients being often of low income groups get pushed out on left out of formal education. As the demand for science/ technology knowledge and skills increase with the general public NFE programmes would come in very effectively to meet these needs. Further the courses or training programmes can be held in areas or locations where there is a demand and at a low cost. Local talent is often used and while training is in session or not the trainers can themselves undergo further training to meet specialized training needs. The curricula of courses will of course be designed to meet the needs of the clients and they will have to be regularly updated via a strong curricula development facility. Resource centres will always be associated with NFE programmes which often cater to a variety of educational needs (in addition to science and technology programmes). Courses will often be practical and applied, bringing a vast array of information, knowledge and skills to meet the demands of many client groups, specially the young who would not have their needs met via formal means. In the future the more 'practical' or 'applied' nature of NFE programmes will have to be strengthened with more 'educational' concept with courses being multidisciplinary, open ended and pupils led on to be more creative in outlook yet retaining their functional characteristics. Of course there will be many different types of NFE Courses.

Economic activity in rural areas are often concentrated in agricultural of technical areas. Of course many services always develop alongside such activity. Investments in human resources in the areas of sciences and technology will itself act as a catalyst to provide for further developments in economic tasks. NFE programmes unlike formal systems will predominantly cater to those who would stay back in the rural areas themselves and provide the knowledge as well as the interests and utilize available local resources for the improvement of their own areas. Rural areas would often be content to carry on with traditional economic activities mainly concentrated on agriculture and low volume traditional technology. Changing the structure of secondary schooling to include NFE programmes as well as inclusion of such programmes outside formal schooling may well be a means of meetings rural unemployment under employment youth dissatisfaction, needs of economic improvement and restructuring of rural areas.

Further, societies in rural areas will face situations of environment protection, conservation of resources, use of alternative sources of energy (renewable as much as possible) and science and technology knowledge both basic as well as in their applied forms will be much in demand. The concept of popularizing science and technology will therefore be implied when we have to meet such situations. Formal systems are much criticized these days and their curricula are often focused to meet needs of pupils proceeding or more professional avenues. Teaching systems still follow basics ignoring needs of societies on social fronts, e.g. health, local technology or local questions of technology introductions. NFE can now look into such areas too, along with the more applied skills that need to be generated at the village level, NFE Programmes can in fact provide for continuing assistance to a wide range of clients to meet their demands for knowledge and skills in or after their initial training under formal or NFE programmes—for adults, housewives, or even the elderly. It is now recognized that in the evolutionary process of education, non-formal education has an increasingly important role to play. Structures, organization, management, supervision, evaluation procedures along with curricula and their educational material production specific to NFE situations as well as learning/teaching methodologies will be the areas to be looked into and progressively researched and developed. At the moment, NFE in Sri Lanka in the area of science and technology is restricted mainly to skills development programmes for youth. It should certainly take on a wider role in the days to come.

*3. Informal Sector—Mass Media*

So far as popularizing of science and technology is concerned the informal sector will of course play an important role. The mass media will come in prominently and will be a powerful tool to bring in information, knowledge, skills and importantly attitudes both scientific as well as humanistic to the whole range of client groups. Informal scientific and technical information is perhaps a very rapidly advancing area and is certainly contributing tremendously to popularizing this important area. In the recent past the commercial value of preparing material and putting it across through the mass media in a way most people find interesting has come in and regular documentaries like "Towards 2000" are very popular bringing in scientific and technical information to the general public.

Science and Technology has always been attractive to the human mind. The rapidity of its growth is indeed fascination to most people. Futuristic novels of present day writers like Arthur C. Clark, as well as H.G Wells of an earlier period continue to fascinate most people. Films on future fiction are screened in many countries and the people both young and old eagerly view videos, documentaries or even read the comics of things to come. The informal scenario is today both a source of interest entertainment and information.

However, it would be relevant for us to 'formalize' the mass media and utilize its vast potential for more specific ends. While this is needed ongoing and there is much good work done to popularize science and technology, this informal sector could come in to help both the formal as well as non-formal education sectors more constructively in our different countries. Educationists may well have to map out the different roles of all such areas when we consider an 'education' for most individuals.

## Aspects of Science/Technology Development and the Future

### *1. Directing Knowledge/Information*

Along with the popularization of science and technology directing relevant knowledge and skills to correct areas and to the people concerned will have to be looked at purposefully. Further, progressive build up of knowledge in science and technology, both through the schooling system, non-formal means as well as informally, is a challenging task. There will be many gaps to be filled, weak points to be strengthened and relevant and new information to be brought in. The vast build up of knowledge must be looked at from these different points of view so far as the users are concerned, and made available in their correct forms, utility wise, information wise or even entertainment or general interest wise. Popularising will therefore have to be viewed in these contexts and management systems along with their evaluation systems called in to assist this process.

### *2. Relevant Technology*

The question of relevance in science and technology is often discussed. Popularising not only new technology but also existing technology, if it suits the local conditions, will have to be looked into. Some countries would wish to adopt certain models already developed or are being developed, may be perhaps by other countries. Some would wish to build up alternate models or develop indigenous models. It all depends on a variety of situations and these factors will have to be recognized in popularising suitable systems in our different countries.

*3. Technology and Social Needs*

Apart from economic needs social needs of different countries will have to be supported through advances in science and technology. These areas include health, sanitation, energy requirements, housing, food and nutrition or even education. In popularising of science and technology via formal, non-formal or informal education, the social needs will need special attention for most of our countries. Conservation and environment aspects will also need to be looked at specifically. Control of population growth, a serious problem to our countries, would need scientific and technological support. All these efforts would contribute to bringing in desirable standards of living to communities in many countries and popularising the relevant technologies will add to practical efforts.

*4. Cultural Patterns*

The culture of a people will be the unseen foundation of which most people live, work and relax. Sudden influx of too much technology has both its good and bad effects. Some feel that technology shrouded in consumer gadgets and devices are often forced on people through devious means. Technology can often influence the ways of living for most people, who often lead satisfied well balanced and healthy lives (mentally and physically). In these situations rapid 'modernization' should be looked at from a long range point of view. Popularising of aspects in science and technology should therefore be subjected to wise judgements and control. On the other hand we also come across communities in dire distress for a variety of reasons. Technology in these circumstances linked up with other social and economic measures will assist to improve their lot. Popularising in this context with practical efforts may be a necessity.

Life styles of people are built up over many decades through trial and error and also through a process of natural selection. Modernization through technology invasions will bring in both the good and the bad. With the powerful tools of communication with us, we will bear a moral responsibility to consider the well being of the recipients and should not be guided by purely economic advantages alone. Social tensions often develop within communities when suddenly submitted to uncontrolled perhaps unwanted technology invasions. Perhaps many modern 'diseases' will be avoided if we learn to select control, and proceed within social norms.

*5. Technology and Peace*

Perhaps no other problem has drawn the attention of nations than the quest for peace on this planet. Science and technology on the other hand has along with its good work, inadvertently though, aided in the process of production of destructive weapons to a point where destruction of our planet completely in a short time is now a possibility. Many countries continue to produce destructive equipment and tools and other countries too, continue this process as a safeguard. Science and Technology has branched out in this awful direction which many will end in our complete annihilation. Many countries which intend fighting others as well as fighting groups within countries could conveniently purchase these items of destruction which modern science and technology continue to develop and improve, spending vast resources for this purpose. Aren't leading nations popularising these technologies covertly and as a result hundreds perhaps thousands of peoples get killed or maimed daily? It may therefore be our task to popularize the negative effects of this technological mutation harmful to all people.

Science and technological development always face this dilemma of enhanced destructive capacity build up, contributing to the enhancement of man's ferocity in contrast to his humanitarian and gentle ways. These capabilities never existed earlier and only become possibilities with technological advancement. Should we therefore not consider seriously of a simultaneous popularization effort of all ill effects that science and technology has forced on mankind and pursue a policy to ban or reduce such developments progressively?

Man's technological advancement have given him skills to lead a well adjusted and comfortable life, if he could use such skills with wisdom. Let us therefore in our popularization effort focus on these positive aspects and send the message through in our formal schools/institutes, non-formal classes, as well as informally. This is perhaps our biggest challenge, perhaps our best achievement.

# 21

# Country Paper: Thailand

SOMCHAI PANCHAWAT

Before 1979, non-formal education in Thailand was carried out by Adult Education section, Department of General Education. However, on March 24, 1989 Non-formal Education Department was founded and combined the Centre for Educational Museums as one of its sections.

In 1963, the Bangkok Planetarium was opened to Thai people, and 15 years later the Bangkok Science Museum was serviced to visitors. Although popularization of science and technology has been carried out by some groups of people for a long time, the non-formal and formal educators are aware of the necessity of science and technology which influence the ways of life for people especially in the rural areas. It can affect their incomes, health, and social welfare. In fact, there are a lot of Thais who have no opportunities to study in secondary level. These people are the majority. How we can popularize science and technology to them is a question to be answered. In order to promote effective non-formal education programme in science and technology, the Non-formal Education Department has set the following policies to solve these problems:

1. To develop science and technology curriculum and texts for adult learners, both classroom system and remote education system.

2. To organize interesting activities which are short course training for adult learners to improve their occupations, incomes and better quality of life. Some knowledge of science, and technology such as planting, husbandry, repairing engine, cloth making, etc. are provided.

3. Let the Centre for Educational Museums be the organizer of science and technology activities in Bangkok, and there will be five centres in the region, Pisanuloke, Nakornsrithamarat, Prachaubkeereekum, Kornhaen and Rayong or Chandhaburi. These centres will have its structure and activities organizing as the same as the Centre for Education Museums. Moreover, there will be a centre of science and technology in each province. It is a source of information to serve students, youths and people in that areas. That centre is a place to popularize arts, culture, occupations and information for tourism in each province. The people in the area can exchange their ideas and popularize some techniques for agriculture and selling local goods as well.

**Popularization of Science and Technology Through Science Museum**

Life-long education is necessary for every people in the changing world today. Formal education may be gained in schools and colleges in a limited period of time, but an informal education takes much longer periods. Science museum is one of the institutions that serves both formal and non-formal education. Everyone can learn freely in a museum, on one's own interests and abilities with equal opportunity at one's own convenience. It is a good laboratory for students whose school does not have a complete science laboratory and other facilitation for science education. Learning in a science museum is a basic step towards fulfilling an ability to serve any problem through thoughful consideration and careful action.

Consider education, which is a continuing process that one must obtain throughout his life. Thus, formal and non-formal education should be provided simultaneously. At present, non-formal education is playing an important role. Formerly schools and families were important sources of education. Nowadays, technology has been developing, but education through the mentioned sources is not sufficient. Self learning process education should be developed so that it would encourage public both in and out of school to seek knowledge forever. In order to live wisely in this changing world, we should urge our populace to continue their education. Education institutions such as national museum, science museum, historical museum and other private collections would increasingly play their roles. It will lead to an important step of upgrading the quality of education, offering freedom to learn and create habitual self-learning.

At present popularization of science and technology through science museum is acceptable to be an effective learning media throughout the world. Although establishing science museum needs a very big budget, in comparing with the very big target groups who visit the museums each year, not less than 200,000 people, it is worthwhile. The promoting for science activities in Bangkok Science Museums are following:

1. To display permanent exhibitions to visitors. These exhibitions include: basic knowledge of science and mathematics, health and human body, energy, solar energy, history of time, communication and transportation, natural history, science museums, popular science, and science park.
2. To promote temporary exhibitions in a special occasion such as Non-formal Education Day, National Science Week, National Children Day, etc.
3. To organize science experiment, science demonstration, and science lecturing in the auditorium.
4. To have a science show.
5. To collect and display natural specimens and artifacts.

According to philosophy of life-long education, science activities are focused on self-studying, depending on visitor's abilities, limit on time, age, sex. Science activities in Bangkok Science Museum will fulfil knowledge of science by using drama, model, real equipment which students, youths and people can understand easily, because the process of learning is direct experience.

**Science and Technology Centre in Provinces**

To disseminate science and technology more effectively, especially in the rural area, Non-formal Education Department set up Science and Technology Centre in each province. At initial stage, 18 appropriated projects were expected to carry out for this goal. Three centres in Chieagmai, Pitsanuloke and Nakoznsachasima were opened and serviced to the public already. The others are going well and expected to be opened soon.

Science and Technology Centre supplies information in various fields, such as occupation, applied technology, basic science and its has come to act as a small museum. Non-formal Education Department plans to erect the centres in every province.

# 22
# Country Paper: Zimbabwe

S. DUKE NDLOVU

The University of Hong Kong and UNESCO Conference on the Popularization of Science and Technology in Distance Teaching has come at opportune time when the whole world is making strides in the use of science and technology to meet the ever growing educational needs that no longer can be met through formal education system. This is of particular importance to developing countries as they are still facing ever increasing population and increasing educational needs at all academic levels, business and management areas.

It is now generally accepted that formal teaching and training can no longer meet all educational and training needs.

Science and Technology geared to facilitate teaching and training are essential at this time of great need. Our countries are crying loud for technological transfer in order to meet the educational demands and national development.

## Zimbabwe Case for Science and Technology

### *Brief Country Background*

Zimbabwe is a former British Colony that gained independence in April 1980. The country has 8 million population and is 390,759 sq. mls. with a population growth of 3.1 and current population density of 19.3.

Zimbabwe is situated in Southern Africa bordered by South Africa on the South, Botswana on the South West, Zambia on the North, Malawi on the North East and Mozambique on the east.

Given Zimbabwe's growing population there is a great need to provide education and training for the people in order to cope with future demands—what is urgently needed is the training of trainers in order to have multiplier effect on the use of technology.

Zimbabwe attaches great importance to education as such the Ministry of Education received the largest budget allocation for the year 1989-90. Education is regarded as an index of national development and as an inalienable right of all citizens. Therefore any efforts by Zimbabwe citizens and by international institutions to popularize science and technology to increase education and training are welcome.

There is greater need to develop education and training through distance education using science and technology so as to reach the largest numbers of the population.

In accordance with the provisions of Manpower Development Act, Zimbabwe aspires to attain self-sufficiency in manpower hence various efforts are made for training in technical areas and in upgrading unskilled manpower and training for middle level managerial skills. We realize that middle level manpower are the backbone of national development. We are committed to the development of manpower training by distance teaching. Ministries of Higher Education, of Primary and Secondary Education and of Manpower Planning Labour and Social Welfare and supportive of various efforts both by the government, by individual institutions and international agencies in the provision of science and technology for education and training.

For example: the following statistics show the intake of students for apprenticeship in technical training under the Ministry of Higher Education Polytechnic Colleges.

**Apprenticeship intakes: 1980 to 1984**

| Industry | Year and number of students | | | | |
|---|---|---|---|---|---|
| | 1980 | 1981 | 1982 | 1983 | 1984 |
| Aircraft | 20 | 55 | 79 | 25 | 50 |
| Building | 86 | 165 | 158 | 121 | 60 |
| Electrical | 238 | 350 | 391 | 260 | 254 |
| Mechanical | 411 | 715 | 797 | 478 | 436 |
| Automotive | 198 | 382 | 350 | 242 | 142 |
| Printing | 49 | 89 | 64 | 60 | 38 |
| Hairdressing | 11 | 59 | 29 | 8 | 18 |
| Total | 1013 | 1815 | 1848 | 1194 | 999 |

**Appenticeship intake 1984/85 by race**

| Industry | European | African | Coloured | Others | Total |
|---|---|---|---|---|---|
| Aircraft | 7 | 43 | – | – | 50 |
| Building | 4 | 51 | 2 | 3 | 60 |
| Electrical | 29 | 217 | 6 | 2 | 254 |
| Mechanical | 77 | 333 | 22 | 4 | 436 |
| Automotive | 47 | 85 | 10 | 1 | 142 |
| Printing | 10 | 26 | 1 | 1 | 38 |
| Hairdressing | 7 | 9 | 1 | 1 | 18 |
| Total | 181 | 764 | 42 | 12 | 999 |

The numbers have been on the increase since independence and the demand is growing. There is therefore a great need to increase science and technology to meet the demand and as such avoid the crisis of confidence. The numbers for training could increase if science and technology were available. The training is still on a textbook and manual demonstrations.

## Agriculture and Technical Colleges

Agricultural training is still mainly labour intensive and formal training in schools of agriculture. Empirical observations have shown that agricultural students tend to want to go and work in town agricultural offices as administrators instead of going back to the land.

There is therefore need for distance agricultural training for those who are committed to agriculture and who are already in the fields as this will upgrade their skills and increase agricultural productivity.

| Year | Institution | | Total |
|---|---|---|---|
| | Agricultural colleges | Technical colleges | |
| 1979 | 171 | 3663 | 3834 |
| 1980 | 173 | 3469 | 3642 |
| 1981 | 169 | 6048 | 6217 |
| 1982 | 539 | 6962 | 7492 |
| 1983 | 528 | 7791 | 8319 |
| 1984 | 745 | 9352 | 10197 |

*Private technical and commercial colleges are governed by the National Manpower Advisory Council Act (1984).*

*Private technical and commercial colleges provide formal training whereas correspondence and distance education college use the correspondence and distance teaching modes.*

*There is nevertheless a problem for courses that require practical training being taught only by the correspondence mode.*

*The distance teaching mode on the other hand provides for supervised practical training since examinations include practicals.*

**Evening Adult Education Classes**

The Ministry of Education through its nonformal division runs evening classes at various schools. The numbers attending have been on the increase each year. The following are figures for 1983, 1984.

**Evening classes: Staff and enrolment**

| Region | No. of centres | Enrolment | No. of teachers |
|---|---|---|---|
| Harare | 75 | 24000 | 1055 |
| Manicaland | 18 | 1705 | 100 |
| Mashonaland | 22 | 2930 | 139 |
| Matabeleland | 120 | 13840 | 750 |
| Midlands | 42 | 3690 | 286 |
| Masvingo | 5 | 641 | 34 |
| Total 1984 | 282 | 46806 | 2364 |
| Total 1983 | 227 | 35847 | 1632 |

**Study groups: Staff and enrolment**

| Region | No. of study groups | Enrolment | No. of mentors |
|---|---|---|---|
| Harare | 54 | 14000 | 200 |
| Manicaland | 79 | 3925 | 105 |
| Mashonaland | 80 | 3150 | 98 |
| Matabeleland | 250 | 12520 | 315 |
| Midlands | 36 | 2524 | 57 |
| Masvingo | 121 | 5020 | 134 |
| Total 1984 | 620 | 41139 | 909 |
| Total 1983 | 840 | 41050 | 1005 |

Considering the increase in Adult Education evening classes the use of science and technology could increase the participation even more.

**Development of Distance Education in Zimbabwe**

From 1954 up to 1980 the main thrust was on the traditional correspondence education. In 1954 the Central African Correspondence College was founded. The Rapid Results College of UK opened its branch in Zimbabwe in 1955, and during the same year the School of Careers of the Cleaver Hume Group was also opened. The International Correspondence Schools branch was opened in 1958. More correspondence colleges such as the Transworld Tutorial College and the I.C.B.A. were opened later.

In 1980 after independence, the Zimbabwe Distance Education College was founded. Its distance teaching approach is a departure from the traditional correspondence teaching mode in that it utilises occasional contiguous teaching for dialogue and audio cassettes, video teletutorials and radio.

**Correspondence Colleges Council**

Due to the need for the control and registration of correspondence colleges, the correspondence colleges act chapter 81:1971 was passed. The new education act of 1984 replaced the correspondence colleges act. The act provides for the establishment of the correspondence colleges with the registrar from the Ministry of Education, and two other members are appointed by the Minister of Education and four other members by election among the correspondence/distance education colleges. The council monitors distance education development and the registration of new colleges. It provides a platform for discussion on matters of educational policy and of mutual interest between government and the private distance education sector.

Distance education colleges have a curriculum development committee that reviews the Ministry syllabii in relation to distance teaching requirements.

Correspondence Colleges and the only one distance education college have a substantial number of students most of whom have come from the formal education system after failing to get the required number of five O levels or two A levels for entry into the job market or into the university. Some candidates are those who due to employment and family obligations cannot go to formal education or vocational training schools therefore distance education is not necessarily for school leavers or dropouts.

On the whole correspondence/distance education colleges have made a considered contribution to Zimbabwe Education over the years of their operation. It is estimated that over a million students have received correspondence education in one form or another from correspondence and distance education colleges over the years. The popularization of science and technology and making it affordable and accessible would greatly enhance the development of the country.

**Background on Zimbabwe Distance Education College—ZDECO**

ZDECO was found in 1980 by Dr. Sikhanyiso Duke Ndlovu and is directed and owned by Drs. S.D. and R.J. Ndlovu.

The college is registered under the Ministry of Higher Education and Ministry of Primary and Secondary Education. The college started with two branches, Harare and Bulawayo, and has expanded to establish branches in Masvingo 300 km from Harare, Mutare 260 km away, Gweru 320 km and Kwe Kwe 250 km away.

Each branch is run by a Resident Tutor and has Administrative Staff and Distance Tutors who mark students, assignments and conduct tutorials locally.

The college further has rural learning centres with rural distance education co-ordinators.

Students are supplied with lesson materials and selected audio cassettes to study at home. In addition students are required to go to their nearest branch or rural learning centre for face to face tutorials in the evening, weekends or day for those not working or sponsored students or refugee students.

***Students Statistics***

Registration of students is continuous.

| | | | |
|---|---|---|---|
| Harare | 5 000 | Kwe Kwe | 1 500 |
| Bulawayo | 3 000 | Masvingo | 1 500 |
| Gweru | 2 000 | Mutare | 1 000 |

We also have a few students from Zambia, Botswana, Mozambique and Malawi and have received applications from Ghana and Sieraleon.

**Tutors**

The College has 120 tutors distributed throughout its branches. Their qualifications range from B.A. to Ph.Ds.

**Examinations**

ZDECO is an examinations centre for the University of Cambridge O & A levels, University of London, Institute of Administrative Management, Zimbabwe Junior Certificate,

London Chamber of Commerce and Industry, Pitmans Examinations, Institute of Marketing and Association of Business Executives.

The Principal is the Custodian of Examination Question papers and Superintendent of examinations for ZDECO Exam Centres.

Examinations take place in January, June and November each year.

**External Degrees**

In conjunction with Wolsey Hall Oxford, ZDECO offers the University of London B.Sc. Economics, LL.B., Diploma in Education and the Masters in Business Administration MBA for the University of Warwick.

**ZDECO on air**

The College provides lectures by radio on various selected subjects every Sunday morning. Efforts are being made to provide video taped lessons for group study at branches. Final constraints and foreign exchange problems have made it impossible for us to implement our video programmes.

**Evaluation of tutor effectiveness**

Every tutor is evaluated by his/her students and by the Principal's Assistant for Academic Affairs and the Principal's Assistant for Teacher Supervision and Student Advisor.

The tutor is evaluated on a scale:

| | | | | | |
|---|---|---|---|---|---|
| a | : | excellent | d | : | fair |
| b | : | better | e | : | poor |
| c | : | good | | | |

and other . . . to be specified.

Areas evaluated are:

1. Knowledge of the subject
2. Delivery
3. Clarity
4. Concern for the students' needs
5. Relevance to subject
6. Other to the specified

See attached evaluation forms and feedback analysis form on evaluation.

**ZDECO Publishing House**

The Publishing House was instituted a year ago and has the objective to encourage Zimbabwean authors to write textbooks and other books based on research in Law, Health, Fiction, Economics and other Social Sciences.

Already three books have been approved for publication:

1. Introduction to Company Law in Zimbabwe by Dr. Nkala & Mr. T. Nyapadi.
2. History for O Level by Dr. Moyana & Dr. Sibanda.
3. Nursing Scene in Zimbabwe by Dr. Rose J. Ndlovu.

**Possible Southern African Student Enrolment**

In conjunction with Wolsey Hall Oxford and other external Universities, we are in a position to enrol students in the Southern African Region or throughout Africa and to have lesson materials delivered directly to the students by our Associates instead of us sending our lesson materials from Zimbabwe.

**How Best Science and Technology Can be Used**

As a developing country Zimbabwe faces the manpower shortage in teaching and training as well as the resources and foreign currency to utilize science and technology. It would be essential to first look at ways of overcoming this problem.

There is a need for a firm policy on distance and nonformal education. Resources and manpower should then be provided in order to implement the policy.

Foreign currency or commodity aid have to be provided. There is further need to identify the science and technological areas to be developed. Science and technology can be approached in two ways:

(1) Training of trainers in and

(2) Training the users.

## Farming and Agricultural Science and Technology

Education and training should be development oriented since hunger, poverty, disease and mortality are on the increase. In Africa and other developing countries, attention should be given to food production, hence farming and agriculture using scientific methods and technology can increase our food basket and we will be able to export food to other African and developed countries.

Computers for agriculture and monitoring of climatic conditions would be a major contribution to development.

Most African countries including Zimbabwe have been affected by draught hence scientific approach to farming and experimentation of draught resistance crops, and veterinary medicine would increase both the food basket and the beef basket to a large extent.

Zimbabwe has been one of the major exporters of beef to the EEC market before the outcome of cattle foot and mount disease which could have been avoided had there been sophisticated scientific diagnostic methods.

## Teaching Agriculture by Computer Conferencing

Sincere farmers or agriculturalists are usually distributed in various areas of the country, computer conferencing would be ideal. Computer conferencing refers to communications between or among individuals separated by time and space via computers. It will also enable farmers to carry on conversations and share ideas on common problems (G. Burt May 1989 ICDE Bulletin).

## Teleconferencing

Interactive radio or teleconferencing are essential in that information is exchanged and problem solutions given immediately to the users. Teleconferencing provides for a tutor or trainer to be able to talk to a group of people at the same time at one location by telephone and to have a feedback interaction without having to travel to the distant places (David Kirby and Cathy Boak 1989). For teleconferencing to succeed, the country must have good telephone system.

## Audio Cassettes

Audio cassettes recorders could be useful instruments for transmitting information particularly in areas where there is no electricity nor telephone. Audio cassettes recorders using batteries and can be affordable to low income people.

## Video Cassettes

Video cassettes can be more effective in that the learner will be able to actually see the demonstrations. Group listing would be ideal at various learning centres hence there is a need to decentralize distance learning facilities in order to reach the greatest number of people.

## Computer Assisted Instruction (CAI)

Distance learners have always been forgotten by education policy makers. Most computer instruction has been made available to formal education system. Computer Assisted Instruction can reach out to large number of people.

Various industries have embarked mainly on computer training. That training is mainly concerned with computer appreciation, computer languages, systems analysis and programming, word processing, typesetting for publications, company informal management, etc.

## Training of Trainers for CAI

What is lacking is the aspect of Computer Assisted learning of the various skills. This area requires training of trainers. Instead of training programmers there is a need to train trainers of programmers, to train trainers of systems analysts, etc. Those trained on how to use computer or how to operate various functions should be trained on how to train others. Such training as I stated before will have a multiplier effect.

## Summary and Conclusion

We have presented a brief background on Zimbabwe, its various training activities, distance education development with special emphasis on the Zimbabwe Distance Education College. We have further given various science and technological possibilities such as utilization of audio cassettes, video, teleconferencing, computer assisted instruction and computer conferencing. We have further stressed the need for the training of trainers in order to achieve a multiplier effect on the development of science and technology in distance education.

Given the large numbers of people that require training due to the limitations of the formal schools and or formal training institutions, there is a great need for the popularization of science and technology to meet the training demands and developmental needs.

The Zimbabwe Distance Education College which has become one of the largest distance teaching institutions in Africa will need international support to implement science and technological training programmes up to university level.

UNESCO, the World Bank, other International Organizations and nations could all contribute to the setting up of a viable experiment on the utilization of science and technology for training of trainers in distance education for development.

## REFERENCES

1. Kirby David and Boak Cathryn, "Investigating Instructional Approaches in Audio Teleconferencing Classes" in *Journal of Distance Education,* Vol. IV, No. 1, Spring 1989 Canada.
2. Matshazi M.J. (Dr) "Distance Education: A Conceptaul Framework", in *The Educational Crisis in Zimbabwe,* Distance Education Workshop, University of Zimbabwe, Oct. 8-9, 1988.
3. Naidu Som, "Computer Conferencing in Distance Education" in *International Council for Distance Education Bulletin,* Vol. 20, May 1989.
4. Ndlovu S.D (Dr) "The Role of a Distance Education Developer", in *Development Design and Distance Education*—Michael S. Parer (Ed) Centre For Distance Learning, Gippsland Institute, Victoria, Australia.
5. Rwambiwa J.P. (Dr) "Trend In Media Distance Education", University of Zimbabwe, Workshop on Distance Education, Oct. 8-9, 1989.
6. Republic of Zimbabwe, Ministry of Education, Secretary Report—1984.

# Part II

# SCIENCE, TECHNOLOGY AND OUTREACH COURSES BY DISTANCE EDUCATION

# Preface

This report is the outcome of a regional workshop on development of science, technology and outreach courses held at Sri Lanka Foundation Institute, Colombo from 19 to 23 September 1988. The Workshop was organized jointly by Unesco Principal Regional Office for Asia and the Pacific and the Open University of Sri Lanka under UNDP funded Project RAS/86/171—Regional Technical Co-operation in Higher Education. Nine senior academics from eight countries, six observers from the host country and a staff member of UNESCO participated in the Workshop (List of participants is at Appendix B).

The Workshop emanated from UNESCO's commitment and continued effort to promote co-operation among the distance teaching universities in this region through the sharing of their experience and expertise. To that objective, a series of regional and national training activities on various aspects of distance and open education had been organized over the years. The present workshop was one that had been identified during such activities and addressed itself to the specific issues related to science, technology and outreach programmes and courses.

Distance education and open university systems are emerging as a major means of broadening access to higher education particularly among the disadvantaged groups. They have proved to be cost effective in improving educational opportunities. It has also been demonstrated that it is possible to teach science and technology courses effectively through the distance teaching mode. The rapid development of communication technology should facilitate further development in distance education.

The purpose of distance education at tertiary level is not only to provide an opportunity for people to complete degree or diploma programmes. It also provides an important means of acquiring new knowledge as a part of continuing education. While courses have been developed in a number of discipline areas, need for such courses is still great in science and technology. The teaching of science and technology courses involving practical work, by distance education, requires special techniques and materials. While such aids have been developed, special orientation of administrative and academic staff is required to conduct these programmes.

Distance education and open university system particularly lend themselves to the running of short programmes. This provides extension work and continuing education to benefit the community. Training in the management and methodology for the conduct of extension courses at different levels and designed for different target groups is essential.

The workshop in particular analysed the present status of science, technology and outreach programmes in the participating institutions and discussed strategy and methodology for the development of such courses. The workshop also discussed policy and measures needed to augment science, technology and outreach courses and suggested ways and means for increased co-operation among the participating institutions in promoting such courses.

# 1

# Issues, Problems and Trends in the Development of Science, Technology and Outreach Programmes and Courses

The workshop sought to identify common issues, problems and trends associated with the development and implementation of science, technology and outreach programmes and courses by distance education. Despite the wide variations in the environments in which the institutions operated and differences in the range and level of courses that were offered, the workshop participants were able to define a number of shared concerns. These general aspects of programme development and implementation are presented in this section of the report.

It should be noted that the range of issues of common concern identified by the workshop participants was quite large. However, many of the issues were characteristic of distance education in general and were not peculiar to courses or programmes in science and technology. Only those issues that have a significant impact upon the development and implementation of courses or programmes in science and technology have been noted in this section. For convenience the issues are considered under six headings.

### Practical Work

Practical work is a major component of most courses in science and technology. In this regard programmes in science and technology differ markedly from other distance education programmes. All institutions had encountered difficulties in the provision of practical work in distance education programmes.

### Staff Recruitment and Training

In many areas of science and technology there has been a traditional difficulty of recruiting teaching staff with appropriate scientific or industrial experience. This situation is often exacerbated for institutions offering courses by distance education. In these institutions there is often an emphasis on teaching and consequently less opportunity to engage in research and development activities than in traditional universities. Teaching staff are also expected to have or to acquire considerable knowledge and skills in the areas of curriculum design and distance education technology and practice.

Also, where institutions require students to undertake practical work at regional study centres under the supervision of a tutor or laboratory assistant, difficulties have been encountered with the recruitment and training of suitable people. These personnel need to be competent in the use of all of the equipment at the centre, as well as being able to assist students with their studies, they must also fulfil a technician's function and ensure that the equipment is maintained in good working order.

### Recognition of Courses

Problems noted concerning the recruitment of academic staff for distance education courses in science and technology may be worsened by the perceived lack of recognition for such courses and programmes. Whilst the use of distance education for non-science and technology courses has become widely accepted in recent years, there is still considerable scepticism concerning the offering of science and technology courses by this mode of study. Much of this uncertainty stems from members of the scientific and technological academic and professional community. Participants felt that more promotion of science and technology courses and programmes by distance education is required to increase awareness of their quality and cost effectiveness.

**Student Enrolment**

All participants noted that enrolment in science and technology programmes available by distance education had tended to be lower than in other discipline areas, such as arts and humanities. The reasons for this disparity are not clear. There are often real disincentives such as increased fees for students enrolling in science and technology programmes. However these discipline areas may be perceived by prospective students as being more difficult to study by distance education, and lacking suitable compensating rewards upon completion.

**Financial Considerations**

The cost of developing and implementing courses in science and technology by distance education is significantly higher than for courses in other discipline areas. The major contributing factor to the high cost is the requirement of most programmes for a large component of practical work. Participants considered a number of alternative methods of providing practical work experience to students, for example, through regional study centres, attendance at a central facility, home experiment kits and computer simulation. However, each involved a significant development or implementation cost. Other factors also contributed to the high cost of these courses. Because of the lack of availability of suitable low-cost textbooks, there was generally a need to develop comprehensive study materials which then required to be updated on a more regular basis than those for other subject areas. Also computer access, whilst highly desirable in many discipline areas, is an essential prerequisite for study in most science and technology courses.

Most institutions were dependent upon government funding for the continuation of distance education programmes. If this source of funding is to be increased, governments must be made aware of the needs for courses in science and technology, and of the quality and cost effectiveness of such courses by distance education. However, all participants recognized the need to seek alternative sources of funding for these programmes. The potential problems associated with passing the higher costs on to students in the form of higher course fees have been noted previously. Therefore, this action could only be justified where increased rewards, in the form of employment or advancement opportunities, were accrued by students on completion of their studies. However, science and technology courses could be targeted to meet the needs of industry and several institutions were investigating the adoption of this approach to obtain increased revenue. Co-operative ventures between participating institutions were also seen as a major opportunity to significantly reduce the costs of offering science and technology courses and programmes by distance education.

**Co-operative Ventures**

Co-operative ventures between institutions engaged in distance education activities were perceived to offer considerable potential for cost reduction, in particular for programmes in science and technology. The conventional economics afforded by the creation of data banks of study materials would be greater for science and technology courses because of the greater development and recurrent cost of study materials and practical work programmes in such courses. Further, savings may accrue from the exchange of staff with specialist subject knowledge and appropriate experience in distance education, the standardization of home experiment kits that would allow for their mass production, and the possible utilization of shared practical work facilities.

# 2

# Approaches to the Development of Science, Technology and Outreach Programmes by Distance Education

In the previous section, some of the major problems commonly associated with the conduct of science, technology and outreach programmes by distance education have been identified. In this part of the report a strategy and methodology for the development of such courses is proposed. The development of programmes in science and technology is a complex and dynamic process with many unique problems. It is imperative therefore to provide a framework or structure to facilitate this task. The methodology in this section has been formulated from the experiences of all of the delegates participating in the workshop and represents an ideal and comprehensive approach to programme development. It is recognized that many institutions may not be able to adopt this approach to programme development in its entirety. However, the proposed methodology identifies many of the factors that are important in the development of science, technology and outreach programmes and provides a structure or framework for their consideration. If it can be used as a guide, many of the difficulties they may be encountered in offering such programmes by distance education may be avoided or minimized.

It should be noted that the proposed strategy and methodology is equally applicable to all types of programmes. Whether the programme of study is extensive and leads to the award of a degree in science or technology, or it is a condensed programme designed to suit the needs of a specific industry, the same factors need to be taken into consideration, and this should be done in a logical sequence.

Finally the methodology outlined in this section applies not only to the development of new courses but should also be used to analyse the viability of existing courses. It is essential to review existing courses frequently and to compare their merits with those of the proposed new courses. When funding is limited, it may be necessary to discard some existing courses in order to provide the resources to undertake new ventures.

The proposed strategy and methodology follows closely the analysis that would be made by any business organization when considering new and existing projects. Increasingly higher education establishments are required to be more accountable and productive, so it is appropriate the techniques of business analysis are utilized when considering the introduction of courses. These institutions are concerned with the development of a "product" or "education service" in much the same fashion as any commercial enterprise.

**Identification of Programmes to be Offered**

The first stage of the process is concerned with the identification of programmes that should be developed. The workshop considered that this identification process should occur in two stages:

*Market Analysis:* It is necessary first to establish where there are needs or perceived demands for programmes in science and technology by distance education. In other words, an institution must endeavour to identify possible markets. It is not essential to substantiate the need for a programme at this stage as it is more appropriate to do this during the evaluation phase, when the nature of the proposed programme has been established in more detail.

As with any business, it is advantageous to be forward looking rather than reactive. Future demand may be predicted by studying industry manpower requirements, economic reports and developments in other countries. Formal surveys of industry in an effort to establish future needs have also been used extensively by Sukhothai Thammathirat Open University.

It is also important to be quite clear about whose needs are being considered. It may be the perceived needs of industry for certain types of employees, the needs of governments or the personal needs of individuals. This will have a major influence on the objective of the programme as well as programme design and evaluation.

Consideration should also be given to the promotion or stimulation of demand for a programme. Institutions of higher education have a social responsibility to identify the future needs of a community and to endeavour to cater for them. Within this context it is possible to lobby governments, industry and the general community in order to create an awareness of the need for a particular programme.

*Analysis of the Capabilities of the Educational Institution:* The second stage of the process involves an analysis of the educational institution to establish its strengths and limitations. Business experience has shown that there is a high rate of success for ventures in which perceived needs can be satisfied using the strengths of an organization. Equally, attempting to satisfy needs in areas where the organization has significant limitations will often result in failure.

This dual process for the identification of science and technology programmes to be offered by distance education has been used with considerable success by Sukhothai Thammathirat Open University and Darling Downs Institute of Advanced Education. In the case of Sukhothai Thammathirat Open University, formal surveys of industry revealed the need for many programmes; the decision on which programmes would be considered for further development was then based on an analysis of the University's capabilities. For example, whilst the need existed for programmes in civil and mechanical engineering, these options were discarded in favour of programmes in industrial technology and information systems where the existing infrastructure could be used and extensive laboratory facilities were not required to be developed.

Darling Downs Institute of Advanced Education was able to build on its experience of offering associate diploma programmes in engineering by distance education and of offering a bachelor of engineering programme by full-time, on-camps study, to develop a degree programme in engineering that is primarily undertaken by distance education.

Delegates at the workshops considered that it was important to guard against the development of programmes where there was no clearly defined need or perceived demand. Also the duplication of programmes that are better accommodated by full-time, on-campus study should be avoided. The latter course of action should only be contemplated where existing conventional establishments are incapable of satisfying the demand for a particular programme. Two of the institutions represented at the workshop derive the bulk of their recurrent income from student fees and this provided a clear and immediate indication of the continuing need for a programme.

The workshop noted that there would be some instances where the need for programmes was dictated by governments. This obviates the need for the identification process but poses other problems.

At the conclusion of the identification process, it should be possible to indicate several programmes that warrant further investigation. No attempt to prioritize the programmes should be attempted at this stage, since more detailed analysis is required before this is feasible.

**Development of Programmes**

When several possible programmes have been identified, it is necessary to investigate each programme in more detail. This process may be broken down into three stages, namely: (a) the nature of the proposed programme; (b) recognition of the programme; and (c) programme design and implementation.

*The Nature of the Proposed Programme:* It is essential to specify the major objective of the programme clearly and in some detail.

It is not sufficient to state that the programme is "intended to train technologists for the manufacturing industry", for example. This is too vague. Participants also considered it necessary to indicate for whom the programme is intended, the level of prerequisite skills and knowledge that are assumed and what is required of students to complete the programme. This information is essential for programme design and implementation. It will assist considerably with the specification of the nature of the programme if the market analysis has been done correctly.

In many countries, open universities distance education courses and often it is a policy of these establishments to have "open entry" to their programmes. This is an admirable concept but may result in significant problems for programmes in science and technology. Many institutions have adopted flexible structures that include courses that provide knowledge and skills at a basic level, in an effort to cater for the diversity of the educational standard of students entering their programmes. But participants noted that there were special difficulties in science and technology programmes. Whereas the prerequisite skills needed to successfully study programmes in business, for example, may be further developed after leaving school, this was not the case in science and technology. Analytical and mathematical skills are not utilized routinely in everyday life and these skills therefore deteriorate rapidly after leaving school. The participants from institutions in India and Pakistan, in particular noted that some students may never have been provided with these particular skills at school in the first instance. These weaknesses were not overcome by flexible programme structures and were a contributing factor to the high attrition rates in science and technology programmes. Whilst data are not available for science and technology programmes in many countries to date, it was revealed at the workshop that in Sri Lanka and Australia attrition rates of the order of 45-65 per cent were experienced. Participants from other countries indicated that attrition rates for non-technological courses were approximately 33-50 per cent.

It is essential to reduce these attrition rates if the

programmes in science and technology are to be attractive to students, and acceptable in terms of progression rates. Therefore careful attention must be given to the aspirations of students and the level of their knowledge and skills. Programmes must not only clearly indicate the knowledge of basic science and mathematics and of communication skills that is assumed, but also indicate precisely what is expected of the student in terms of workload. At Allama Iqbal Open University prospective students are often provided with brief examples of study materials and self assessment instruments. Students may therefore gain an indication of their chance of success in a course or programme before they formally enrol. Many participants also expressed the concern that students are unaware of the rigours of study at the higher education level and of the impact that it will have upon their lives. So it is not only necessary to provide courses in basic sciences social and mathematics, it is also vital to include courses on how to study by distance education successfully.

*Recognition of the Programme:* For a programme of study to be relevant it must be acceptable to one or more of the following bodies: (a) professional bodies; (b) employers; (c) government instrumentalities; (d) prestigious educational establishments; and (e) the general community.

For short programmes designed to suit the needs of a specific employer for in-house training of employees, only the recognition of the employer is necessary. However programmes normally must be acceptable to more than one of the above groups. In general terms, the more a programme is acceptable to these groups, the greater will be its attractiveness and hence its demand.

Acceptance of a programme will depend to a large degree upon the extent to which it is believed that it can achieve its stated objectives and this will depend upon programme design. Several participants at the workshop have indicated that this process can be facilitated by inviting representatives of professional bodies and major industries to serve on programme development and evaluation committees.

*Programme Design and Implementation:* It is of primary importance that the programme is designed and implemented so that the programme objectives are capable of being achieved by an acceptable proportion of participants. However it is also necessary to balance this aspect of programme design with the attractiveness of the course to students. The latter aspect is important because it influences demand for the programme and ultimately the cost effectiveness and viability of the programme. Also the programme design and implementation must take cognizance of the existing infrastructure for distance education that exists at the institution, since the development of new media for delivery may be expensive.

There are a number of particular difficulties that are associated with the design implementation of programmes in science and technology by distance education. Firstly, suitable textbooks are only produced in a few countries and are often expensive and difficult to obtain. Further, the nature of science and technology is such that textbooks are constantly being updated. For science and technology programmes therefore, there is usually a greater need to produce composite study materials for students, that do not require any specific textbook. Secondly, courses in these programmes tend to involve high levels of practical work. Which often requires access to sophisticated or expensive equipment. Lastly, programmes in science and technology require increasing access to computing facilities.

The high cost associated with the preparation of comprehensive study materials for each course in a programme can be defrayed by co-operative ventures between distance education centres. Darling Downs Institute of Advanced Education has undertaken an evaluative study for the Australian Commonwealth Tertiary Education Commission on the implication of sharing the costs of preparation of study materials with other institutions.

The cost of preparation of the study materials may also be alleviated if the materials can be used in courses of other programmes offered by the same institution. For example, study materials for a course in introductory computing may be utilized in both degree and diploma programmes, and in outreach programmes. Preparation of study materials in modular form will considerably assist in either of the two situations outlined above.

The most significant of the difficulties of conducting science and technology programmes is that of practical work. There are several factors that should be considered in this regard.

It may be possible to select programmes in science and technology that by their nature have very low levels of practical work. For example Sukhothai Thammathirat Open University has targeted to upgrade extension programmes for students who have already completed programmes that were heavily practical work oriented. Such students have extensive practical experience and are therefore primarily in need of theoretical knowledge. This approach allows funding from student fees without the necessity to establish expensive laboratory facilities and provides an ideal method of introducing science and technology programmes into an institution.

When such an approach is not possible, it is first necessary to question the level of practical work that is required in the programme. Many programmes in science and technology evolved in an environment where practical work could be undertaken with comparative ease. The workshop considered that it was necessary to attempt to evaluate carefully the requirements for practical work in any distance education programme rather than just to accept an existing situation.

One must accept, however, that some practical work is essential in science and technology programmes. There are a number of ways of accommodating practical work in distance education programmes. These include:

*Residential School:* Several factors should be considered with regard to the use of residential schools. It is important to establish the number of days of residential school that are acceptable to students and their employers. This must then be balanced against the educational requirements of the programme. The length of residential schools will vary depending upon the level of the course, the requirement to develop practical skills and the local conditions within each individual country. For programmes offered by the Open University of Sri Lanka a period of approximately 20 days per year seems to be acceptable with an additional period of 21 days once during their programme for students in technology programmes. For diploma and degree programmes offered by Darling Downs Institute of Advanced Education, residential school periods of five or six days per year are more prevalent.

The location of the residential schools is a related matter. A central facility may necessitate students travelling large distances; they may also have difficulty in finding suitable accommodation when numbers are large. A central facility is very cost effective for the education establishment but expensive for the student. Generally residential schools using this approach will be short and held only once a year. Where residential schools are arranged at regional centres, the cost and inconvenience to students is reduced and residential schools may be longer and more frequent. However, the cost of duplication of equipment and of staffing may be high unless the facilities of other appropriate institutions can be utilized.

*Home Experiment Kits:* These have been used successfully by several institutions. They are not appropriate however for foundation level courses where students may have no prior experience of scientific method.

*Computer Simulation:* This requires access to a microcomputer but is particularly effective in certain types of courses, for example, electronics, microprocessor system design and engineering drafting. Microcomputers may be available at regional study centres or students may have access to a computer at their place of employment. In some countries, it is realistic to expect students to purchase or lease microcomputers and peripheral hardware, as the cost is reasonable and is likely to fall substantially. Many students will continue to utilize microcomputers after graduation from their programme.

It is necessary to decide at an early stage whether access to a microcomputer will be a programme requirement as this can profoundly influence the nature of study materials developed in various courses in the programme.

*Use of Facilities in Industry:* This has traditionally been accomplished through the use of "sandwich" type programmes. It is unlikely that any commercial organization would make its facilities available to significant numbers of students. However, as industry is increasingly the repository of much of the more sophisticated technological equipment, it may be feasible to allow credit in programmes for in-house training on such equipment undertaken at a student's place of employment, and exempt the student from attendance at residential school.

It is essential to look at the structure of the programme when considering any provision for practical work in science and engineering programmes. Students should not be required to invest large amounts of time and money in the course, nor should institutions establish practical facilities for large numbers of students at the first level of a programme until both parties have had the opportunity to assess the students' chance of successfully completing the programme.

**Planning for Implementation**

When the preliminary programme design and method of implementation has been established, it is necessary to consider the human and physical resources necessary to implement the programme.

*Physical Resources:* To some extent this topic has been covered in the section on residential schools. For science and technology programmes and outreach programmes containing a major component of science and technology, establishing laboratories or workshops and purchasing equipment must require considerable expense. The workshop identified the following possibilities of reducing this cost.

The facilities can be established at one central location. In effect this passes some of the cost to the students, who must travel to the central facility and pay for accommodation there. This may be acceptable where the distances involved are not great and the educational establishment has surplus or cheap residential accommodation.

The facilities can be established at a number of regional centres. This involves considerable expense for the institution but reduces the cost and inconvenience for students. In science and technology programmes, where equipment is expensive and may have to be updated on a regular basis, the cost of this approach could be prohibitive. This would be especially true if the facilities were to be idle for long periods of time between residential schools. Further, in many instances, trained technical staff will be needed to operate the equipment and this expertise will not be readily available in some cases. Even if suitable people are available, it may not be possible to employ them on a causal basis.

Existing facilities may be used in total or in part. The most promising venues would be other educational institutions offering full-time, on-campus programmes in science and technology. This is because both the equipment and expertise to supervise students in its use, reside in one place. With the cost of a single numerical control machining centre approaching US$250,000, co-operative ventures between educational establishments would seem to be the most promising approach. These facilities exist in industry of course, but it is unlikely that any commercial organization would allow the use of any of its equipment by anyone other than its employees. So this avenue is not very promising where significant numbers of students are involved.

The students may be able to purchase or lease equipment suitable for some courses or programmes. For example, both Sukhothai Thammathirat Open University and Darling Downs Institute of Advanced Education are likely to require students to have access to microcomputers and peripheral hardware for some courses. Leasing of this equipment offers obvious advantages for most students, but this would generally require the educational institution to work in co-operation with a manufacturing or supplier of such equipment, as the institution is unlikely to be able to afford the establishment cost of such a programme.

*Human Resources:* Recruitment of suitable staff is a major problem for several institutions. It is common for open universities in the region to rely on academic staff from other institutions to prepare the textual subject matter of study materials. In this context many participants have indicated that it is difficult to obtain staff with expertise in the subject area and a commitment to the production of high quality materials within an agreed schedule. It is also necessary to recruit staff for regional study centres.

The training of staff is also an important consideration. Many participants noted that the academic staff of institutions conducting courses by distance education needed not only to have a good knowledge of their own discipline area but must also be familiar with an extensive range of instructional media and have good management skills in order to supervise the preparation of study materials and conduct of the courses. Staff members needed to be supportive of distance education and aware of the external constraints that impact upon the conduct of courses offered by distance education. In order to function effectively within constraints, staff members needed to be innovative and flexible in their approach.

To instill such skills in members of staff requires extensive training. To date most institutions have been fully occupied in the preparation and provision of distance education courses and have been unable to devote sufficient time to the education of their own staff. This results in inefficiencies of operation as many staff members continue to learn a substantial part of their job by experience. Formal training is not only given insufficient emphasis within individual organizations, but formal network among organizations is also absent offering no means for staff members to benefit from the experience of other institutions. This is particularly unfortunate because in science and technology programmes the cost of mistakes is often very high.

*Organizational Aspects:* The final stage of planning for the implementation of programmes is the consideration of amendments to the organization for distance education that may be necessary or desirable to accommodate its new programmes.

In some institutions all of the necessary expertise and facilities exist to design, prepare, produce and conduct programmes by distance education. Such institutions may also offer their programmes by full-time, on-campus study. More often institutions have a comparatively small core of academics staff and must rely heavily upon external agencies for the preparation of course materials and the conduct of distance education courses. It is evident from the reports of participants that the greater an institution has to rely on external agencies, the less control it has over the process. In this scenario, management of the process assumes a greater importance. It has been noted previously that increased co-operation between institutions engaged in distance education activities and other bodies is of major importance when developing programmes in science and technology.

It is necessary to consider the organizational aspects associated with all phases in the design and conduct of distance education programmes because it may have a profound influence on curriculum development and implementation. For example, the difficulties associated with simultaneous examinations of large numbers of students at various locations can be a major organizational problem. Central Radio and Television University of China limits such examinations to four per year. Thus it is evident that organizational difficulties can determine the method of assessment of student performance. The implications for conducting assessments of students' practical abilities must be evident.

**Evaluation of Courses**

After consideration has been given to the development and implementation of programmes by distance education, it is necessary to cost and evaluate each programme in order to establish a priority listing. A major consideration in this process is the anticipated number of students who will enrol in the programme and at this stage it is appropriate to conduct surveys of prospective students in order to ascertain the demand. An accurate indication of demand can only be obtained after details of the programme design and proposed method of implementation are enunciated. The Allama Iqbal Open University also conducts pilot programmes to assess demand for courses.

When a reliable estimate of the number of enrolled students is obtained it may be necessary to review the nature of the proposed programme, the programme design and the implications for implementations. Thus it can be seen that not only are components of the methodology interactive but also the process itself is reiterative.

In evaluating the proposed programmes, methods of cost reduction should also be analysed and additional sources of revenue should be investigated. Several ways of reducing costs have been cited in the body of the section. They include: (a) targeting of science and technology programmes that are most appropriate to offer by distance education; (b) co-operation with other institutions in the development of study materials, dissemination of information and utilization of physical facilities; and (c) increased productivity through training of staff.

It is pertinent to recall that this analysis should be applied to existing programme in order to free resources for the introduction of a new programme that will benefit a greater number of students. Institutions that offer science and technology programmes by distance education have a unique opportunity to raise revenue by utilizing courses within these programmes to service specific needs of industry and to provide continuing education opportunities for practising scientists, technologists and engineers. A general trend exists for professional societies within these fields to insist upon evidence of continuing education in order to retain membership. Study materials of higher quality may also be sold to other educational establishments for conduct of full-time, on-campus programmes. This may be beneficial to such institutions where they are understaffed or are unable to obtain academic staff with appropriate expertise in narrow, but important subject areas.

# 3

# Policy Alternatives and Measures for Augmentation of Science, Technology and Outreach Courses

There are a number of different ways in which this can be viewed. The workshop classified matters relating to policy in a functional manner as follows: choice of programmes (outreach, diploma or degree, or postgraduate programmes); staff development (special needs, separate unit); funding and course fees (state funding and non-traditional source); and investment alternatives (development of printed course materials, audio-visual materials, delivery system, regional networks, or laboratory and computing facilities).

Policy can also be made at different levels. For the purpose of this report, two levels have been considered: university level and national level.

## Choice of Programmes

At university level, decisions regarding the choice of programmes have to be made by the academic community. Different mechanisms for implementing these are available and have been tried out in different institutions. Satisfactory arrangements have to be evolved, taking into account the peculiarities of each situation. Universities should actively investigate co-operation with other institutions, local, regional and international, in the matter of the choice of courses. At the national level, especially in cases where new or additional resources are required, the university will have to convince funding agencies of the desirability of selecting a particular programme for development. When such proposals originate from them, they would in turn have to convince the relevant university academic body (such as the senate).

*Outreach Programmes:* There is a great need for the open universities in the region to offer courses that are aimed at providing very necessary skills and even information to either the mass of the people or to specific identified groups. In most of these countries, which do not possess a well developed market economy, the identification of programmes to be offered has to take into account the social accountability of the university. It would be very disirable if at least some of these programmes, especially those that have to be offered at comparatively short notice, be developed from existing long-term programmes by suitable adaptation.

Universities should develop sufficient visibility to attract outside organizations, whether they be government institutions and departments or private industry, when they have a need for an identifiable teaching or training programme, especially where distance teaching methods are more suitable. However, the university should accept such an assignment only when it fits into the overall development plan of the university, or in very exceptional cases, when there is an urgent national need.

*Diploma/Degree Programmes:* A diploma or a degree programme in a science based area needs a large amount of resources. It should only be offered when resources will certainly be made available. Even though, ideally, such a decision can only be made when the university has actually got the required resources within itself, this is not practicable in the context of the real situation prevailing in most of the countries in the region. A more viable approach would be to first identify the necessity to offer a particular course by an academic committee within the university, augmented by suitably qualified persons from other institutions. Once a project is identified, it will then be possible to seek funding, staffing and other necessary facilities while the planning process is in progress.

In developing programmes of this nature, great care has to be taken to ensure that the course developed is suitable for distance education and that the curriculum is relevant to the needs of the prospective students. This task is made more difficult by the fact that public expectations would tend to direct the planners to conform to the pattern of existing conventionally taught courses. This is even more so in the case of professional courses, such as in engineering, where acceptance by professional institutions will be a requirement.

It is necessary that the position of an open university as an organization that promotes the democratization of education be emphasized when new programmes are proposed, especially at this level. In most countries in the region, tertiary education is still a luxury and only a comparatively small proportion of the population has access to it. It is also one of the few means of social mobility that is available to the poorer sections of the people. This rigid structure of the conventional tertiary education system does not, however, allow much scope for all those who would wish to take part in this process. Hence, the open universities carry a heavy social responsibility in providing such opportunities. Further discussion will be under the heading of 'funding and course fees'.

*Postgraduate Programmes:* The choice to offer postgraduate programmes in an open university will be made in a manner similar to that of a degree programme.

Research based postgraduate programmes are necessary for yet another reason, namely, for the establishment and maintenance of a qualified academic community. If a faculty is to attract and retain quality academic staff, they have to be provided with adequate research opportunities. When the university itself finds it difficult to provide the necessary facilities, joint programmes with established research institutions may be undertaken.

The open universities should also both encourage and recognize research in the methodology of education, with special reference to the teaching of science and technology programmes at a distance.

### Staff Development

Each open university should establish a separate unit for the selection, recruitment and training of academic staff, with special emphasis on the needs of science and technology programmes. Training will take into account the requirements in respect of: distance education, science and technology education, guidance for tutors, and course specific training.

### Funding and Course Fees

Funding is a very important aspect in the operation of any institution. In the case of open universities, at least in some of the countries, there is a noticeable more away from the tradition of state funding that is prevalent in the conventional universities in the region. There are a number of understandable reasons for this tendency. However, there is a case to be made for a higher level of state funding, in view of the role that the open universities have been called upon to play: in meeting national educational needs, in providing opportunities for the underprivileged and in providing science, technology and outreach programmes.

In those countries where a substantial part of the cost of a programme has to be generated by the university, the fees charged from the students tend to be rather high. This is particularly so in the case of courses in science and technology, because of the higher cost of production as well as delivery, including laboratory classes. In these cases, it is necessary that the principle of fees being related to the average earning power of the target population rather than to the cost be accepted by the funding authorities.

### Investment Alternatives

The relative importance of the computing demands on available resources is to be determined by the academic authorities, in respect of each course. Some of the more important factors are: medium (printed material, audio-visual aids, computer based teaching material); delivery system (regional centres, tutoring, teleconferencing); and laboratory and computing facilities.

*Medium:* The cheapest medium is print. This is also the most important and most widely used medium. The workshop was of the view that the print media will continue to occupy this pre-eminent position in the foreseeable future in the teaching of science and technology courses. There are some situations where audio-visual media have an advantage over print. One such case is when it is necessary to reach a very wide audience of low educational background. In some cases, the target audience may even be illiterate. Special arrangements need to be developed with the national broadcast and television media, especially for the delivery of the outreach programmes.

Audio-visual media are also useful in presenting certain parts of a course which is otherwise taught mainly through the print media. For very specific applications, such as the teaching of elementary language (English) skills and also in some sophisticated simulation studies, computer based teaching material are of interest. The course teams should be responsible for selecting the correct mix of the different media available to them.

*Delivery System:* Regional centres play a pivotal role in the operation of the open universities. Given the high cost of transport, both in terms of money and time, a good regional network is an essential component of the delivery system. Emphasis should also be placed on the development of a satisfactory tutoring system, including personal tutoring, based on the regional or study centres. Given the state of the tele communication networks in the region, it is unlikely that sophisticated tele-conferencing and other modern communication systems will be of any significant importance in the near future. Institutions should be wary of investing in such facilities, especially in the light financial situation that all the open universities find themselves in.

*Laboratory and Computing Facilities:* Laboratory experiments are an integral and compulsory component of almost all courses in science and technology. This is also an expensive component. In an open education system, it is also a constraint on the students as they have to make arrangements to participate in this activity. Every effort should be made to make maximum use of the time spent by the student at a centre for the purpose of taking part in laboratory work. Provision of in-house residential facilities will help to reduce the duration of residential courses, and this should be given high priority. The use of the facilities available at other universities and colleges should be actively pursued.

With the dramatic reduction in the cost of computing equipment, it is now becoming possible to provide access to computers at regional and/or study centres, and advantage should be taken of this to augment the laboratory classes by suitable simulation experiments. This will help to keep the costs down, without compromising standards but will only be possible for the diploma or degree and post-graduate programmes, and for selected outreach programmes. It may not be feasible in the case of outreach and certificate level courses conducted through the national languages.

# 4

# Co-operation Among Institutions

The workshop noted that the annual budgets allocated by governments for supporting educational purposes in the participating institutions are rather insufficient. It was of the view that the universities should endeavour to augment existing resources by requesting the co-operation of various agencies, both in the public and private sectors, to assist in the university's operations. Apart from the local agencies, they should also co-operate with international organizations, both regional and international. In particular, they should seek co-operation among the open universities.

Science, technology and outreach programmes are new to most of the open universities in the region. Even though some open universities have commenced offering science and technology programme, they are still at the very early stages and need further development. It is anticipated that co-operation will result in the improvement of the quality of the programmes and that better cost effectiveness can be achieved. Co-operation can be bilateral among the existing institutions or multilateral, through associations. It can also be at different levels: national, regional and international.

Introduction and administration of programmes in science and technology is more difficult than those in social sciences. This is because they involve practical work and special teaching media. Co-operation with external agencies is necessary in order to obtain resources, experience, know-how and assistance for strengthening the programmes. The main objectives of such co-operation would be to improve the quality of the programmes, achieve better cost effectiveness and get wider acceptance of the programmes.

The workshop was of the view that co-operation should be based on mutual benefits. Since the science and technology programmes of these institutions are new and not well-known to the general public, it may not be easy to get co-operation at the beginning. The workshop felt that the universities should actively seek co-operation with existing institutions and agencies by the following strategies:

Institutionalizing multilateral co-operation by establishing suitable linkages to interact with the relevant agencies.

Establishing good public relations at the national level, to ensure wider acceptance, participation and co-operation. Needs and demand assessment will help in the identification of potential partners.

The potential agencies for co-operation can be broadly classified into three. Firstly, at the national level, institutions that possess facilities that are useful to the university are good potential partners. Use of facilities available at other agencies is to be encouraged since the resources of the open universities are limited. On the other hand, these agencies can benefit from the academic services of the open university as well.

At the regional level, co-operation among the open and distance teaching universities in the region is important for their future developments. They can make use of the services of the existing distance education agencies, e.g. Asian Association of Open Universities and the Regional Resources Centre in Distance Education (both located at STOU, Thailand). These organizations have been established recently in co-operation with UNESCO.

Lastly, co-operation can be at the international level. Since the open university concept has an international character, co-operation with the open universities in other regions, international agencies and associations will be of great benefit to the development of open learning systems in the region. Among potential partners for international co-operation are: UNESCO, The British Council, Japan International Co-operation

Agency, Canadian International Development Agency, International Development Research Centre, International Council for Distance Education, University Without Walls International Council and the newly established Commonwealth for Learning.

Areas of co-operation among the open universities in the region can be in utilizing existing facilities and equipment and in sharing staff expertise. Establishing joint-venture programmes in producing learning materials, exchange of existing materials, and sharing and exchanging experiences in teaching science, technology and outreach programmes should be encouraged.

# 5

# Summary and Conclusions

The Workshop identified a number of difficulties in the design and implementation of programmes by distance education that it believed were exacerbated for programmes in science and technology. These particular problems are noted below.

All participants encountered problems with the provision of practical work which is an integral and often compulsory component of science and technology programmes.

Difficulties with the recruitment and training of suitable personnel to prepare instructional materials and to conduct programmes were experienced by most participants.

The Workshop noted that, whilst the use of distance education for non-science and technology courses has become widely accepted in recent years, there is still considerable scepticism concerning the offering of science and technology courses by this mode of study.

Participants indicated that enrolment in science and technology available by distance education has tended to be lower than in other discipline areas. This may be because they are perceived by prospective students as being more difficult to study by distance education, and lacking suitable compensating rewards upon completion.

It was noted that the cost of developing and implementing courses in science and technology by distance education is significantly higher than for courses in other discipline areas. The higher cost was associated with a number of factors including the provision of practical work, the lack of availability of suitable, current textbooks which necessitated the development and maintenance of comprehensive study materials, and the need to provide access to sophisticated equipment, including computing facilities.

By way of conclusion, the Workshop was able to make a number of suggestions concerning the development and provision of science and technology programmes by distance education. It was hoped that the adoption of these recommendations would alleviate many of the problems that were identified. A summary of the principal recommendations contained within the body of the report is presented below:

*Increased Recognition:* The workshop reiterated that there is a need for increased recognition of the importance of offering science and technology programmes by distance education. Institutions should promote these programmes vigorously.

*Sound Methodology:* Because of the high costs and organizations difficulties associated with the provision of science and technology programmes by distance education, the Workshop considered it essential to adopt a sound methodology for the development of such programmes and to establish a planned pattern for their introduction.

Participants at the Workshop considered that it was important to guard against the development of programmes where there was no clearly defined need or perceived demand. Also the duplication of programmes that are better accommodated by full-time, on-campus study should be avoided. This latter task was often made difficult by the fact that public expectations tended to direct planners to conform to the pattern of existing conventionally taught courses. This may be more evident in the case of professional courses, such as in engineering, where acceptance by professional institutions is normally a requirement.

*Practical Work:* Practical work is an integral and often compulsory component of all programmes in science and technology and the participants of the Workshop considered the relative merits of a number of alternative methods of providing practical work experience to students. These included the use of regional study centres for practical work, attendance at a central facility, leasing of equipment, home experiment kits, co-operative ventures with industrial and scientific organizations and computer simulation. The perceived advantages and limitations of each of these approaches are detailed within the body of the report.

Prior to evaluating the most appropriate avenues for providing students with practical work experience, the Workshop recommended that the level of practical work required in the programme should first be investigated. Many programmes in science and technology evolved in an environment where practical work could be undertaken with comparative ease and the requirements for a similar level of practical work in a distance education programme should carefully evaluated, rather than just accepting and adapting an existing practice.

The participants felt that the dramatic reduction in the cost of computing equipment, warranted serious consideration of the use of computer simulation to reduce the level of practical work of distance education programmes. Students should not be required to invest large amounts of time and money in the course, nor should institutions establish practical facilities for large number of students at the first level of a programme until both parties have had the opportunity to assess the students' chances of successfully completing the programme.

The cost of preparation of study materials may be reduced considerably if the same materials can be used in courses of other programmes. For example, study materials for a course in introductory computing may be utilized in degree and diploma programmes, in outreach programmes and probably in programmes offered by other institutions. Preparation of study materials in modular form will considerably assist with this approach.

*Staff Training:* It was noted that to date most institutions offering science and technology programmes by distance education have been fully occupied in the preparation and provision of distance education courses and have been unable to devote sufficient time to the education of their own staff. This results in inefficiencies of operation as many staff members continue to learn a substantial part of their job by experience. Formal training is not only given insufficient emphasis within individual organizations, but in the absence of any formal network, staff members are unable to benefit from the experiences of other institutions. Each open university should establish a separate unit for the selection, recruitment and training of academic staff, with special emphasis on the needs of science and technology programmes.

*Careful Selection of Students:* In many countries, open universities operate distance education courses and often it is a policy of these establishments to have "open entry" to their programmes. This is an admirable concept but may result in significant problems for programmes in science and technology. In particular attrition rates for such programmes may be very high. It is vital that attrition rates are reduced if the programmes in science and technology are to be attractive to students, and acceptable in terms of progression rates.

The Workshop emphasized that careful attention should be given to the aspirations of prospective students and the level of their knowledge and skills programmes in science and technology by distance education must not only clearly indicate the knowledge of basic science and mathematics and of communication skills that is assumed, also indicate precisely what is expected of the student in terms of workload.

*Funding:* Most institutions were dependent upon government funding for the continuation of distance education programmes. If this source of funding is to be increased, governments must be made aware of the needs for programmes in science and technology, and of the quality and cost effectiveness of such programmes by distance education. Governments should be lobbied to provide differential funding for science and technology programmes in recognition of the higher costs incurred by institutions offering such programmes.

*Alternative Sources of Funding:* The Workshop recognized the need to seek alternative sources of funding for these programmes. Institutions that offer science and technology programmes by distance education have a unique opportunity to raise revenue by utilizing courses within these programmes to service specific needs of industry and to provide continuing education opportunities for practising scientists, technologists and engineers. There is a general trend for professional societies within these fields to insist upon evidence of continuing education in order to retain membership. Study materials of higher quality may also be sold to other educational establishments.

*Profile Development:* Institutions should develop a profile that is attractive to external organizations that have needs for specific teaching or training programmes, especially where distance education methods are appropriate. It was noted that this process can be facilitated by inviting representatives of professional bodies and major industries to serve on programme development and evaluation communities.

*Consideration for Fee Increase:* Passing increased costs on to students in the form of increased fees may be counterproductive and may decrease the number of enrolment in a course or programme. This action could only be justified where increased rewards in the form of employment or advancement opportunities were accrued by students on completion of their studies.

*Institutional Co-operation:* Co-operative ventures between institutions engaged in distance activities and between other public and private organizations were perceived to offer considerable potential for reducing the costs of offering science and technology courses and programmes by distance education, and for improving their quality. Areas of co-operation could include the exchange of staff with specialist knowledge, the utilization of shared practical work facilities and equipment, the development of standardized home experiment kits, and the joint development of study materials and exchange of existing materials.

*Research:* Open universities should both encourage and recognize research in the methodology of education with special reference to the teaching of science and technology programmes at a distance.

## Part III

# POPULARIZATION OF SCIENCE AND TECHNOLOGY: DELIVERY SYSTEMS FOR OUT-OF-SCHOOL SCIENCE ACTIVITIES

# Preface

This source book on Popularization of Science and Technology comes in a series. This publication is on Delivery Systems for Out-of-School Science Activities Including Regional Science Olympiad.

The first part is the result of two workshops, one, the Regional Training Workshop on Improvement of Delivery Systems for Out-of-School Science Activities, and two, the Technical Working Group Meeting on the First Asia and the Pacific Regional Science Olympiad, both held at SEAMEO-RECSAM, Penang, Malaysia, during the dates 15-25 March 1988.

The Regional Training Workshop on Improvement of Delivery Systems for Out-of-School Science Activities had 11 participants, two resource persons and one observer, the names and office bearers of which are in Annex 1. The Technical Working Group Meeting for the Planning and Organization of the Regional Science Olympiad for Asia and the Pacific had four participants and three resource persons; the names of those involved are in Annex 2. In both workshops, UNESCO-PROAP was represented by Mr. M.A. Qureshi.

As for the method of work for the workshop on delivery systems, the participants from the various countries had been asked to prepare a report describing the development of out-of-school science activities in their countries. Their reports include:

- the main issues and problems in developing and implementing out-of-school science activities;

- recent advances and trends in the development of delivery systems for out-of-school science activities; and
- explore training materials on a selected out-of-school science topic.

During the discussion sessions, topics taken up with reference to out-of-school science activities were on (1) identification of problems and issues; (2) identification of appropriate delivery systems; (3) development of guidelines and strategies for improving delivery systems; (4) development of exemplar training materials; and (5) guidelines for co-operation and collaboration on the improvement of delivery systems. These five topics form the Chapters in part I of the source book.

The second part is on the Regional Science Olympiad for Asia and the Pacific. It provides a general information as well as the draft regulations for the conduct of the olympiad.

The reports of the two workshops were recompiled/edited and made part of this publication. The ideas and opinions expressed are those of the participants and resource persons, and do not necessarily represent the views of UNESCO. The designations employed and the presentation of materials throughout the publication do not imply the expression of any opinion, whatsoever, on the part of UNESCO concerning the legal status of any country, territory, city or area, or of its authorities its frontiers or boundaries.

---

# 1 Introduction

Science and technology have always been important factors in shaping human society. Technological efforts have tended to manipulate and control the physical world while scientific pursuits have primarily attempted to comprehend it. These separate efforts have now joined into an inseparable whole and has helped improve the economy and quality of life of many nations and individuals. It has also brought about crises such as resource depleting and environmental pollution.

The rapid advancement of science and technology in modern times can bring benefits such as greater productivity and better quality of life, but only if the general populace can comprehend and keep pace with the changes being made. As people are helped to develop better living skills through the practical application of scientific principles, they will also develop scientific and technological awareness.

In the early 80's it was recognized that many out-of-school science activities and many extension programmes were being carried out in the Asia and Pacific regions. In order to assess the existing situation and to plan for future coordinated action, and Asian Centre of Educational Innovation for Development, UNESCO Principal Regional Office for Asia and the Pacific, Bangkok, organized a "Workshop for Key Personnel Concerned with Out-of-school Scientific Activities by Young People" in collaboration with the Science Society of Thailand (Bangkok, August 1982). The workshop recommended the development of a "Training Handbook for Key Personnel Organising Out-of-School Scientific Activities". This was developed by a team of authors identified by the National Council of Educational Research and Training, New Delhi, India. The draft manuscript was reviewed by another group of key personnel at a regional workshop organized in Delhi (Regional Workshop for Key Personnel Concerned with Out-of-School Science Activities and Extension Work for Young People, New Delhi, October 1986). The participants of the workshop also contributed case studies and exemplar activities. The revised manuscript "Handbook for Organizers of Out-of-School Scientific Activities and Extension Work" (1987) has been sent to the countries of the region for their consideration. This handbook was developed as the starting point for future coordinated efforts towards out-of-school activities.

In continuance of these efforts, delivery systems to various target groups need to be examined. What delivery systems are currently being used? How effective are they in achieving their aims and objectives? Do these programmes improve the quality of life of the target groups?

Broad target groups as identified under the "Science for All" programme are as follows:

A. The formal school population. Science and Technology education should be an integral part of the primary and secondary education of all children, including those who will proceed further in science and technology.

B. The out-of-school population which includes:

  (i) out-of-school children and youth, including those who should have been in school under the universalization of education process;

  (ii) the work force, including vast numbers of functional illiterates;

  (iii) the educated adult section of the populace.

The "Regional Training Workshop on Improvement of Delivery Systems for Out-of-School Science Activities" met in Penang, Malaysia from 15-24 March 1988 to deliberate on this issue. The workshop was to produce guidelines and strategies, which would benefit adults and adolescents in the Asia and Pacific Region, who may be functionally illiterate or may have had a minimum of education at the elementary school level, and who form a sizeable work force in their national economy. Such guidelines and strategies would help provide this group of adults and adolescents with knowledge and information, which they may not have acquired in their formal schooling. It would also enhance their well-being economically, socially and culturally.

The purposes of the workshop were to:

1. Review existing delivery systems for out-of-school science activities.
2. Identify problems and issues relating to delivery systems for out-of-school science activities.
3. Identify appropriate delivery systems for out-of-school science activities that help to meet the needs of present-day living.
4. Develop guidelines, strategies and training programmes for the identified delivery systems.
5. Propose recommendations for regional/international co-operation and collaboration on the improvement of the delivery systems for out-of-school science activities.

# 2

# Some Factors Influencing the Delivery Systems of Science Education to Out-of-School Learners

It is important to consider the nature of the learner when preparing to deliver science education to out-of-school learners. This chapter examines some factors about learning, in general and of the target group in particular. It then attempts to draw implications for consideration by those who are involved in designing and implementing delivery systems. Many of the concepts mentioned will be developed further in later chapters.

## 2.1 Understanding the Nature of the Target Group

Before designing or preparing delivery systems, it is necessary to be fully aware of the group you wish to influence.

Out-of-School learners are generally those who:

- are likely to be early school leavers;
- have little formal learning, including science learning;
- have relatively poor learning skills and/or abilities;
- have a weak command of vocabulary, and may not fully understand nuances of meaning;
- lack resources, both material and financial; and
- lack public utility services, perhaps including:

- electricity
- a reliable source of clean safe drinking water
- adequate garbage and sewage disposal services
- roads and other communication infrastructures
- have long working hours or little time left after multiple jobs, or have much time available because of unemployment or underemployment
- have an unsophisticated approach to coping with life

The target group's personal environments may dictate additional constraints on learning because of social, cultural, economic and political factors. Some of these which directly affect the out-of-school target group are:

- long-held cultural practices and taboos;
- religious practices and philosophic constraints;
- socio-cultural peer group pressures;
- racial interaction concerns; and
- political limitations.

For practical purposes, we may consider the bulk of the target group to be functionally illiterate.

**2.2 The Nature of Learning and Communication**

In order to focus on the nature of the learner, first we should focus on how each person learns. To this end, we shall take as a working guide that, "Learning occurs in the learner when it results in a permanent change of behaviour".

The learning process has three distinct aspects or domains:

- cognitive (knowledge),
- affective (attitudes), and
- psychomotor (skills).

In order to reach the functionally illiterate target group we must deal with all three domains. For example, no matter how well the material is presented by the delivery systems, the learner must have a positive attitude about accepting new ideas, before any meaningful learning can take place.

In addition, we must recognize that different people learn in different ways, largely because of the different set of abilities that each learner has.

The delivery system used should be the one most appropriate to the likely abilities of most of the target group.

The "channels" of communication are the human senses. Each of the five senses has a role to play in learning (as do some of the other senses, such as the sense of balance). A study of several years ago showed that we learn more through some senses than through others:

| | | |
|---|---|---|
| taste | 1 | per cent |
| smell | 1.5 | per cent |
| touch | 3.5 | per cent |
| hearing | 11 | per cent |
| seeing | 83 | per cent |

This is, of course, partly skewed toward seeing because of the importance of reading, particularly in higher learning.

Another, less precise, study showed that we retain:

10 per cent of what we READ,

20 per cent of what we HEAR,

30 per cent of what we SEE, but

50 per cent of what we SEE and HEAR.

A third study, shows that the extent to which learning is retained by the learner depends on the method of communication, and that using more than one "channel" is far more effective than using only one channel.

| Methods of Communication | Recall 3 hours later | Recall 3 days later |
|---|---|---|
| Telling, when used alone | 70% | 10% |
| Showing, when used alone | 72% | 20% |
| When a blend of Telling and Showing is used | 85% | 65% |

It has also been noted that there are three basic levels of learning experiences:

- the *direct* purposeful "hands-on' experience, using concrete materials and concrete examples.
- the *vicarious* or indirect experiences, especially for those experiences too dangerous, remote or expensive for direct experience. This is often accomplished through film, video and other visual media.
- the *symbolic* which provides learning experience through symbols, such as chemical and mathematical symbols, but also visual symbols such as flags, catch-phrases, images, abbreviations and even works themselves.

Science, of course, has traditionally been communicated through all of these learning experiences. However, the medium of communication to be used is influenced by the type of experience desired.

Communications theory is based upon a sound understanding of the nature of learning. It has implications for learning which strongly reinforce those derived from our knowledge of how people learn.

In brief, simple uncomplicated communications sent to out-of-school learners should contain clear messages transmitted through various "channels", preferably by more than one "channel".

**2.3 Implications for Delivery Systems**

(a) The target group of out-of-school learners is likely to contain:

- illiterates, semi-literates and functional illiterates;
- those who tune out messages, and those whose attention must be striven for, e.g. through strong motivational efforts;
- those whose attitudes toward formal learning are often very negative and who try to avoid it;
- those whose attention span is limited, and therefore require short messages;
- those whose background knowledge (especially scientific knowledge) is limited, and who must be given basic information;

- those who for socio-economic, cultural or political constraints may not be able to attain education beyond primary school.

(b) To meet the needs of the target audience, the delivery system should:

- be pictorial, or use key words or catch phrases;
- be inexpensive and widely distributed;
- deliver a clear, attention-demanding message;
- be delivered by a "hands-on" medium;
- be multi-sensory, or attempt to appeal to the senses;
- show immediate benefits to the learners, or at least show how results can be obtained in short term; and
- involve direct experience if possible; if not, then vicarious experience is beneficial.

(c) In essence, the *message* communicated should:

- be short, direct, clear, uncomplicated and unsophisticated

With a thorough understanding of the nature of learning and communication, those involved in the delivery of science education to out-of-school learners can effect great changes in their target group through the wise use of effective messages and media.

**2.4 Science Education and the Quality of Life**

An urgent problem confronting developing countries is societal development. It is generally acknowledged that development should involved integrated change in all aspects of society including its technology, beliefs and value systems. It also means adoption of new technology, economic growth, socio-cultural upliftment, modifications or changes in value systems, and thus an improvement in the quality of life.

Many of those who show concern about recent developments have serious doubts, however, as to whether some of the developments are likely to be beneficial to the target groups they were designed for.

Ideally, development activities should aim to improve the people's resource-base and provide more income from employment. If the construction of infra-structures could answer the basic needs of the people, then there would be no reason for concern. But some important questions need to be asked:

- What thinking processes went into the planning of development activities before decisions were made?
- Were the people for whom the development is targeted involved in the planning?
- Have these people been given enough information so they understand why the development activities have to be undertaken?

As science educators, and as concerned citizens, our belief is that one way to enhance development is to harness science and technology so that they will directly benefit the community and its people.

This can be done by providing scientific literacy. It entails providing the population with avenues by which they can become scientifically literate, self-reliant, self-sufficient and responsible as members of society. To be scientifically literate means that people understand the basic scientific principles governing the world around them, that they are open-minded about ideas and experiences, and that they are critical-minded in securing or dealing with information. Furthermore, they are able to use simple scientific process, e.g. practical skills, problem-solving and decision-making in dealing with phenomena occurring in everyday life.

When scientifically literate, the general populace should have a better understanding of science and technology, together with proper scientific attitudes and technological skills, which can be used in their day to day activities which will help prepare them for the future. Furthermore, the target population should have an awareness of scientific knowledge, skills and attitudes which are needed for living in the so-called modern world.

**2.5 The Problem of Early School-leavers**

Many of the youth in developing countries are out of school: either early school leavers or drop-outs. Many of these youths were able to enter primary school because most countries have adopted a policy of universalization of education, but at a certain point in time, they leave school. Some reasons are:

- They found formal education to be irrelevant so far as community and working life were concerned.
- Their families found it difficult to shoulder the indirect costs of sending their children to school.
- Children have to help parents as additional farmhands, or have to earn a living to augment family income.

### 2.6 Considerations in Promoting Out-of-School Science Activities

Many out-of-school science activities are organized in this part of the world. It is mainly school children who participate in them as part of their extra-curricular programmes. These activities are undertaken in science technology clubs, science societies or circles, camps, fairs, exhibits, museums, science centres, nature and field centres. Olympiads, apprenticeship and intern programmes, excursions, guided visits, lecture-meetings and so on.

Sometimes out-of-school youths have opportunities to participate in these activities, but mostly there are no opportunities for them to participate because of lack of resources. Often they don't see the value of joining the activities anyway.

The people who are involved in organising out-of-school science activities should:

- have an understanding of the basic socio-cultural and economic aspects of the society which the activities are likely to influence;
- be knowledgeable about the benefits that the activities could provide, so that these can be explained to the target groups, for their greater awareness and better understanding;
- plan activities considering the needs, levels of understanding and comprehension of the target group, with the purpose of motivating them to join the activities; and
- involve the target group in the planning of the activities so as to ensure their active participation.

To consider all the above is not an easy task, especially if the activities are intended to change behaviour and life long habits. If people lack awareness and understanding of the activities planned for them, it can be a barrier to their involvement, or it may result in resistance or antagonism. In that case the efforts would be futile.

The important factors to consider therefore, in organising out-of-school science activities with reference to the specific target groups, are:

- relevance to their needs;
- resource availability (human, financial, material); and
- benefits to the larger sector of society, e.g. employment generation which will lead to improvement in the quality of life.

**2.7 Strategies for Planning the Activities**

To plan strategies for out-of-school science activities, planners have to be sensitive to the types of community for which the project or activity is addressed. This should involve the carrying out of:

- an inventory of the community's physical, socio-cultural and natural resources;
- an identification of its social organization, e.g. family types, age groups, traditional beliefs and practices;
- an identification of people's economic conditions, including sources of income and types of employment.

Having background information about available resources and the hierarchy of needs of the people will help in the selection of appropriate activities.

**2.8 Scientific and Technological Directions: Some Suggestions**

Considering the resources available in the environment of developing countries, activities which will possibly enhance scientific and technological progress should emphasize:

- self-sufficiency and environmental development;
- balanced agro-industrial development which encompasses improved productivity in agriculture,

forestry, fisheries, mining, etc., and also includes import substitution and export development;

- development of skills related to industry, e.g.,
    - food production, processing and preservation,
    - garments, textiles and leather products,
    - coal and petroleum production,
    - tin, iron and steel production, and
    - commodities like coffee, tea, cocoa, sugar cane, coconuts, plam oil and rubber;
- outreach programmes related to health, e.g.,
    - biotechnological research and development, and
    - pharmaceutical research and development with emphasis on indigenous resources, e.g. herbal medicines;
- research and development of health services, e.g.,
    - combating malnutrition,
    - awareness about communicable diseases, e.g. hepatitis, AIDS, and
    - immunization programmes;
- provision of basic knowledge and techniques in science and technology which help to create a better quality of life; and
- creation of an awareness of the importance of science and technology in everyday life.

## 2.9 Planning, Implementing and Assessing Delivery Systems

Many programmes have been attempted which seek to improve the quality of life of the out-of-school sector of society. Reports of meetings organized by UNESCO, ICASE and other agencies have been circulated; yet many people, especially in developing countries, still have very low socio-economic status.

Some reasons, the activities may not be very effective, are:

- There has been a lack of coordination in government and non-government efforts to promote out-of-school science activities. Many programmes/activities organized, overlap or duplicate each other.

- Some activities rely heavily on economic aid. Once the aid stops the activities also stop.
- Some activities are person-dependent. Once the person in charge is removed from the project or is transferred to another, the activities stop, and most often are forgotton.
- There is a lack of infrastructure necessary for the promotion of science and technological activities, especially for the out-of-school target group.

**2.10 Summary**

Delivery systems for out-of-school science activities for the target group specified should consider:

- the target group's cognitive level and learning abilities;
- the relevance or appropriateness of the delivery system to the needs of the target group;
- the availability of human, financial and material resources;
- the benefits derived by the target group's society, especially those which would generate employment and improve the socio-economic status.

In addition delivery systems for out-of-school science activities for school leavers and dropouts should make the target group aware of the advantage and benefits that will be derived from their involvement in the activities. The planners and organisers of such activities should have a commitment to the programmes themselves before expecting the involvement or commitment of the target group.

Finally, there should be co-ordinated efforts among the agencies concerned with promoting out-of-school science activities so that the resources available can be utilized effectively.

# 3

# Out-of-School Science Programmes in Various Countries of the Region

Many different out-of-school science programmes are taking place in the various countries of the Asia and Pacific region. Some countries have been carrying on these programmes for some time, while others are just beginning.

Each of the participants at the Workshop presented a "Country Paper" describing the state of development of out-of-school programmes in their country. The paper described the activities which are taking place and highlighted various problems and issues.

Summaries of each of the Country Papers are given below:

## SUMMARIES OF COUNTRY REPORTS

### 3.1 India

Out-of-school activities in India have been a part of the scene for a long time. They include Science Museums, Science Exhibitions, Mobile Exhibitions, Science Parks, Science Clubs, Science Quizzes, Writing and Poster Competitions, Science Camps, Science Seminars, Street Theater, TV and Radio. These activities are carried out by both government and non-government organizations, which include Trusts, Science Associations and small individual organizations. The main government agencies are the National Council of Science Museums (Calcutta), National Council of Educational Research and Training (New Delhi), the National Council of Science and Technology Communication of the Department of Science and Technology and their counterparts in individual Indian states. Funding for activities is mainly from government sources.

The programmes which have been running most successfully are those addressed to children in school. Here also, the urban population derives much more benefit from them than the rural people. Programmes for the functionally illiterate are currently far fewer and not well designed. The news and entertainment media (TV, radio), do produce programmes, but most of them are not in the prime time slot. Sometimes, even when they are in this slot, they are the last programmes to be put on. The other problem in the delivery of out-of-school science activities is the lack of properly trained planners and designers, as well as facilitators. Not enough scientifically literate persons take an interest in such activities. Lastly, monitoring and feedback, as well as evaluation, are not always done.

### 3.2 Indonesia

Awareness of the importance of science and technology among the people in Indonesia is strongly increasing. Indonesians are very much aware that science and technology are important to increase productivity and to improve the quality of life of each community.

At present, science is taught not only in schools and universities, but also in non-formal education. Less attention is paid to non-formal education than to formal education.

There are many out-of-school science activities taking place. They can be categorized into "captive-audience activities" and "non-captive-audience activities". Examples of captive-audience activities are: rural radio listeners groups, Science Clubs for Youth and Literacy Classes. Examples of non-captive audience activities are museums, television, exhibitions, Olympiads.

### 3.3 Republic of Korea

Korea currently has 14 science museums and two non-governmental agencies which serve as the major organizations related to out-of-school scientific activities. The major projects are as follows:

1. Permanent Exhibits
2. Science Film Service
3. Saturday Science Lectures
4. Main Events of Science Week
5. TV Programmes
6. Publications
7. Science Fairs
8. Student Science Invention Contests
9. Special Activities
10. Various Contests
11. Special Projects
12. Science Classes
13. Computer Classes
14. Science Garden Projects

In Korea, the National Science Museum carries out major out-of-school science activities. It is unable to perform its function in all areas of scientific development as the building and facilities are inadequate for exhibitions. Accordingly, what is most urgently needed is a new facility to meet the requirements of a complete science museum. As such, there have been plans for the construction of a new "Integrated Science Museum", the first stage of which will be completed at the Daeduk Science Town by 1989.

Two student science museums, a forest museum, a traffic museum, an aquarium and professional museums of industry have been established in Korea since 1984.

Also, the National Science Museum is closely co-operating with eleven existing student science museums to promote exchange of information and exhibition materials; to discuss common interests about the National Science Fair, Student Science Invention Contests, Events of Science Week and the Science Garden Project. These are discussed with the advisory committees, directors of student science museums, and science inspectors.

### 3.4 Malaysia

The clientele of out-of-school scientific activities falls under two major categories: the school population and the out-of-school population. The National Educational Policy provides the impetus for the development of the current form of out-of-school scientific activities. In 1970, several of these activities were given special attention, and were co-ordinated separately at the national level. In 1987, these activities were carried out collectively during the National Science Week.

The major out-of-school scientific activities brought together during the week included: National Science Quiz, Scientific Essay Competition, Science and Mathematics Exhibition, Software Writing and the Young Scientist Programme. Three other activities will also be included during the National Science Week 1988, were Inventors' Camp, Science and Art Camp and a Computer Seminar.

Other out-of-school scientific activities that are ongoing at the local level are: tours/visits, excursions, video-making, animal rearing, nature walks, science forums and science talks. In addition, there are regular activities for the out-of-school population. Examples of these activities are: Youth Club competitions, technology demonstrations related to people's daily activities, study visits to scientific institutions or science centres, and open-dialogue sessions. Science is treated in a much wider perspective in the out-of-school population, than in the school population.

As in any dynamics of change, new trends in out-of-school scientific activities bring in additional needs, issues and problems. Funds, facilities and equipment/materials are the major ones. Other issues and problems include:

1. lack of networking and co-ordination among agencies involved in delivering the activities,
2. expertise in the local schools is yet to be fully utilized at community levels,
3. little consideration is being given to needs-analysis, with the flow of information normally going from top to bottom,

4. the lack of evaluating/monitoring to further modify or improve the existing out-of-school scientific activities.

There is, however, a growing interest among non-governmental bodies to provide inputs, and to be directly involved in helping the government support scientific awareness and applying its principles to society.

**3.5 Nepal**

Nepal is an enchanting mountainous country. Scientific and Technological Development is one of the country's major problems. No nation can progress without the development of Science and Technology. With only 33 per cent literacy, it is very difficult to develop a science literacy programme for out-of-school children and illiterate adults. It has therefore become imperative that along with formal science education, out-of-school science activities should be launched on a larger scale so that a wider section of the community can benefit. According to the needs of the target groups, there are various agencies involved in carrying on out-of-school activities in Nepal. A few of them are listed below:

1. Royal Nepal Academy of Science and Technology (RONAST),
2. Research Centre for Applied Science and Technology (RECAST),
3. Two University campuses, schools and CDC,
4. Natural History Museum, and
5. Science Education Development Centre (SEDEC).

Besides the above-mentioned organizations, several other governmental and non-governmental agencies are working for the promotion of science activities in the rural and urban areas, and are following these programmes:

a. Science Exhibitions,
b. Science Quiz Contests,
c. Science and Technical Publications,
d. Science Radio and Television Programmes,

e. Travel Grants,
f. Grants to Science and Technology Societies,
g. Awards, and
h. Conferences and Seminars.

Since the start of out-of-school science activities it has been found that there are several practical hindrances, such as:

- Accommodation problems,
- Poor financial support,
- Inadequate workshop facilities,
- Lack of motivation and supervision,
- Poor attention being given to the organization of out-of-school science activities,
- Shortage of trained, experienced and skilled teachers/ experts,
- Shortage of adequate resources, materials, equipment, maintenance work and short-term training programmes, and
- Need for much more audio-visual media.

Ongoing out-of-school science activities, through careful planning, will continue to be developed in the future. The country expects to continue making progress through the earnest co-operation of all.

### 3.6 New Zealand

New Zealand's relatively low population density enables all people to have easy access to the natural environment. Children often gain their first understanding of science through observation of their environment. As they look for cause and effect situations around them, they begin to develop a scientific way of thinking; science comes to be seen as a part of life, an everyday reality rather than a body of knowledge.

As a result, New Zealanders participate in a wide range of out-of-school scientific activities and the climate of scientific awareness is high. Various scientific activities are provided through both formal and non-formal education programmes. These include:

- Camps and field trips,
- Visits to parks, botanical gardens, zoos, museums, planetariums, scientific industries, open days, etc.
- Focus on Science Week which seeks to get the whole community to focus on science,
- Science fairs,
- Department of Conservation's 'Arbor Day' and 'Conservation Week',
- The Women in Science Education programme, which encourages girls and women to be involved in science,.
- The New Zealand Science Teachers Badge Award Scheme, which encourages students to study a science topic in depth, and
- The Correspondence School's work for students in an out-of-school environment.

New Zealanders' expect that whatever scientific and technological information is needed will be available and can be accessed easily. Many organizations are involved in transmitting this information: radio, television, newspapers, adult education programmes, community groups, government departments, private companies, entertainment centres, hobby clubs, etc.

While it is true that New Zealanders are involved in many out-of-school scientific activities, there is still a need for a continuing promotion of scientific and technological education as an economic necessity. This will ensure that New Zealand can generate sufficient technological skills to develop the economy, and to support the social and welfare programmes being undertaken.

### 3.7 Pakistan

Science Fairs, Science Exhibitions, Science Quizzes, Science Clubs, Village Workshops, Mobile Workshops, Mass Media

Productions, Zoological and Botanical Gardens, Science Museum and Planetariums are part of the ongoing activities in Pakistan. These programmes are being delivered through: the Open University, the non-formal education system, literacy centres, the Educational Equipment Centre, and the Literacy and Mass Education Commission.

Among the problems and issues of concern in Pakistan are: low literacy rate (26.4 per cent), lack of finance, lack of co-ordination between different agencies and different industrial enterprises, lack of motivation, low per capita income, lack of communication infrastructure, lack of implementation facilities, low qualifications of teachers generally and a lack of qualified science teachers and out-of-school science personnel.

Some suggestions for the future include: improvement of literacy, more funds for science programmes, motivation of teachers, better co-ordination between different agencies and ministries, and inducement of industry and scientific organizations to corporate in educational activities.

### 3.8 Philippines

Various out-of-school science activities have become effective means for promoting science and technology among the youth. Some government agencies now take the lead in conducting science activities. The private sector has also kept pace with the education system's renewed emphasis of science and technology.

The Department of Education, Culture and Sports (DECS) and the Department of Science and Technology (DOST) continue to coordinate out-of-school science activities through their regional offices. Some of these activities are: science clubs, science camps, film forums, youth apprenticeship action programmes, and science and technology exhibits. Privately-sponsored activities include science and mathematics quizzes as well as TV and radio programmes.

The University of the Philippines Institute for Science and Mathematics Education Development (UPISMED) undertakes various projects designed to:

1. promote scientific and technological literacy,
2. arouse interest in science, mathematics and computers,
3. improve the quality of life through science and technology, particularly in the deprived sector.

Some of the projects of UPISMED include the development of Science Readers, the Open Labs Programme, "Beyond Classroom Science and Mathematics" (BCSM), and Project Link.

Science Readers are comic-style short printed materials on a single topic or concept. The target users are children 9 to 11 years old so topics are those that naturally arouse children's curiosity. "Beyond Classroom Science and Mathematics" (BCSM) is an enrichment programme for children from kindergarten to high school level. This programme provides children with science and mathematics experiences not normally given in school due to time and resource constraints. Project Link looks into ways of linking formal education with out-of-school activities in science and technology for the youth.

### 3.9 Sri Lanka

The tropical island of Sri Lanka, "The Pearl of the Indian Ocean", is an enchanting small island with 9,914 schools and a school-going population of 3,625,897. Science education begins at year 4 of school. In years 6 to 11, science is taught to all, and in years 12 to 13 a selected group of students studies science.

Out-of-school science activities are carried out in Sri Lanka with the objectives of improving the quality of education, popularising science, and making children aware of scientific ways and methods. There are three main types of activities:

1. School-based activities,
2. Activities sponsored by the Ministry of Education, and
3. Activities sponsored by other agencies.

School-based activities are carried out through societies in schools. The Ministry of Education has three institutes with which they carry on this programme:

(a) Curriculum Development Centre,

(b) Field Study Centres, and

(c) Science Support Centres.

At the field study centre, students and teachers undertake environmental studies.

There are many other agencies in Sri Lanka which carry out science activities, including the Sri Lanka Association for Advancement of Science, the Institute of Fundamental Studies, the Natural Resources Energy and Science Authority, the Sri Lanka Association for Science and Mathematics Education, the Central Environmental Authority, and others.

Problems experienced in Sri Lanka include:

1. Students are reluctant to take part in extra activities as the school syllabus is examination-oriented, and these activities are time-consuming,
2. Lack of funds and facilities,
3. Lack of motivation, and
4. Lack of training for teachers to undertake such activities.

### 3.10 Thailand

There are many well organized out-of-school scientific activities taking place in Thailand. The main trust of these activities occurs each year between the 18th and 24th of August during "Youth Science Week". This week is organized by the Science Society of Thailand together with the Ministry of Science and Technology; the Ministry of University Affairs and the Ministry of Education in co-operation with the private sector. Activities held during the Science Week include exhibitions; science quizzes; science and computer camps; and also competitions in various areas of science: projects; inventions; art; oratory; process skills and compositions.

The Centre for Educational Museums promoters out-of-school science activities through its exhibitions, lectures and demonstrations and through multi-media shows in its planetarium and observatory. The Centre has also established a Mobile Museum Unit in an attempt to decentralize education services and provide equal education for people in rural areas.

In 1987, the first Science Olympiad was held in Thailand involving 80 students from throughout the country.

Although Thailand is blessed with an abundance of natural resources, it is still a developing country in many respects. It is recognized that there is a need for more scientific and technological specialists so that the country can develop more rapidly.

## TRENDS IN THE REGION

While each country has its own approach to out-of-school science activities and its own types of programmes, some trends can be identified.

Programmes in the last few decades were mainly addressed to children in school and literate adults, particularly those living in urban areas. This is still so in countries just starting to develop out-of-school science activities. In other countries the trend is towards reaching the functionally illiterate masses, particularly in the rural areas and urban slums.

In the past, materials were developed centrally and distributed all over the country. The current trend is to involve local people in planning, and to pay heed to local socio-cultural considerations. In other words, it is the target group which is being given the opportunity to decide what they would like to know about.

Keeping pace with the change in target groups and with the determination of needs, the delivery systems are also changing. Science museum activities, science fairs, science quizzes, science contests, science clubs and such activities continue to proliferate, and there is a deliberate attempt to draw the literate rural population into these activities. Education of parents through their children, both in urban and rural areas, is also being tried. Since a major target group is functionally illiterate and semi-literate adults, more use is being made of posters, comics, radio, television, and illustrated booklets using very simple language.

After the country reports had been presented the Workshop participants spent time identifying the various problems and issues which are occurring in out-of-school science activities in the region. These problems and issues are described in Chapter 4. Identification of these problems and issues in the light of the above trends enabled the Workshop to develop guidelines and strategies to make delivery systems for science programmes more effective.

# 4

# Problems and Issues Relating to Delivery Systems for Out-of-School Science Activities

A wide range of out-of-school scientific activities is being carried out in the various countries in the region. Many of these activities were highlighted in the various country reports described in Chapter 3.

The workshop was asked to identify some of the problems and issues pertaining to these activities.

It considered the problems and issues occur in three related areas:

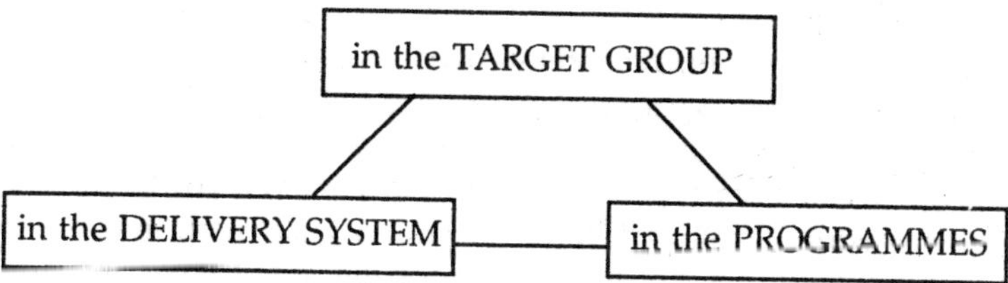


These three areas will be considered separately:

### 4.1 The Target Group

Before any effective scientific education programme can take place the target group needs to be identified and its particular needs defined. Questions such as the following need to be considered and answered:

*(a) What is the target group?*

Is it - school children?
- school dropouts?
- illiterate adults?
- literate adults who are scientifically illiterate?
- people in urban areas?
- people in urban slums?
- people in rural areas?

*(b) How can the target group be identified?*

Is it - by age?
- by level of education?
- by locale?

*(c) What are the characteristics of the target group?*

- What occupations do they have?
- What is their income level?
- What kind of lifestyle do they have?

*(d) What are the needs of the target group?*

- Who these needs perceive?
  - the target group themselves?
  - the programme implementors?
  - the public?
  - the scientific community?
- Are the needs short- or long-term?
- Can the needs be met using existing learning skills and indigenous technology?

*(e) How can the target group be motivated?*

- Does the programme build on their existing interests?
- Will it provide them with some reward or benefit?
- Will the benefits be direct, short-term or long-term?
- Can they see how it will give them a better understanding and a better way of life?

*(f) Where is the target group located?*

Once the nature of the target group has been established appropriate programmes can begin to be developed. There may still be problems, however, which must be addressed if the programmes are to be effective, especially if the target group is people who are scientifically disadvantaged or underprivileged.

This group may make up to 80 per cent of the population of some countries in the region.

Some of the problems identified for the scientifically disadvantaged target group are as follows:

- Large number of people to be reached;
- Poor literacy of the people;
- Many languages, dialects, races, ways of dressing;
- Resistance caused by taboos, beliefs, customs, norms;
- Indifference, apathy, poor motivation;
- Low priority given to scientific activities;
- Poverty;
- Lack of basic equipment;
- Existing work habits;
- Lack of time;
- Family structures;
- Age structures;
- Societal decision-making processes;
- Sexual mores; and
- Poor accessibility especially for rural and island people.

The target group for the workshop was defined as being "those adults and adolescents in the Asia and Pacific regions who may have had the minimum of education at the elementary school level, and who form a sizeable workforce in their national economy". Because this target group is scientifically disadvantaged it exhibits may of the problems cited above.

The second area where problems and issues arise in out-of-school scientific activities is in the organization of the scientific programmes being carried out.

**4.2 Organization of Out-of-School Scientific Programmes**

The workshop considered that all scientific programmes should have the following goals:

- an understanding of the nature of scientific knowledge;
- an understanding of the key concepts of science;
- an understanding of the processes of science and their acceptance in people's daily lives;
- an understanding of scientific values like honesty, respect for logic, truthfulness, tolerance, concern for people, concern about consequences;
- a development of problem-solving and decision-making skills;
- a development of respect for the environment;
- an understanding of the link between science and national development; and
- a development of the skills needed for science and technology.

Scientific programmes for the workshop's target group should particularly aim at developing scientific literacy and creating a climate of scientific awareness. As so many countries in the region are developing countries, the scientific programmes should highlight the economic and social benefits which can be achieved through science and technology.

**4.3 Problems in the Development of the Programmes**

Problems in the development of out-of-school programmes can come about at various levels:

(a) at the Government-policy level,

(b) at the programme organization level, and

(c) at the training of facilitators level.

Some of these problems at different levels are described as follows:

### 4.3.1 Problems at the Government-Policy Level

The problems include:

- little commitment to the programmes;
- the social and educational policies of the Government may be in other directions;
- lack of two-day communication between the Government and the programme facilitators;
- the Government policy may not address the needs of the target group;
- decision-making may be slow;
- politicians, administrators, planners etc. may not themselves be scientifically literate; and
- the official Government policies may target specific regions or groups and miss others.

### 4.3.2 Problems at the Programme Organization Level

The problems at the level include:

- lack of co-ordination between facilitators and other agencies involved;
- the same group may continue getting the benefits of a programme and others miss out;
- lack of finance; the finance may not reach the target group; the finance may be misappropriated;
- lack of suitable facilities;
- lack of suitable resources or an overlap or misuse of resources;
- the target group may not be involved in the planning;
- a total dependence on particular resource people;
- lack of administrative support;
- lack of incentives, or a reward system; and
- lack of monitoring of the effectiveness of the programmes.

### 4.3.3 Problems at the Training of Facilitators Level

The problems at this level include:

- lack of expertise in the trainers;
- training programmes may be poorly presented;
- the personality, age, sex, class, dress, language, jargon, etc. of the trainer may detract from the programme;
- lack of basic equipment;
- the trainers may not have had a balanced exposure to the target group;
- the training needs may not have been properly identified;
- the training programmes may not meet the needs of the target group; and
- lack of evaluation, assessment and follow-up in the training programmes.

The third area where problems and issues were identified was in the delivery systems used.

## 4.4. Problems and Issues in Delivery Systems

The main thrust of the workshop was in the improvement of delivery systems for out-of-school science activities. It was felt that if problems and issues in delivery systems could be clearly identified, it would help in the development of appropriate strategies and training programmes. The workshop's suggestions for improvement of delivery systems are described in Chapter 5.

Problems and issues in delivery systems were identified as those of:

### 4.4.1 Human Resources

Suitable committed people are required as facilitators for out-of-school science programmes at different levels: leaders, workers, helpers, trainers. There are not enough suitable people available, so those potential facilitators need to be identified and approached personally. One way they can be trained is by working alongside existing facilitators. One problem here is the indifference of many people and their unwillingness to be involved in scientific education programmes. If community leaders won't support the programmes or participate in them, this will also have severe negative consequences. In areas where few suitable facilitators are available, the only volunteers may be people whose personality, age, sex, class, behaviour, dress, language, etc. are not accepted by the local community. This problem is magnified in areas where there are many different cultures.

**4.4.2 Other Resources**

Lack of suitable materials, equipment, facilities, services (especially electrification), etc. can be a major problem in the delivery of out-of-school science programmes. Sometimes these resources can be supplied by better inter-agency co-ordination or by seeking the sponsorship of various industries or non-government organizations. Care should be taken in approaching such institutions so only those which are genuinely seeking to promote out-of-school scientific activities are involved. Problems have occurred where some organizations have not had a holistic approach, or where commercial interests have run counter to a proper conservation of the environment.

**4.4.3 Finance**

Many out-of-school science activities cannot take place successfully because there is lack of finance. Governments must see that funding of scientific and technological education programmes will benefit their national economy in the short- and long-term. Funds are required for personnel, space, materials, administration, and for the delivery systems used.

**4.4.4 Communication Systems**

Poor communication between groups involved in out-of-school science activities can come about in many ways. Some of it is caused by the target group being in isolated areas where there is poor access, difficult transport, lack of electrification and unreliable communication networks. Other co-ordination problems arise because the various agencies involved in preparation of programmes tend to work in isolation. There is much overlap with similar programmes being developed by the different agencies. This is time, resource and cost ineffective. A clearing house is needed where programmes which have been developed can be stored and accessed easily. Materials which have not been effective can also be included, so future programmes will not make the same mistake again.

This chapter has highlighted some of the problems and issues which were identified by the Workshop pertaining to out-of-school scientific activities. In future chapters, ways of overcoming some of these problems will be described so that the various delivery systems used can take place more effectively.

# 5

# Identification of Appropriate Delivery Systems for Out-of-School Science Activities

If out-of-school science activities are to be an effective medium for bringing about scientific literacy and improving the quality of life, they must be related to the basic needs of the target group. They must also be implemented through appropriate delivery systems. This chapter describes some of the basic needs which scientific activities can address and suggests appropriate delivery systems.

## 5.1 Basic Human Needs

Individuals have similar basic needs, regardless of which part of the world they come from. These needs are described in Maslow's hierarchy of needs:

Sharing, service, contribution to others

Recognition, rewards, motivation, incentives

Love, acceptance, family, to be part of a group

Peaceful environment, shelter, education (including scientific and technological literacy)

Food, clothing, health, employment

Generally when the basic physiological needs are satisfied people can have their needs at higher levels met. Out-of-school science activities can have a major role in meeting these basic human needs. Some of the "needs" which should have priority in out-of-school science programmes are the needs for:

- FOOD
- WATER
- ENERGY
- HEALTH AND SANITATION
- CLOTHING
- DEVELOPMENT OF APPROPRIATE TECHNOLOGY
- PREVENTION OF DRUG ADDICTION AND ALCOHOLISM
- SAFETY
- POPULATION EDUCATION
- ENVIRONMENTAL CONCERNS
- GENERATION OF EMPLOYMENT AVENUES

("Health" cuts through all of the above areas and could be built into most out-of-school science programmes.)

Materials which can be developed to meet each of these identified needs are very varied, depending on the particular target group.

An example is given below for "food".

*Food* is one of mankind's most basic needs. The food production technology used in many countries of the region is often very primitive, resulting in low productivity. Scientifically and technologically literate people are able to produce more per hectare because they have knowledge about tools, finances, fertilisers, pest control, breeding, concern for the environment, etc.

In agriculturally-based countries food production is a matter of national economic survival. In an industrialized country like USA only 6-7 per cent of the population are involved in agriculture. These few not only provide food for the whole country but also export some. This is because they use efficient agriculture practices and apply advanced technology. In many countries of the Asia-Pacific Region, 60-80 per cent of the population are engaged in agriculture, yet many are still net importers of food.

In these countries agricultural extension centres may provide information on the latest technology but often it is not used by farmers. Each region needs to get information about efficient production in their area and then put it into practice. This may involve overcoming beliefs, superstitions and inefficient current practices.

Any programme that is designed must be holistic in its approach. It must involve care for the environment, a concern for health, respect for community beliefs, and a proper application of technology together with a recognition of its widespread benefits.

The chart on the next page gives an idea of the wide range of problems that can be addressed under the broad umbrella of "FOOD". It is by no means complete. The section under 'production' is given in greater detail for one area only: 'agriculture'. Each of the areas delineated can form the basis for one or more multi-media packages.

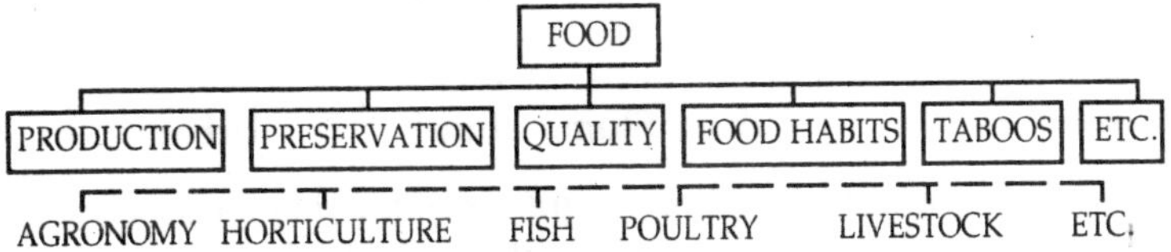


- Proper use of Fertilisers,
- Insecticides, Pesticides,
- Soil and water management,
- Harvest technology,
- Seed production,
- Maintenance of farm implements,
- Waste disposal,
- Farm management, etc.

The other sections, preservation, quality, food habits, and taboos can also be similarly spelt out. The same principles may also be applied in all the basic areas mentioned above.

## 5.2 Identification of Target Groups

It is not enough to identify just the needs of the target group. The actual target group must be identified as well.

Broad target groups were listed in Chapter 1. A large number of out-of-school science programmes are being carried out for literate children and adults. A large per cent of the functionally illiterate population is thus left out. Within this group it is the girls and women who often get the least benefit from educational programmes. If the female population receives adequate attention, it will ensure that future generations will get a modicum of scientific literacy in their early years from their mothers.

The target group of the functionally illiterate population can be further divided into sub-groups, as shown below:

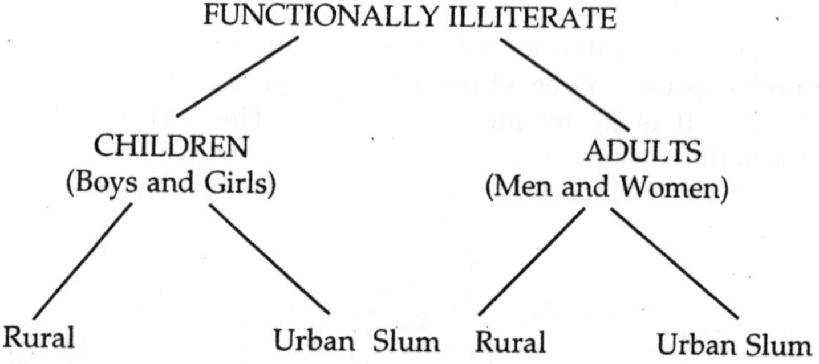


The aim of out-of-school programmes for this target group is to improve their quality of life through the application of science. (Some of the basic physiological needs of this target group are not being fulfilled at present.)

The ultimate goal will of course be "scientific literacy". This entails awareness of scientific and technological developments, ability to understand cause and effect and development of problem-solving skills. In other words the goal is to produce scientifically conscious citizens.

## 5.3 Identification of Delivery Systems

The ultimate goal of the delivery systems used for out-of-school science activities is scientific literacy. This is much easier to achieve if the target group is functionally literate. It is still possible, however, to impart a certain amount of scientific literacy to the functionally illiterate.

The delivery systems currently in use for various out-of-school science programmes are:

- Television*,
- Radio*,
- Films/VCRs*,
- Printed materials*:
  - (a) Pictorial—wordless,
  - (b) Pictorial with few simple words,
  - (c) Books, comics, modules, etc.
  - (d) News media,
- Lecture/demonstrations,
- Street plays/puppetry/songs/folk media,
- Club/group activities,
- Exhibitions,
- Museums/science parks/zoos*, etc., and
- Person to person.

(Those that are marked (*) may operate without facilitators being present on the site.)

Since the identified target group is in most part functionally illiterate, the delivery system should rely mainly on seeing, hearing, doing and following models, rather than on reading. If reading is required the material must be in simple language, use large prints and include a large number of pictures.

There are various possible strategies for delivery:

1. Facilitator-mediated learning, e.g. using elders, teachers, para-professionals, influential people in the village and volunteer youth leaders. Science kits or multi-media packages could be used by these facilitators.

2. Peer-mediated learning—This is where people learn from each other, e.g., farmer to farmer, child to child, housewife to housewife. It often takes place in interest or hobby groups.
3. Mass media—radio, television, computer, print and folk media.

The delivery systems which are most suitable for the functionally illiterate are:

- Word—Pictorial,
- Pictorial with few words,
- Radio, and
- Television.

These methods may be used with or without a facilitator on site.

Other methods which may adopted are:

- Club and group activities,
- Street plays/puppetry/folk media/songs,
- Demonstrations,
- Exhibitions (mobile and temporary) at community centres, markets, festival sites, places of worship, community centres, and
- films and videos.

Planners and designers must keep the following things in mind as they choose appropriate delivery systems for particular target groups:

- language, dress and other local socio-cultural aspects,
- mixing and identifying with the target group,
- involving target groups in planning,
- involving non-governmental organizations as well as governmental agencies,
- recognizing levels of learning,

- starting from the level of learning of the target group,
- using a learner-centred approach (andragogy) instead of teacher-centred (pedagogy),
- ensuring a good distribution system, and
- ensuring that there are ample materials for reinforcement.

In order to do this, planners and designers must have certain competencies. They must:

- be sensitive to target groups and local needs,
- be scientifically knowledgeable,
- have good communication skills,
- be able to visualize the whole programme, and
- have monitoring and evaluation skills.

The facilitator (person on site) needs to have a different set of competencies. He or she must:

- preferably be a local person or be fluent in the local dialect,
- be familiar with socio-cultural aspects of the scientific target group,
- be a committed, out-going person,
- be acceptable to the community,
- be able to assess the needs of the community and communicate the needs to planners and designers,
- be able to transmit the planners, and designers, ideas to the community, and
- be a role model for the community.

In this chapter we have emphasized that the needs of specific groups within a community must be met using delivery systems particularly applicable to them. Some examples are given below for various target groups.

### 5.4 Examples for Various Target Groups

**5.4.1 Target Group:** Squatters and people in slums and ghettos.

**Facilitators:**

The work could be carried out by strong, committed social workers, of recognized status, who are willing to live among the target group. They would also need to be competent to train field workers.

(a) *Specific target group: children with limited schooling,* (therefore having little scientific awareness.)

The educational packages used should impart basic knowledge about hygiene and sanitation to the target group. It should also show them the economic benefits of healthy living.

(b) *Specific target group: dropouts*

This group has a very strong peer influence and often forms gangs. Individuals in the group need recognition by others. If they are encouraged to do things which are seen to be of value by the community, it may motivate them to do better.

The strategies adopted for this group could be to organize them into group/clubs. A social worker could start a group based on things they are interested in e.g. music, drama, sports. Scientific literacy should not be imposed but introduced naturally e.g. a sports person would benefit by knowing first aid, hygiene and proper diet. Peer-mediated learning can be the most effective delivery system here. A reinforcement strategy would be to bring in ex-dropouts who have done well in areas which the target group respect, e.g. basketball pros.

(c) *Specific target group: Females* who drop out of school to become domestics/housewives, or who have little opportunity for further schooling.

This group needs scientific awareness about family planning, pregnancy, and factors involved in being a housewife, including sex education, nutrition, breast-feeding, hygiene and sanitation. The husbands also need to be taught about family planning.

This group could be encouraged to form clubs where they can socialize, share problems and discuss things related to the home. This will help create scientific awareness. To achieve this there is a need for networking of existing agencies and para-professionals in rural health centres.

**5.4.2 Target Group:** Agricultural Sector

Some scientific awareness has been created through agriculture extension workers. Often, however, their ideas are not put into practice.

The needs of this group are:

- to learn about natural ways of improving food production;
- to use fertilisers/pesticides with greater understanding;
- to use raw materials more efficiently; and
- to learn how to process and market efficiently and how to diversify into new products.

Some strategies to meet these needs are:

- additional training and reorientation of extension agents and existing agencies;
- peer group training for farmers;
- local schools being provided with horticulture/ agronomy sections to train children who will become farmers in the future;
- radio programmes which are followed by discussion groups;
- village seminars;
- community centres with comics, posters, wall charts, kits, models, etc.;
- model farms, demonstrations, etc.; and
- wider use of agricultural extension centres.

**5.4.3 Target Group:** The whole country, i.e. a general national campaign.

Politicians, ministers, presidents, kings, etc. (i.e. people with influence) would introduce the campaign giving it credibility.

They would be asked to particularly emphasized the importance of science and technology.

e.g. *Focus on Science Week*

Use of media: radio/TV/print/meetings/rallies, etc. to promote scientific awareness and the importance of scientific literacy for the economic development of the country. Get comic writers to include scientific principles in their comic because so many read them.

This chapter has highlighted the main requirements of an appropriate delivery system. It is to identify the basic and specific needs of target groups and use delivery systems which are appropriate and feasible. Sensitivity to the socio-cultural milieu and the needs of the target group forms the basis upon which an appropriate delivery system can be designed.

# 6

# Strategies and Guidelines to Improve Delivery Systems for Out-of-School Science Activities

Delivery systems play a key role in all out-of-school science activities. Even when human and material resources are available many programmes have failed because they have not used appropriate delivery systems.

Previous chapters have described various delivery systems which are in operation in the region, together with problems and issues which have arisen. In this chapter strategies and guidelines are given for improvement of these delivery systems so that out-of-school activities can take place more effectively.

### 6.1 Human Resources for Delivery Systems

Most out-of-school science activities require at least a 3-tier system for their operation.

*(a) Planners and designers*

These people design the programme according to a base-line survey of the target group's needs. They can develop and disseminate materials, gather resources and train implementors. They also have responsibility for overall monitoring and evaluation of the programme.

*(b) Implementors*

Their role is to manage the programme in operation. They train the facilitators and survey personnel, adapt materials if necessary and liaise between the planners and the facilitators. They may also monitor and evaluate on-going programmes.

*(c) Facilitators*

These are the people who actually deliver the programmes to the target groups.

**6.2 Assessment of Needs**

The choice of a particular delivery system is based on such factors as the identified needs of the target group; specific community directions and national priorities. The following strategies may be adopted to help in assessment of needs so that appropriate delivery systems are used.

- establish a close relationship with the community, especially its leaders;
- careful training of survey personnel;
- carry out a base-line survey of the target group. The survey should enquire into such things as:
  - local knowledge, attitudes and practices,
  - facilities available,
  - identified needs,
  - demographic information,
  - family structure,
  - power structure,
  - age/sex distribution,
  - occupations,
  - sources of information,
  - traditional methods, beliefs, taboos, norms;
- seek out funding agencies; and
- establish priorities and feed information back to the planners and designers.

Once the base-line survey of the target group has been carried out so their needs are clearly identified, appropriate delivery systems can begin to be designed, and materials developed.

**6.3 Development of Materials**

This may involve:

- identification of suitable experts or resource people to develop the materials;
- a survey of existing materials which can be adopted, adapted or modified;
- development of trial materials; and
- production of materials on a pilot scale.

**6.4 Carrying Out a Pilot Programme**

A small-scale tryout is necessary to validate the materials which have been developed. The pilot programme will include:

- training of facilitators;
- dissemination of the material;
- a check on the management side of the programme;
- carrying out the programme on a small-scale with the target group;
- formative and summative evaluation;
- refinement of materials; and
- validation of materials.

**6.5 Delivering the Programme**

Once all of the planning and organization describe above been carried out, the out-of-school science programme can be implemented with the target group.

This will involve:

- full-scale production of validated material;
- training of implementors and facilitators;
- setting up of a management infrastructure;

- distribution of materials;
- selection of suitable facilities;
- establishment of a monitoring and evaluation system and finally;
- implementation of the programme.

### 6.6 Follow Up

At each stage in the development of the delivery system there has been monitoring and evaluation. An analysis should be carried out and the programme modified, if necessary. The success of the programme may mean that the characteristics of the target group have changed somewhat, so a new base-line survey will need to be carried out, and the process begin again.

The materials which have been developed, together with their evaluation and any recommendations should be sent to national and regional clearing houses, so that the materials can be available for others to use as well.

The guidelines suggested above for the development of delivery systems for out-of-school science activities and summarized below:

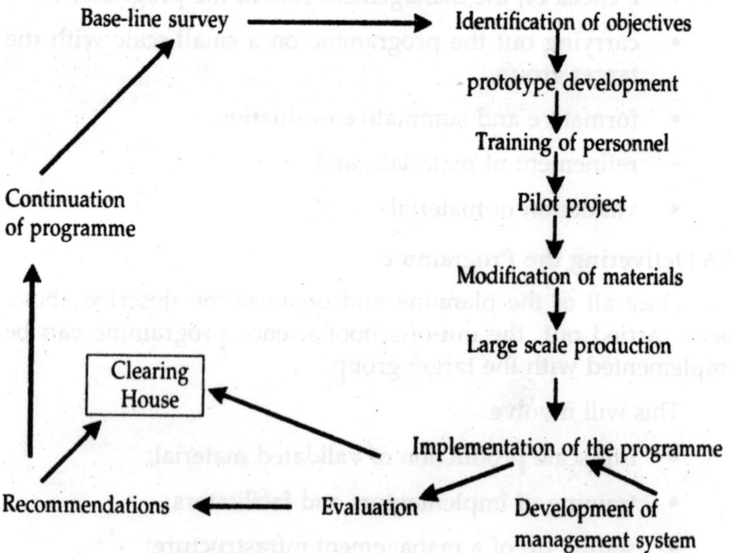

## 6.7 Guidelines for Implementation of the Various Strategies

In order to follow the strategies outlined above certain general guidelines are suggested below. These will have to be adapted according to the conditions in a particular country. The guidelines given are for:

1. finding finance;
2. funding suitable resource people;
3. training of survey personnel;
4. training of implementors;
5. training of facilitators; and
6. development of materials.

### *6.7.1 Guidelines for Finding Finance for Out-of-School Science Programmes*

Finance is often a major limiting factor in delivery systems for out-of-school science activities. Some strategies for obtaining finance at various levels are given here:

- Approach international or national agencies which provide finance for country development programmes, e.g. ADB, UNESCO, World Bank, FAO, IDRC, WHO, UNICEF, UNDP.
- Approach Government or regional agencies. For finance to be forthcoming from this sector the officials involved need to be convinced that the programmes will be economically or socially worthwhile.
- Approach community organizations to help fund local programmes.
- Approach private companies. Some companies have a very good record of providing sponsorship, materials or finance. A much wider range of companies could be involved. Assistance may be provided as funds, as services or as goods they produce.
- Community cooperatives have funds which could be used for out-of-school science activities. A tariff could be introduced to gather a continuous source of supply,

e.g. a science institution could be funded by revenue obtained from stamp sales.

- Local fund-raising activities could be held, e.g. work-a-thons, science-a-thons, science marches, science days, etc. Sometimes activities like these will require an official permit.

- Those who benefit from the programme could be charged a minimal amount. The reason for this must be carefully explained so they see that it is for their own benefit, or for the community's benefit. This would help science programmes become more self-sufficient.

- National science days could be established similar to national literacy days. They would include fund-raising for specific science projects.

- Coin boxes at airports, hotels, shopping centres, etc. could provide a "fund for scientific literacy".

*6.7.2 Guidelines for Finding Suitable Resource People for Out-of-School Science Programmes*

The resource people who are to be involved in organising and facilitating out-of-school science activities need to have qualities such as: proficiency on their subject; respect by the community; commitment to the programme; credibility; flexibility; resilience; adaptability; willingness to learn; open-mindedness pragmatism; practicality; dynamism; and an understanding of the needs of the target group. Very few people have all the qualities. As most programmes are organized and facilitated by teams, rather than by individuals, the resource people in a team can complement each other in the various qualities and capabilities.

Some guidelines for finding such people are:

- People resources are best tapped from existing local agencies, including universities; schools; scientific institutions; development agencies; local industries, and associations as well as village officials; retired people; para-professionals; volunteer workers etc.

- Regional centres for improving scientific literacy should be staffed by competent resource people who are able to relate to people in other regions. These centres can act as a resource base for people, as well as for programme and material resources. What is needed is people who can relate well to the target group, not just experienced teachers.
- Networking between resource people in various agencies and countries should be encouraged, both formally and informally.

*6.7.3 Guidelines for training of survey personnel*

Some steps involved in the training of people who will carry out the base-line surveys are:

- Acquaint them with the primary aims of the programme and give them an overview;
- Spell out the specific objectives of the survey;
- Go through the various features of the survey form and the purpose of each item;
- Demonstrate techniques of asking probing questions and paraphrasing questions in the survey form;
- Discuss various modes of assessing the needs of the households without resorting to a formal interview, e.g. by observing their lifestyle, work habits, eating habits, personal hygiene, leisure;
- Discuss how they can identify the needs, problems, etc. of certain groups of people by listening in on their conversations;
- Describe some basic tenets which are important when conducting interviews—e.g. tactfulness, diplomacy, politeness; and
- Point out the importance of recording immediately to avoid losing valuable information.

*6.7.4 Guidelines for Training of Implementors*

Implementors are the people who manage the programme while it is in operation. Some guidelines for training implementors are:

- Discuss the programme; its goals and its rationale;
- Discuss the specific objectives for the implementation of the programme; i.e. what the planners want to be implemented;
- Identify the infrastructure needed by the target group and the facilitators;
- Acquaint the implementors with the nature of the materials to be used by the target group and the facilitators; and
- Discuss methods of monitoring the use of the materials (Some implementors may be involved in carrying out this monitoring.)

*6.7.5 Guidelines for Training of Facilitators*

A training programme for facilitators could be sequenced as follows:

- Aquaint facilitators with the aims and the rationale of the programme;
- Explain the objectives of each learning package and the corresponding activities that target users will go through to attain the objectives;
- Demonstrate strategies for presenting the leading materials;
- Discuss how to motivate the target group so they gain as much benefit as possible from the materials;
- Describe how they can evaluate the target group's learning. This evaluation can take place during or after the use of the material. It can be done using written or verbal response, and by observation of the target group's behaviour;

- Point out the importance of recording any deviation from the material (for consideration during revision of the programme); and
- Discuss how people learn, the cognitive levels at which individuals perform; the importance of transforming concrete operations to formal thinking.

*6.7.6 Guidelines for Development of Materials*

- The materials selected must focus on the nature of the learner in the target group;
- The materials selected must attempt to be the most cost-effective means of reaching the target group;
- More than one delivery system may be selected for one topic to provide reinforcement;
- The delivery system chosen should be capable of carrying many subsequent messages to the target group. Once a system has been established it should be able to be used again; and
- An attempt should be made to identify materials which have been previously designed or used:
    - with the target group,
    - with other target groups,
    - in other local situations,
    - in other languages, and
    - using other delivery systems.

Such materials can be adopted as is; adapted; modified, or rejected.

- Both innovative and proven materials should be considered.
- Consideration should be given to the material being a *model* for other materials, or one of a series.
- Materials should be designed to present:

- new information,
- old information in new ways,
- reinforcement of information,
- the possibility of information at higher levels.

- Materials for the functionally illiterate target group should be wordless, or use for words.
- Wherever possible target groups should be involved in the planning of the materials.
- Pilot development of material may be on a small-scale, but production quality should be high to avoid duplication of initial costs.
- Design materials so that modifications can be made after pilot-testing, without too much difficulty.

If the various strategies and guidelines in this chapter are followed; it will mean that the delivery systems used for out-of-school science activities in the region will take place more effectively.

# 7

# Exemplar Materials for Out-of-School Science Activities

The workshop considered various areas where exemplar materials could profitably be prepared. These are areas where out-of-school science programmes are particularly needed by the target group.

The areas suggested were:

- food and nutrition,
- water,
- energy,
- health and sanitation,
- shelter and clothing,
- environmental concerns,
- domestic and technical living skills, and
- food production.

The workshop decided to concentrate on preparing exemplar materials for two of these areas only. These are on environmental concerns and food and nutrition.

**7.1 Area: Environmental Concerns and Food and Nutrition**

Described below are the kind of materials which could be used to present out-of-school science activities which are relevant to the target group. The exemplar materials are in prototype form the would have to be developed into final forms which are appropriate for target groups in each country.

For each of the exemplar materials the target group and some of its problems are identified and the objectives of the programme are given as well. There is an outline of an appropriate delivery system and a discussion of how it could be organized.

*7.1.1 Exemplar A*

*Delivery System:* RADIO PROGRAMME "Using pesticides properly"

*Target Group:* Farmers in rural areas

Problems related to the target group:

- Many farmers don't use pesticides at the recommended rate, e.g. they use too little to save money or too much in a mistaken belief that this will be more effective.
- There is a reliance on chemical control without an understanding of natural methods.
- Safe storage and use of pesticides.
- Not using pesticides for appropriate pests.
- Lack of caution in spraying pesticides.
- Using of banned pesticides.
- Lack of understanding of how pesticide use can affect the environment.

*Objectives*

To be able to demonstrate that farmers can use pesticides safely, at the recommended rate and with understanding.

*Delivery System*

Radio programmes would be broadcast regularly, e.g. at a fixed time each week. Each programme would be 3-5 minutes in duration and would use a variety of communication methods, e.g. drama, dialogue, story, song, interview, etc. The radio programmes could be supported by posters, banners, etc., which would give a visual representation of what is described in the radio programme. T-shirts could be used as "mobile posters".

A possible outline for a series of programme is:

1. Interview with victim to hospital who has been poisoned while·using pesticides.
2. Drama where farmer describes how a new pesticide was applied (not following instructions). Neighbour gets upset and explains how it could have been applied properly.
3. Talk by an expert explaining how pesticides work and how they should be used.
4. Poems, songs which emphasized safe use of pesticides.
5. Dialogue between farmer and field-worker discussing dangers of pesticides, and how they can be stored and used safely.
6. Pesticide quiz where farmers are the participants.
7. Interview with a famous farmer who has improved productivity and earned a bigger income by using pesticides properly.

*Organization*

- The programmes should use simple language and be interested and appealing. They should also use dialects. (This might mean that local radio stations would be involved in the preparation.)
- The programmes should use language, examples, ideas, etc. which the target group is familiar with, and are relevant to them.
- After scripts have been drafted, expert radio script-writers would prepare them for broadcast.
- The programmes should be professionally produced so they are of a high standard.
- The programmes should be scheduled if possible during free time of farmers. Timetables should be clearly displayed in community centres, reinforced by regular

announcements. They could also be displayed in places where pesticides are sold.

- The programmes should be repeated so those who miss them can hear them later on.
- Pesticide manufacturers could be charged a tariff to help fund the programmes.

*7.1.2 Exemplar B*

*Delivery system:* Wordless mini-poster "A balanced diet"
Large posters
Radio advertisements

*Target group:* Women

*Problems related to the target group:*

- many families have a monotonous starchy diet
- many women who prepare meals have a lack of understanding of food types, and what constitutes a balanced diet.

*Objectives*

To assist the target group plan and prepare means which provide a balanced diet.

*Delivery System*

A multi-media package would be presented with each part reinforcing the others:

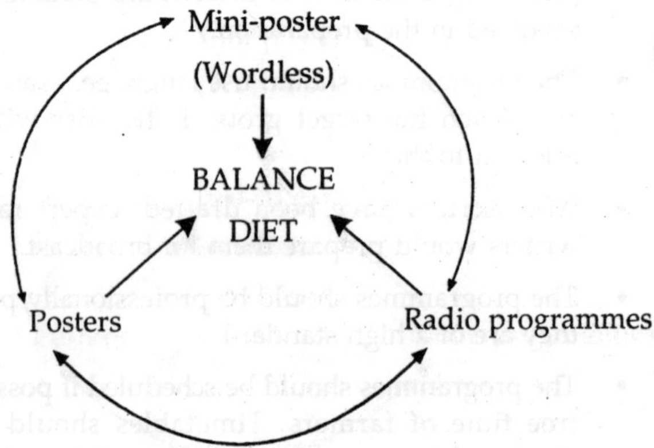

*(a) Wordless mini-poster*

This would show:

- a child with a large stomach eating only starchy foods. Afterwards the child still has a large stomach.
- a child with a small stomach eating a balanced diet (including proteins). Afterwards the child has a normal-sized stomach.
- a child with a large stomach eating a balanced diet (including proteins). Afterwards the child has a normal-sized stomach.

*(b) Posters*

A series of posters would be prepared showing:

- pictures of foods which constitute a balanced diet.
- too much of one kind of food is not a balanced diet.
- too little of one kind of food is not a balanced diet.
- a balanced diet is needed if people are to be healthy.

*(c) Radio Programmes (Advertisements)*

These would be of two types:

- 30-second programmes introducing the need for people to have a balanced diet.
- 10-second programmes for reinforcement.

*Organization*

- This programme makes minimum use of facilitators, but there is a lot of work to be done by planners and implementors.
- The posters should be distributed widely through the target group.
- The mini-posters would be produced cheaply so they could be available in large numbers. They would be distributed by hand.

- The large poster series would be produced more professionally and would be displayed in public places, meeting halls, etc.
- Both sets of posters would be wordless, or contain few words.
- The artwork in the posters would be in a simple, cartoon style.
- The radio programmes would be presented concurrently with the distribution of the posters.
- The radio programmes would be repeated regularly, especially at times when the target group is free to listen.
- A catch phrase like "Always eat a balanced diet" would link the posters and the radio programmes. The catch phrase would be part of every presentation of the programme.

The two exemplar materials described above are examples of delivery systems for out-of-school science activities which will help bring greater scientific literacy to the identified target groups. This will hopefully then help the members of the target group improve their quality of life.

# 8

# Guidelines for Regional and International Co-operation and Collaboration for Improvement of Delivery Systems for Out-of-School Science Activities

In order to clarify the task of preparing guidelines for regional and international cooperation and collaboration, the workshop first established the objectives of such activities.

## 8.1 Objectives of Regional and International Co-operation and Collaboration

1. There should be a sharing of:
   - materials, methods and delivery systems (including successes and failures);
   - problems encountered and successful solutions;
   - strategies for needs assessment, validation, and formative and summative assessment; and
   - expertise.
2. There should be coordination of effort among nations, organizations and agencies; both government and non-government.
3. There should be encouragement for the co-ordination of all agencies involved in out-of-school science activities within each nation.

4. Adult education organizations should become further involved in co-operative efforts with out-of-school science education organizations.
5. Professional science education organizations should be encouraged to participate in co-ordinated efforts with out-of-school science organizations.

### 8.2 The Role of UNESCO

UNESCO is already involved in coordinating and implementing many of these objectives. It has a vital role in promoting co-operation and collaboration, both at regional and international levels.

Some of the major thrusts of UNESCO are:

- sponsoring of meetings, seminars and workshops;
- training of key personnel;
- co-ordination within the regions to avoid duplication of effort;
- the "Build Bridges of Peace and Understanding" approach to the development of advisory and regional consultations;
- the "Education for All" programme is one of the major programmes which includes adult and literacy education;
- the "Science for All" programme for improving scientific and technological literacy;
- at the regional level APEID publishes a newsletter which goes to all areas of the region and a special newsletter for science and technology education. Both of these include information useful for those involved in out-of-school science activities; and
- the publishing, dissemination and exchange of appropriate materials.

UNESCO APEID publications and information can be obtained from:

ACEID Clearinghouse
UNESCO-PROAP
Bangkok
Thailand

### 8.3 Guidelines for Implementation of Programmes of Co-operation and Collaboration

Programmes for co-operation and collaboration must consider funding, organization and staffing, if they are to be implemented effectively. Some guidelines for this are:

- establish a working group at the national level to link with UNESCO/ACEID. This working group should include members from various agencies involved in out-of-school science education. It should be accountable to the appropriate government department.
- establish information-dissemination procedures for those involved in planning, preparing, producing, implementing, facilitating and evaluating out-of-school science activities.
- provide exemplar or prototype materials to those working in out-of-school science programmes.
- establish national clearing houses which liaise with a central international clearing house.
- train personnel who will be involved in planning, implementing, facilitating and evaluating delivery systems for out-of-school science activities. This training could take place on a national or an international basis.
- involve non-governmental organizations in the planning and implementing of out-of-school science activities.
- hold appropriate consultations at regular intervals for planers and implementors of out-of-school science activities.
- ensure that information about out-of-school science activities and their delivery is part of the relevant curriculum in pre-service and in-service teacher training activities.

# 9

# The Regional Science Olympiad: General Information

## 9.1 Introduction

*Rationale*

Although about two-thirds of the world's population live in the region, only a few of the member states have sent participants to the International Olympiads in Mathematics, Biology, Chemistry or Physics. This may be because of cost or because of a perceived inappropriateness of content. Whatever the reason, it is seen to be important to mount an Olympiad to which all countries in the region will have reasonable opportunity to attend and whose content, format and regulations will be designed to suit the countries of the region.

## 9.2 Subject Matter of the Olympiads

It was decided that the Olympiads should be science Olympiads, rather than specialist-subject Olympiads (in chemistry, physics, mathematics or biology only).

*Rationale*

Increasingly science has become a multi-disciplinary field of endeavour. Indeed the distribution between science disciplines is rapidly blurring. The able scientist of tomorrow will necessarily have a good knowledge across more than one of the specialist science areas. Thus, the notion of a Science Olympiad will represent the modern nature of the field more truly than specialist-subject Olympiads. Some new sciences (such as environmental sciences, biophysics and space science) are essentially interdisciplinary.

- The organization of two, three or four specialist-subject Olympiads simultaneously is regarded as both too difficult and too costly.
- Organization of Olympiads which rotate amongst the separate science disciplines is unsatisfactory because of the very long time interval between Olympiads in any one discipline.
- Science Olympiads will discourage specialization in separate science disciplines at too early an age.
- In summary, we accept the view that science is one discipline.

**9.3 Objectives**

The objectives of the Olympiad are:

1. to arouse interest in science in the member states;
2. to encourage striving for excellence in science;
3. to provide opportunities for uncovering the most talented science students in the member states;
4. to encourage an appreciation of the interdisciplinary nature of science;
5 to promote meaningful and relevant science education; and
6. to encourage the spirit of cooperation, friendship and international understanding.

**9.4 Description of the Olympiad**

The Olympiad shall provide various learning experiences including a competition.

**A. Tne Non-competitive Learning Experiences**

The learning experiences will be decided by the host country and may consist of one or more of the following:

(i) lecture by scientists,

(ii) visits to laboratories/industries,

(iii) field visits,

(iv) students working with scientists,

(v) cooperative tasks in a scientific environment,

(vi) visits to historical and cultural interests, etc., and

(vii) others.

**B. The Competition**

1. The competition shall consist of three parts,

   (i) Theoretical,

   (ii) Practical, and

   (iii) Communication on a socially-relevant science topic.

2. In all the sections, the participants shall tackle the task as a team. All the responses to be assessed shall be the result of a co-operative team effort. That is, in each section, there will be one joint response from the participants of each country, to be arrived at by a process of discussion among the participants.

*Rationale*

- The Olympiad should, above all, be a learning experience. Co-operative team efforts involving discussion, negotiation, defence of opinions, testing of opinions, weighing-up of alternatives and decision-making will provide more opportunities for the participants to learn (from the interaction with the other Team members) than would individual responses.

- Almost all scientific progress occurs as a result of interaction between groups of people. The team format of these Olympiads will therefore represent the nature of scientific advancement more truly than if based on individual tasks.

- The team format allows greater opportunity for achievement of the Olympic ideals of co-operation, character building and development of interpersonal relationships.

3. The time allocation and relative weightages for the various components will be,

   (i) Theoretical— 4 hours— 40 per cent

   (ii) Practical— 6 hours— 50 per cent

   (iii) Communication— 1 hour— 10 per cent

**9.5 Language**

1. The official language of the Olympiad will be English.
2. Where necessary, the task maybe translated by Leaders or Deputy Leaders from English into the working language of the participants.

**9.6 Delegations to the Olympiad**

**A. Participants**

1. Each participating country state should send a team of not more than 3 students.

*Rationale*

- Larger teams may lead to the selection of specialists in each of the science areas, each specialist working alone on various parts of a task. This would be country to the objectives of the Science Olympiads. It is preferred that each of the participants will be able to make effective contributions in more than one area of the tasks.
- Larger teams would increase the costs to member states.

2. Students eligible to participate must be attending secondary (or higher secondary) schools or schools at an equivalent level (e.g. technical, vocational correspondence, etc.).
3. Students at the tertiary level are not eligible to join the competition.

4. The participants should not be more than 18 years of age on the first day of the competition.

*Rationale*

- This maximum age will include most of those in the final year of secondary schooling in the majority of countries.
- The higher the maximum age is set, the more inappropriate the competition would be for those countries in which students are only 16/17 in their final school year.
- Although some countries may have students who reach the age of 20 in their final school year, once the competition is running regularly, every student will have the opportunity to participate in the Olympiad or the Olympiad selection processes at some stage of their schooling.

**B. Accompanying Persons**

1. Each delegation will be accompanied by a Leader (head of delegation) and a Deputy Leader.
2. The Leader and Deputy Leader should be scientists or science educators who are capable of understanding the task and their solutions, and evaluating the participant's performance.
3. The Leader and Deputy Leader should be proficient in English and be able to express themselves accurately and clearly on scientific and technical aspects of the Olympiad.
4. The Leader and Deputy Leader should be able to translate tasks from English into the language of their participants and to translate the responses of the participants into English, if necessary.

**9.7 The International Council**

1. The International Council shall consist of the Chairman, and the Leader (or in his absence the Deputy Leader) of each delegation.
2. The Chairman shall be appointed by the organizers.

3. The responsibilities of the International Council are the following:
   (i) to be the final arbiter of any decisions related to the competition component of the Olympiad.
   (ii) to approve at the beginning of the competition the qualification of the participating students.
   (iii) to familiarize themselves with the competition tasks selected by the organizer, their solutions and the prepared assessment guidelines, as well as to comment and to decide in the case of proposed changes.
   (iv) to assess participants' responses and ensure that all participants are judged by equal criteria, as far as possible.
   (v) to determine the recipients of the awards.
   (vi) based on the experiences of the Olympiad, to recommended changes of regulations, organization and content of future Olympiads.
4. The members of the International Council are obliged to maintain professional discretion with respect to their knowledge of the tasks and not to assist any participant, directly or indirectly.

**9.8 The Organiser**

The Olympiad will be organized by one of the member-states (the host country) in collaboration with UNESCO. It will be the responsibility of the host country to appoint the organizing committee. The responsibilities of the organizers are the following:

1. to be responsible for the organization and conduct of the Olympiad.
2. to ensure that the competition is conducted in accordance with the Regulations.
3. to produce a set of Guidelines based on the Regulations and sent to the participating countries, giving enough time. These Guidelines shall give details of the Olympiad not covered in the Regulations, and give the

names and addresses of the institutions and persons responsible for the Olympiad.

4. to establish a programme for the Olympiad (schedule for the participants and the accompanying persons, programme of excursions, etc.) which is sent to the participating countries in advance.

5. to check well in advance the eligibility of the participants.

6. to choose the tasks (according to specifications in the Regulations and the outline of the syllabus specified in the Appendix), and to ensure the translation of the chosen problem and their solutions into the language required.

7. to maintain confidentiality regarding the competition.

8. to prepare the awards which are to be presented at the official closing ceremony.

9. to provide services related to the Olympiad needed by the delegates including the following:
   - accommodation,
   - food,
   - local transport,
   - emergency medical care,
   - secretarial services, and
   - facilities to be used in the competition.

10. to provide arrangements towards an observance of the security regulations.

11. to provide accident and medical insurance for all participants in connection with the organized programme.

## 9.9 Compilation of Tasks

1. Each participating country, except the host country, shall be required to forward at least 3 tasks in English for the theoretical component, and 1 task for the practical component, along with complete solutions for each.

2. The competition tasks shall be chosen by the Organiser from the submitted tasks. Modifications to the submitted tasks may be made as judged appropriate.
3. The competition tasks shall be presented to the International Council along with complete solutions, including alternative solutions, and assessment guidelines.

**9.10 Assessment of Tasks**

1. For the solution of the theoretical tasks a maximum of 40 points will be given, for the solution of the practical tasks a maximum of 50 points, and for communication for socially-relevant science topic, 10 points, all in all a total of 100 points.
2. Each of the competition tasks is independently marked by every member of the International Council.
3. The International Council shall consider the results and decide on the final scores.
4. The original manuscripts of the participants remain with the organizer.

**9.11 Prizes**

1. The International Council decides the recipients of the awards to be presented.
2. The number of gold medals should amount up to approximately 10 per cent, the number of silver medals up to 20 per cent, and the number of bronze medals to approximately 30 per cent of the total number of participants.
3. Each participant shall receive a certificate of participation.
4. In addition to the medals other awards maybe offered. Moreover, special prizes can be granted.

**9.12 Finance**

1. The participating country covers the expenses of its delegation for travelling to and from the venue of the Olympiad.

2. Other expenses in connection with the organized programme, including the cost of food and accommodation for the members of the delegation, will be the responsibility of the host country.
3. The Organizers of the next Olympiad may send a maximum of three observers at their own expense.

**Recommendations Regarding UNESCO Contribution**

1. UNESCO may consider meeting the cost of participation of delegations from the least-developed countries and some of the developing countries upon request.
2. UNESCO may consider assisting the host country to meet a part of the organization expenses.

**Suggested Timetable of Tasks Prior to the Olympiad**

| | | |
|---|---|---|
| As soon as Possible | : | Finalise regulations and syllabus outline |
| 0-15 months | : | Send out invitations to member states along with general advice, Regulations, samples of tasks, Syllabus description and guidelines for formation of problems. |
| 0-12 months | : | Acceptance of invitations by countries and identification of responsible agencies. Possible recirculation of advice. |
| 0-6 months | : | Receipt of tasks/problems from countries. |
| 0-4.5 months | : | Receipt of nomination of participants. |
| 0-3 months | : | Validation/finalization of participants and inform member states on validation of participants |
| 0-1 month | : | Receive travel plans |
| 0-2 months | : | Finalization of competition tasks |

**9.13 Concluding Clause**

Those who take part in the competition acknowledge the Regulations through their very participants.

# 10

# Draft Regulations of the Regional Science Olympiad for Asia and Pacific

## 10.1 Objectives

The objectives of the Olympiad are:

1. to arouse interest in science in the member states,
2. to encourage striving for excellence in science,
3. to provide opportunities for uncovering the most talented science students in the member states,
4. to encourage an appreciation of the interdisciplinary nature of science,
5. to promote meaningful and relevant science education, and
6. to encourage the spirit of co-operation, friendship and international understanding.

## 10.2 Description of the Olympiad

The Olympiad shall provide various learning experiences including a competition.

*A. The Non-competitive Learning Experiences*

The learning experiences will be decided by the host country and may consist of one or more of the following:

(i) lecture by scientists,
(ii) visits to laboratories/industries,
(iii) field visits,
(iv) students working with scientists,
(v) co-operative tasks in a scientific environment,
(vi) visits to historical and cultural interests, etc., and
(vii) others.

*B. The Competition*

1. The competition shall consist of three parts,
   (i) Theoretical,
   (ii) Practical, and
   (iii) Communication on a socially-relevant science topic.
2. In all the sections, the participants shall tackle the task as a team. All the responses to be assessed shall be the result of a cooperative team effort. That is, in each section, there will be one joint response from the participants of each country, to be arrived at by a process of discussion among the participants.
3. The time allocation relative weightages for the various component will be,
   (i) Theoretical—4 hours—40 per cent
   (ii) Practical—6 hours—50 per cent
   (iii) Communication—1 hour—10 per cent

**10.3 Language**

1. The official language of the Olympiad will be English.
2. Where necessary, the task maybe translated by Leaders or Deputy Leaders from English into the working language of the participants.

**10.4 Delegations of the Olympiad**

*A. Participants*

1. Each participating country state should send a team of not more than 3 students.

2. Students eligible to participate must be attending secondary (or higher secondary) schools or schools at an equivalent level (e.g., technical, vocational correspondence, etc.).
3. Students at the tertiary level are not eligible to join the competition.
4. The participants should not be more than 18 years of age on the first day of the competition.

*B. Accompanying Persons*

1. Each delegation will be accompanied by a Leader (head of delegation) and a Deputy Leader.
2. The Leader and Deputy Leader should be scientists or science educators who are capable of understanding the task and their solutions, and evaluating the participant's performance.
3. The Leader and Deputy Leader should be proficient in English and be able to express themselves accurately and clearly on scientific and technical aspects of the Olympiad.
4. The Leader and Deputy Leader should be able to translate tasks from English into the language of their participants and to translate the responses of the participants into English, if necessary.

**10.5 The International Council**

1. The International Council shall consist of the Chairman, and the Leader (or in his absence the Deputy Leader) of each delegation.
2. The Chairman shall be appointed by the organizers.
3. The responsibilities of the International Council are the following:
   (i) to be the final arbiter of any decisions related to the competition component of the Olympiad.
   (ii) to approve at the beginning of the competition the qualification of the participating students.

(iii) to familiarize themselves with the competition tasks selected by the organizer, their solutions and the prepared assessment guidelines, as well as to comment and to decide in the case of proposed changes.

(iv) to assess the participants' responses and ensure that all participants are judged by equal criteria as far as possible.

(v) to determine the recipients of the awards.

(vi) based on the experiences of the Olympiad to recommend changes of Regulations, organization and content of future Olympiads.

4. The members of the International Council are obliged to maintain professional discretion with respect to their knowledge of the tasks and not to assist any participant, directly or indirectly.

**10.6 The Organizer**

The Olympiad will be organized by one of the member-states (the host country) in collaboration with UNESCO. It will be the responsibility of the host country to appoint the organizing committee. The responsibilities of the organizers are the following:

1. to be responsible for the organization and conduct of the Olympiad,
2. to ensure that the competition is conducted in accordance with the Regulations,
3. to produce a set of Guidelines based on the Regulations and sent to the participating countries giving enough time. These Guidelines shall give details of the Olympiad not covered in the Regulations, and give the names and addresses of the institutions and persons responsible for the Olympiad,
4. to establish a programme for the Olympiad (schedule for the participants and the accompanying persons, programme of excursions, etc.) which is sent to the participating countries in advance,

5. to check well in advance the eligibility of the participants,
6. to choose the tasks (according to the Regulations) and to ensure the translation of the chosen problem and their solutions into the language required,
7. to maintain confidentiality regarding the competition,
8. to prepare the awards which are to be presented at the official closing ceremony,
9. to provide services related to the Olympiad needed by the delegates including the following:
    - accommodation,
    - food,
    - local transport,
    - emergency medical care,
    - secretarial services, and
    - facilities to be used in the competition,
10. to provide arrangements towards an observance of the security regulations, and
11. to provide accident and medical insurance for all participants in connection with the organized programme.

**10.7 Compilation of Tasks**

1. Each participating country, except the host country, shall be required to forward at least 3 tasks in English for the theoretical component, and 1 task for the practical component, along with complete solutions for each.
2. The competition tasks shall be chosen by the Organizer from the submitted tasks. Modifications to the submitted tasks may be made as judged appropriate.
3. The competition tasks shall be presented to the International Council along with complete solutions, including alternative solutions, and assessment guidelines.

**10.8 Assessment of Tasks**

1. For the solution of the theoretical tasks a maximum of 40 points will be given, for the solution of the practical tasks a maximum of 50 points, and for communication of socially-relevant science topic, 10 points, all in all a total of 100 points.
2. Each of the competition tasks is independently marked by every member of the International Council.
3. The International Council shall consider the results and decide on the final scores.
4. The original manuscripts of the participants remain with the organizer.

**10.9 Awards**

1. The International Council decides the recipients of the awards to be presented.
2. The number of gold medals should amount up to approximately 10 per cent, the number of silver medals up to 20 per cent, and the number of bronze medals to approximately 30 per cent of the total number of participants.
3. Each participant shall receive a certificate of participation.
4. In addition to the medals other awards maybe offered. Moreover, special prizes can be granted.

**10.10 Finance**

1. The participating country covers the expenses of its delegation for travelling to and from the venue of the Olympiad.
2. Other expenses in connection with the organized programme, including the cost of food and accommodation for the members of the delegation, will be the responsibility of the host country.
3. The Organizers of the next Olympiad may send a maximum of three observers at their own expenses.

### 10.11 Concluding Clauses

Those who take part in the competition acknowledge the Regulations through their very participation.

### Guidelines for Framing Questions/Problems/Tasks

1. Remember that the participants are among the most talented students in the region.
2. The emphasis of the tasks should be on science process skills within a reasonable content-knowledge base.
3. The task should be formulated in simple, concise, clear English.
4. It is the intention that both the theoretical and practical components of the Olympiad Competition will challenge the inter-disciplinary or multi-disciplinary knowledge and skills of the students.
5. The competition should not consist of an accumulation of different tasks, each in a specialist science area (i.e. physics, biology, etc.), as this would allow a team of specialist participants to individually tackle separate tasks.
6. It is not necessary that any one question should attempt to involve *all* areas of science (although such questions would be most desirable). If each question involves two or three science areas then the organizers will be able to frame an overall competition with reasonable balance.
7. Within any one task it would be preferable if the design of the task was such that all sections involve team work rather than allow each participant to individually apply specialist knowledge to different sections.
8. There should be a reasonable likelihood that all students will have some familiarity with equipment and materials necessary to complete the task.
9. Open-ended questions which challenge the imagination and ability to innovate, and which allow participants to proceed in different directions are desirable,

especially in the Practical section. The difficulty of assessing responses to such questions should not be regarded as a deterrent.

10. The tasks should be tested. It may be appropriate to use tertiary-level students for this purpose.
11. The task framers should propose detailed alternative responses and suggest assessment guidelines/checklist for each task.